Zacharias Tanee Fomum

THE ART OF INTERCESSION

Éditions du Livre Chrétien
4, rue du Révérend Père Cloarec
92400 Courbevoie France
editionlivrechretien@gmail.com

All Biblical quotations, unless otherwise noted, are from the Revised Standard Version.

First edition by Vantage Press, New York.

2002 edition under licence from the author
by Crossroads' Communications
C-13 CoziHom 251 PAll Hill
Bandra, Mumbai- 400 050. India
E-mail: crossroadscom@yahoo.com

© Zacharias Tanee Fomum, 1990

All rights reserved. No part of this publication may be reproduced, translated, stored in a retrieval system, or transmitted in any form or by any other means, without the prior permission of the author.

Piracy is theft.

Edité par :
Editions du livre chrétien
4, rue du Révérend Père Cloarec
92400 Courbevoie - FRANCE
Tél : (33) 9 52 29 27 72
Email : editionlivrechretien@gmail.com

Couverture :
Jacques Maré

To Esther Kouonang,

an advancing student in the school of prayer, in recognition of six hours that are currently being invested daily in intercession for world conquest for Christ with the expectation that her goal of fifteen hours of daily intercession will soon be accomplished, to the glory of God and His Christ.

Contents

Foreword 9

Part 1: Introduction 11
1 Prayer 12
2 Prayerlessness 18
3 Intercession 22

Part 2: The Need For Intercessors 25
1 The need for intercessors 26
2 The shortage of intercessors 41
3 Why Is There Such A Shortage Of Intercessors ? 50
4 The Intercessor's Heart : Total Identification 58

Part 3: Daniel The Intercessor 71
1 Daniel's Qualification to Intercede 72
2 The Knowledge of the Art of Intercession 85
3 On the Job Interceding 93

Part 4: Moses The Intercessor 113
1 The power of intercession 114
2 The art of intercession 127

Part 5: Two other old testament intercessors 191
1 Abraham's Ministry of Intercession 192
2 NEHEMIAH's Ministry of Intercession 214

Part 6 Two new testament intercessors 227
1 The Apostle Paul's Ministry As An Intercessor: Unceasing Activity
....228
2 Epaphras'S MINISTRY of intercession: labours for the maturation of the saints 247

Part 7 God in the ministry of intercession 263
1 The Lord Jesus As An Intercessor Whle On Earth 264
2 The Lord Jesus As Intercessor In Heaven 281
3 The Holy Spirit: The Resident Intercessor 294

My Prayer 303

Very Important 305

Foreword

Dr. Zacharias T. Fomum is a minister of the Word, and a scientist. He combines the teaching of organic chemistry at the University of Yaounde, Cameroon, West Africa, with the spiritual ministry of teaching the Word in many countries. He searches out facts and presents them in a teachable format.

In expanded outline form, Dr. Fomum presents the Biblical teaching about who an intercessor is, what intercession is, and how an intercessor intercedes in this book entitled, The Art of Intercession.

An intercessor then ... takes the sin of another upon himself... He pleads and labours with God until the guilty party is forgiven.

Pointing to a great shortage of intercessors, the question is asked, "Does it matter to you ?" Biblical teaching on intercession is covered in both the Old and New Testaments. Perhaps the greatest need of the Church today is that we be intercessors. Dr. Fomum examines the art of intercession as practised by Moses, Abraham, Daniel, Nehemiah, Paul, Epaphras and Jesus Himself.

The challenge is disturbing as the reader realizes how short of the mark is even the most spiritual of Christians.

Dr. Fomum practises what he teaches, as do some Churches in Cameroon. Who of us prays for several hours each day? Who of us fasts and prays in spiritual warfare for from 21-40 days at a time, several times per year?

This book is MUST reading for the serious Christian.

Dr. Lester Sumrall

PART 1

Introduction

1

PRAYER

Unless the prayer life of an individual is revived and kept vigorous, all that may be happening in his spiritual life may just be activities of the soul life, which are bound to be short-lived before man and of no consequence at all before God.

1. Prayer is the most important work on earth.
2. Prayer is very hard work.
3. Prayer is the greatest thing that anyone can do on earth to advance the interest of God, the Church, man, and himself.
4. Prayer is the rail on which the locomotive of God's power moves.
5. A man is only as spiritual and only as important before God as his prayer life is.
6. Prayer is the greatest power in all the world.
7. Prayer has more power locked up in it than the atomic bomb.
8. Prayer is the one thing that puts the devil's kingdom into confusion.

9. God's ablest soldiers are those who pray.
10. Prayer is the priority of spiritual people.
11. Prayer is the way to God's heart.
12. God has committed Himself to answer all prayers that are in His will and that flow forth from pure hearts.
13. Praying people have more power over nations than Heads of States.
14. The world is controlled by praying believers.
15. A prayer meeting of Spirit-filled believers has more power over the affairs of the world than the United Nations Security Council.
16. One praying man can change a life, family, city, nation, and continent.
17. All people are open to being controlled by prayer. They all yield to the power of prayer, even if they do not want to.
18. Men are powerless against the prayers of holy, consecrated people.
19. All things are possible to the one who prays.
20. Praying saints know nothing that is impossible with God.
21. People who pray never accept a "No". They press on with God until their request is granted.
22. Prayer is more important than preaching.
23. Prayer is more important than writing books.
24. Prayer is more important than evangelism.
25. Prayer is more important than teaching the Word.
26. Prayer is more important than helping the poor.
27. Prayer is more important than every other thing in the Christian life.
28. Prayer is the priority of priorities.
29. Prayer is the one thing that Satan dreads.

30. The most important pre-occupation of Satan is stopping the saints from praying.
31. Character is more easily changed by prayer than by all else.
32. World peace will be accomplished faster by prayer than by human peace efforts.
33. The unity of the Church is maintained more by prayer than by talking, boards, and resolutions.
34. Economic situations are altered faster by prayer than by all other means put together.
35. The prayer chamber is the place of victory.
36. Praying is the answer to indulgence.
37. Praying leads to total deliverance from worldliness.

Prayer is work. Get to work. Get to prayer. If you are a real "man," you should pray.

1. Pray silently.
2. Pray aloud.
3. Shout in prayer.
4. Cry out in prayer.
5. Stand in prayer.
6. Lift up your hands while praying.
7. Walk while praying.
8. Kneel while praying.
9. Go on long prayer walks alone with God.
10. Go on a hill or mountain to pray.
11. Withdraw for fifteen minutes of prayer alone.
12. Withdraw for one hour of prayer alone.
13. Withdraw for twelve hours of prayer alone.

14. Withdraw for twenty-four hours of prayer alone.
15. Withdraw for one week of prayer alone.
16. Withdraw for one month of prayer alone.
17. Withdraw to pray in pairs.
18. Withdraw to pray in fours.
19. Withdraw to pray in larger groups.
20. Pray when you have a burden.
21. Pray when you have no burden.
22. Pray when you feel like praying.
23. Pray when you do not feel like praying.
24. Pray when all in you hates praying.
25. Pray when you "feel" the presence of God.
26. Pray when you do not "feel" the presence of God.
27. Pray when you feel like giving up the Lord.
28. Pray when you think you hate God!
29. Pray when you are happy.
30. Pray when you are sad.
31. Pray when you are frustrated.
32. Pray when you have been successful.
33. Pray when you have failed.
34. Pray when you have been encouraged or praised.
35. Pray when you have been rebuked.
36. Pray when you have come to the end of yourself.
37. Pray when answers come quickly.
38. Pray when answers do not seem to come.
39. Pray in the morning.
40. Pray in the afternoon.
41. Pray in the evening.

42. Pray in the night.
43. Pray into the night.
44. Pray throughout the night.
45. Pray when you are tired.
46. Pray when you are hungry.
47. Pray when you have eaten.
48. Pray when you are sleepy.
49. Pray after you have slept.
50. Pray when you are in •an emergency.
51. Pray when all is going well.
52. Pray one-sentence prayers.
53. Pray long prayers.
54. Pray for yourself.
55. Pray for others.
56. Pray for all men.
57. Pray specifically.
58. Pray in a general way.
59. Pray for the glory of God to be manifested in your life.
60. Pray for the glory of God to be manifested in the Church.
61. Pray for the glory of God to be manifested in the world.
62. Pray when you doubt yourself.
63. Pray when you doubt God.
64. Pray when you believe yourself.
65. Pray when you believe God.
66. Pray with tears.
67. Pray with sighs.
68. Pray with groans.
69. Pray with known words.

70. Pray in unknown tongues.
71. Pray without words.
72. Pray when you are fasting.
73. Pray when you are not fasting.
74. Pray until the answer comes.
75. Pray that the Lord may show you His needs.
76. Pray that the Lord's needs be provided for.
77. Pray that the holiness of the Lord be manifested to you and in you.
78. Pray that the holiness of the Lord be manifested in the Church.
79. Pray that the holiness of the Lord be manifested to the world.
80. Pray that the Lord's will be known and accomplished in your life.
81. Pray that the Lord's will be known and accomplished in the Church.
82. Pray that the Lord's will be manifest to the world.
83. Pray that the Kingdom of God should come in full measure.
84. Pray more than any person you have seen give himself to praying.
85. Pray more than any person about whom you have read.
86. Make prayer your one pre-occupation.
87. Satisfy God's heart through praying.
88. Win the Christian race through praying.
89. Pray without ceasing.
90. What I say to you I say to all, pray!

2

PRAYERLESSNESS

1. Prayerlessness is the worst sin.
2. Prayerlessness is a disaster.
3. Preachers who spend more time before men than they spend before God are dangerous men. They will ultimately do more harm to God's cause than any good that they think they are doing.
4. Prayerlessness opens the door for the committing of many other sins.
5. Prayerless men replace praying with singing.
6. Prayerless men replace praying with counselling.
7. Prayerless men replace praying with preaching.
8. Prayerless men replace praying with helping the poor.
9. Prayerless men replace praying with the writing of Gospel books.
10. Prayerless men replace praying with the writing of tracts.
11. Prayerless men replace praying with councils, boards, synods, et cetera.
12. Every sin that has ever been committed can be attributed to prayerlessness on the part of someone.

13. Every act of backsliding is the result of prayerlessness.
14. The Word of God is always dull in the ears of prayerless saints.
15. Prayerlessness is the refusal to know God's will.
16. Prayerlessness is the refusal to do God's will.
17. Prayerlessness is disobedience to God and His Word.
18. Prayerlessness is taking sides with Satan against God.
19. Prayerlessness is giving the devil weapons with which to fight God.
20. Prayerlessness is an attempt to overthrow God.
21. Prayerlessness is a determination to ensure that the lost remain lost.
22. Prayerlessness is a determination to ensure that backsliders remain backslidden.
23. Prayerlessness is a determination to ensure that the Body of Christ never reaches maturity.
24. Prayerlessness is a determination to ensure that the Lord Jesus does not return to take His Bride with Him.
25. Prayerlessness does more harm to God's cause than adultery.
26. Prayerlessness does more harm to God's cause than murder.
27. Prayerlessness does more harm to God's cause than divisions.
28. Prayerlessness does more harm to God's cause than heresy.
29. Prayerlessness is laziness, regardless of how busy one may consider oneself to be.
30. Prayerlessness is purposelessness, regardless of how goal-directed the person may consider himself to be.

31. Prayerlessness leads to godlessness.
32. Prayerlessness results in selfishness.
33. Prayerlessness results in the loss of vision.
34. Prayerlessness results in indulgence.
35. Prayerlessness results in inner and outer disharmony.
36. Prayerlessness is evidence of backsliding.
37. Prayerlessness is evidence of lost glory.
38. Prayerlessness is proof that Satan and a man are establishing a relationship.
39. Prayerlessness is evidence that a man has lost God.
40. Prayerlessness is proof that a person has an idol in his heart, most probably the idol "self."
41. Prayerlessness is proof that the mind is no longer set on heavenly things.
42. Prayerlessness is proof that the mind is now set on earthly things.
43. Prayerlessness says that one is finding God a problem.
44. When prayer times are reduced, prayerlessness has begun.
45. When prayer is boring, prayerlessness is advancing in the heart of a person.
46. When prayer times are infrequent, prayerlessness is being established.
47. The enemies of the Cross commit the sin of prayerlessness with free consciences.
48. The one who stagnates in prayer, praying the same number of hours a day for several years and having no increasing burden, is already committing the sin of prayerlessness.
49. All the prayerless should repent.
50. The sin of prayerlessness must be recognized.

51. The sin of prayerlessness must be confessed and forsaken.
52. The Spirit of prayer must be invited to possess the praying believer.
53. Be stiff-necked no longer.
54. Watch and pray.
55. What I say to you I say to all, "Watch and pray."

3

INTERCESSION

1. An intercessor is a person who takes the sin of another on himself, identifies fully with the sin and the sinner, and then labours with God until the guilty party is forgiven.

2. God has ordained the ministry of intercession so that through it the needs of people that would otherwise not be met are met. It is a part of His great love for man. In intercession, the helpless can receive help, the ignorant can become informed, and the untaught can become taught.

3. If I am not an intercessor, I am the one to blame. Others should not be blamed.

4. Intercessors are needed because they stand in the gap between man and God, causing God to bless man or causing God not to bring well-deserved punishment upon man.

5. Although intercessors are so important, the tragedy is that they are in short supply. God Himself has complained about their shortage, and there is much judgment that could have been averted had He found an intercessor.

6. Calamity befell the people not only because they sinned, but because there was no intercessor.

7. The judgment of God has come and is coming on the world, not only because the world has sinned, but because there is a shortage of intercessors.
8. The people deserved judgment because God takes a hard look at sin committed by people who know better. No one was interceding. No one pleaded before God. No one asked for pardon. God waited in vain for someone to do something about it—intercede— but nothing was done. The Lord, instead of punishing them as they deserved, went out of His way to seek for a man among them who could intercede. He looked and looked, searched and searched, but it was all in vain. There was no one qualified to intercede. Because the Lord found no intercessor, He poured out His indignation upon the people. His indignation was there from the moment the people began to commit sin. However, God held it under control as He waited for someone to intercede. He held it under control as He sought for an intercessor. When after a diligent search He found out that there was no intercessor, He gave vent to His wrath. He acted. He poured out that which He had held under control for a long time.
9. The Lord saw it and it displeased him that there was no justice. He saw that there was no man and wondered that there was no one to intervene (Isaiah 59:15-16).
10. God does not normally wonder. However, He wondered! He did not wonder because of their sin. He wondered that there was no one to intercede.
11. Intercessors are people who intervene between God and a judgment-deserving people.
12. God was not looking for many intercessors. He was looking for only one. One would have been enough! One would have intervened and things would have been different. He wanted one to come forth, but there was none

who came forth. Be¬cause none came forth, He was compelled by divine justice to punish, and that He did.

13. Normally, intercessors will change the situation. The question is, "Where are they?"

14. "*Run to and fro through the streets of Jerusalem, look and take note! Search her squares to see if you can find a man, one who does justice and seeks truth; that I may pardon her*" (Jeremiah 5: 1).

15. "*I looked, but there was no one to help; I was appalled, but there was no one to uphold*" (Isaiah 63:5).

16. Does it mean anything to you? God has not changed. Because there was no intercessor, He brought judgment on the peo¬ple. What He did then He will do today. The sinful condition of men has not changed. His judgment is coming. It is imminent. When it comes it will be devastating. Does it matter to you that He will soon act that way? Does it matter to you that multitudes might soon perish? If it matters to you, will you do something about it?

17. If you intend to do something about it, won't you start today? Tomorrow may be too late. It could be that the sins of your family, assembly, city, nation, continent, and planet have been piling up before God for years and He has been waiting for an intercessor. He has waited for a long time. It could be that today a point will be reached where it will be too late to intercede. While there remain a few hours before the wrath of God is poured out, will you step into the gap? Will you not do something about it?

18. Read the rest of the book and act at once!

19. Praise the Lord!

PART 2

The Need For Intercessors

1

THE NEED FOR INTERCESSORS

"And the Word of the Lord came to me: Son of man, say to her, You are a land that is not cleansed, or rained upon in the day of indignation. Her princes in the midst of her are like a roaring lion tearing the prey; they have devoured human lives; they have taken treasure and precious things; they have made many widows in the midst of her. Her priests have done violence to my law and have profaned my holy things; they have made no distinction between the holy and the common, neither have they taught the difference between the unclean and the clean, and they have disregarded my sabbaths, so that I am profaned among them. Her princes in the midst of her are like wolves tearing the prey, shedding blood, destroying lives to get dishonest gain. And her prophets have daubed for them with whitewash, seeing false visions and divining lies for them, saying, 'Thus says the Lord God,' when the Lord has not spoken. The people of the land have practised extortion and committed robbery; they have oppressed the poor and needy, and have extorted from the sojourner without redress. And I sought for a man among them who should build up the wall and stand in the breach before me for the land, that I should not destroy it; but I found none. Therefore I have poured out my indignation upon them; I have consumed them with the fire of my wrath; their way have I requited upon their heads, says the Lord God" (Ezekiel 22: 23-31).

GOD'S DESCRIPTION OF THE NATION

The Lord said of the nation, "You are a nation that is not cleansed of sin. You are a nation that is not rained upon in the day of indignation." This indignation could be manifested in any of the following ways:

1. Famine
2. Floods
3. Droughts
4. Cyclones
5. Earthquakes
6. Lakes that give up toxic gases that kill
7. Volcanic eruptions and landslides
8. Incurable diseases of all kinds
9. Crop diseases
10. Drastic weather, like very cold winters or very hot summers
11. Crops produced that cannot be sold
12. Lands cultivated but with poor yields
13. Et cetera

Is there any nation in the world where one or more of these evidences of God's indignation do not apply? I do not think so. We may ask why the Lord is indignant.

The answer is plain:

1. Her princes (leaders and important people) are like a roaring lion, tearing the prey. Where in the world do we have national leaders and important people who are not using the people they lead for their own interests? Name one such leader or such a group of leaders, and that nation

will be exempted from what the Word is saying here.
2. They have devoured human lives. Do you know of a nation where the leaders have never caused someone or some people to be killed in order that they could continue to remain in leadership? If you don't know of such a country, you are ignorant. It could be that the human lives devoured were in other lands, but they certainly existed. Some lives are not completely devoured. These people are just shut up permanently in some prison without a fair trial or any trial at all.
3. They have taken treasures and precious things. Where are the leaders who honestly live on their income? Where are the leaders who do not have large accounts in foreign banks? Light a lamp and look for them the world over, and you will have a hard job finding them.
4. They have made many widows in the midst of her. The men are killed or locked up, and the widows remain either to suffer or to be used. This was true of Israel. It is true today of any nation in the world. It may not be true of every leader of every nation, but it is true of some leaders of every nation.

To sum up the attitude of the political and administrative leaders the Lord says, "*Her princes in the midst of her are like wolves tearing the prey, shedding blood, destroying lives to get dishonest gain*" (Ezekiel 22:27). That is the testimony of God's Word. Let anyone who wants to contend with what it says do so.

If the problem was only with political and administrative leaders, it would be different. Alas, the problem is not limited to that class. The Bible says of her priests and prophets, the popes, archbishops, bishops, moderators, superintendents, pastors, teachers et cetera, that constitute the confused religious denominations of the day or the leaders of God's people who have left God and become one

with the world:
1. "Her priests have done violence to my law." Where are the religious leaders who proclaim God's Word without compromise? Where are those who proclaim it and live it out? Are there not many who have decided that sin should no longer be called sin but just a mistake? Are there not some who have decided that the Bible is too out-of-date for today? Are there not many who have run from the Word to seek solutions in psychology, psychiatry, and every other device invented by modern man? Where are the pulpits from which the Gospel goes out clearly? Where are the pulpits from which men of God still proclaim the Gospel, *"Repent, and be baptized every one of you in the name of Jesus Christ for the forgiveness of your sin, and you shall receive the gift of the Holy Spirit"*? (Acts 2:38). Where do we hear the preacher say like the Lord, *"Unless you repent you will all likewise perish"*? (Luke 13:3). Violence has been done to the Word of God. There is the proclamation of God's acceptance of unrepentant sinners. There are programmes of unity away from or without any truth-a unity in the dark.

2. "Her priests have made no difference between the common and the holy." Consecrated preachers are very rare today. They are rarer than ever. Most love the company of men. Few seek the company of God. Many love sleep, food, and all else. Few are separated unto God. Few withdraw to seek God for one hour a day or for two days a week. There are preachers who have never left all the men and the world behind and gone to a lonely spot for one, two, or three weeks just to seek God's face. There are preachers who can go for a week without spending one hour alone with God in prayer. It was said of a certain nation where there are more "full-time" preachers than

anywhere else on Planet Earth that opinion polis showed that the average pastor spent only two minutes each day in prayer. Few spend hours reading the Scriptures. Few fast. It is sad, very sad. They do not know the difference between the holy and the common. They have divorced themselves from all discipline. They eat. They talk. They advertise themselves. They spend money and lust for more. They watch television or go for some other entertainment. They sleep. They yawn; then they sleep again!

3. "Her prophets have daubed for them with whitewash, seeing false visions and divining lies for them saying, 'Thus says the Lord God,' when the Lord has not spoken." In a world on the brink of God's judgement, many are the false prophets who are comforting an unrepentant people who while remaining in their sin, they will see the best and most far-reaching revival and be carried out of the world without any tribulation (which they avoid by carrying out all sinful practices and compromises) to the Marriage Supper of the Lamb! Such men do not spend hours on their knees reading the Word and crying to God for revelation. They are blind to their own sin. They cannot weep for themselves, and so they cannot weep for others. They cannot call people to repentance. They must whitewash the people in their sin, since they themselves are whitewashed sepulchres! They dare not tell the people the truth, for the truth will make them unpopular and possibly reduce their financial profits. This is sad but true. I spent three weeks with a noted evangelist and never saw him withdraw for fifteen minutes of prayer. He talked and talked into the early hours of the morning, not to sinners, but to believers in the evening and late night gossip sprees, and woke up after more serious people had spent

four to five hours with God alone doing the business of the kingdom.

If the problem were only with the religious leaders and the political leaders, it would be bad enough. However, it is worse. It includes the people, perhaps all the people. The Word of God says: "The people of the land have practised extortion and committed robbery; they have oppressed the poor and needy, and have extorted from the sojourner without redress."

The people have just gone ahead and acted as the spiritual and political leaders have done. The people always do what the leaders do. They know that if they commit the same sin with the leaders, they will not be punished.

So they have:
1. practised extortion,
2. committed robbery,
3. oppressed the poor,
4. oppressed the needy,
5. extorted from the sojourner without redress.

They have done these things shamelessly. They cover up every sin with a lie. They have established an eleventh commandment that says: "Thou shall not be caught." In other words, steal, kill, commit adultery, and do any and every kind of evil that you like, but make sure that you are not caught. There is no fear of the God before whom everything is exposed. They try not to get caught, but they are not too worried if caught, because they can always see some big man to intervene on their behalf, or they can use part of the stolen material to corrupt. There is no fear of God. There is no fear of His judgment. They think that God does not exist, or they say that He is too good to punish.

GOD'S RIGHTEOUS JUDGMENT

There is no question about the fact that God sees all that is behind closed doors, in utter darkness, in the totality of human secrecy, in the recesses of the human mind and heart. All is open before Him. He sees all and records all. The Bible says:

"Whither shall I go from thy Spirit?
Or whither shall I flee from thy presence? If I ascend to heaven, thou art there!
If I make my bed in Sheol, thou art there!
If I take the wings of the morning and dwell in the uttermost parts of the sea, even there thy hand shall lead me, and thy right hand shall hold me.
If I say, 'Let only darkness cover me, and the light about me be night,' even the darkness is not dark to thee, the night is bright as the day; for darkness is as light with thee"
(Psalm 139:7-12).

There is no need to hide any sin. All will be revealed. The sin will not only be revealed; it will be judged. All that is secret will come up and be exposed, and then judged. Your sin will be exposed and judged. The Bible says: "*Nothing is covered up that will not be revealed, or hidden that will not be known. Therefore whatever you have said in the dark shall be heard in the light, and what you have whispered in private rooms shall be proclaimed upon the housetops*" (Luke 12:2-3). "*They show that what the law requires is written on their hearts, while their conscience also bears witness and their conflicting thoughts accuse or perhaps excuse them on that day when, according to my gospel, God judges the secrets of men by Christ Jesus*" (Romans 2: 15 -16).

God must judge sin. If He did not judge sin, He would Himself be violating His law, and that is impossible!

GOD'S MERCY

Although God's justice demands that the sinner be punished, God is a God of mercy. He wants to forgive the sinner. He wants to liberate him. He wants to let him go free. If there is anything that God can do to allow the sinner to go unpunished without breaking the moral laws on which the universe hangs, He will do it. God only punishes when He has explored all the routes through which He can set the sinner free and found none. Judgment is the very last thing that God carries out in any situation.

GOD'S ORDINATION OF THE FACT AND MINISTRY OF THE INTERCESSOR

God has ordained the ministry of intercession as part of His great mercy. Normally, He would and He does demand that:

1. If a person has sinned,
2. that person should be punished.

He has also ordained that:
1. A person sins.
2. The one who has sinned repents.
3. The one who has sinned comes to Him and pleads for mercy.
4. He forgives the person and does not punish the person.

He has also ordained that:
1. Many people sin.
2. All those who have sinned repent.

3. All those who have sinned come to Him and plead for mercy.
4. He forgives the people and does not punish them.

It is already evident that the fact that a person can sin and be forgiven because he has repented and asked for forgiveness, shows great mercy on God's part. This means that a person can sin and not be punished, but be forgiven because he has repented. How great God is! If you consider the human legal system, you will see something of the greatness of God's mercy. If a thief is caught stealing and is brought before the judge and he confesses, "I am indeed a thief. I stole. Have mercy on me," will he be set absolutely free? Of course not. He may be punished less severely than he would be if he did not own up, but he will not be set free.

God is different. He sets repentant sinners free and He even forgets the fact that they have sinned. When He forgives, He forgets. He says:

"This is the covenant that I will make with them after those days, says the Lord: I will put my laws on their hearts, and write them on their minds, then he adds: 'I will remember their sins and their misdeeds no more'" (Hebrews 10: 16-17).

God saw that there were very many people who would sin, deserve to be punished, and know how to turn to Him for forgiveness, but not turn to Him for forgiveness and pardon, He would, therefore, be forced to punish them in love and mercy. He ordained the ministry of intercession in which:

1. A person sins.
2. That person deserves punishment for his sin.
3. Another person who has not committed that crime comes to the Lord.
4. He confesses the sin of the guilty one, taking it upon hi

self as if he had sinned, and identifies fully and completely with the one who has sinned and with his sin, in such a way that, although he has not sinned, he considers himself a sinner and pleads for forgiveness.
5. God hears and forgives the guilty person.

This is intercession! The one who takes the sin upon himself is the intercessor.

OR

1. Many people sin.
2. They deserve punishment and will be punished or are already being punished for the sin.
3. One person (or a small group of people who have not committed the sin) has compassion on those who have sinned and will be punished or are already being punished, takes the sin of the people on himself, and identifies fully with the people and their sin; confesses it to God and pleads for mercy until the Lord hears and forgives the people and does not bring on them the intended punishment, or takes away the punishment that is already being meted out on the guilty.

An intercessor, then, is a person (or group of persons) who takes the sin of another or of others on himself, identifies fully with it, and identifies with the one who has sinned. He then pleads and labours with God until the guilty party is forgiven.

Intercession does not always have to do with sin. It can also have

to do with other needs. For example:
1. A man is sick.
2. He may pray or not pray for the Lord to heal him.
3. Someone else has compassion on him.
4. The one who has compassion pleads with God for the sick man's healing.
5. The Lord hears and heals the sick person.

Let us look at another example:
An act of intercession has taken place.
1. A person does not know the Lord Jesus. He may even be comfortable in sin.
2. Another person who knows the Lord Jesus knows the value of knowing the Lord Jesus and the fact that the other person does not yet know the Lord Jesus.
3. He has compassion on him and prays that the Father should reveal the Lord Jesus to that one who does not know Him.
4. The Father reveals the Lord Jesus to the one who then becomes a believer.

An act of intercession has taken place! Let us look at two more examples:
1. Someone does not know the truth about some aspect of the doctrine of Christ.
2. In his ignorance he is teaching something to the contrary and even justifying what he is teaching and condemning the truth.
3. Someone who knows the truth has compassion on him.

4. This second man prays to God that the Lord should open the first man's eyes to see the truth.
5. The Lord opens the eyes of the person, and he is convicted and converted to the Bible position about that aspect of the truth.

An act of intercession has taken place! As another example:
1. Someone is in need of money.
2. He is asking the Lord to give him money, or he may not even be asking God for money but trying to labour on his own.
3. Someone without money knows his need and has compassion on him.
4. The second person prays to the Lord to give the person in need the money.
5. The Lord hears the prayer and answers it, sending money to the person in need in any way that He chooses.

An act of intercession has taken place!

God has ordained the ministry of intercession; so that through it the needs of people which would otherwise not be met, are met. It is a part of His great love for man. In intercession, the helpless can receive help. The ignorant can become the informed, the untaught can become taught, et cetera.

In ordaining the ministry of intercession, God has ordered that one person be in a position of bringing limitless help to multitudes. Our great God has provided that one person can, through the ministry of intercession, change the destiny of
1. One other person,
2. Ten other people,
3. One hundred other people,

4. One village,
5. One town,
6. One tribe,
7. One nation,
8. One continent,
9. One planet.

The Lord has put it very bluntly. He says of Jerusalem: "*Run to and fro through the streets of Jerusalem, look and take note! Search her squares to see if you can find a man, one who does justice and seeks truth; that I may pardon her*" (Jeremiah 5: 1).

The Lord wanted just one person in Jerusalem who met His specification. If such a person were found, God would pardon. He was prepared to pardon the entire city because of one person. He has not changed his mind. One intercessor will do. He says, "*The people of the land have practised extortion and committed robbery; they have oppressed the poor and the needy, and have extorted from the sojourner without redress. And I sought 'for a man among them who should build up the wall and stand in the breach before me for the land, that I should not destroy it*" (Ezekiel 22:29-30).

The people committed many evils, the political leaders, the priests, the prophets, and the entire population. Regardless of this, the Lord was looking for just one intercessor who could change the situation. He did not say, "I sought for men among them," but, "And I sought for a man among them." Yes, He wanted a man. He still wants a man. One will serve the purpose!

God was saying that the political leaders could continue to be corrupt. The priests, and prophets (the religious leaders) could continue to be as bad as they were; the population could continue to be what it was. However, if He found just one intercessor, the nation would not be punished!

A GREAT CHALLENGE

As far as I am concerned, this is one of the greatest possibilities in the Word of God: the fact that God can act so mightily if He finds an intercessor. I also find it as the greatest challenge for me.

I need not complain about the political leadership.

I need not complain about the religious leadership.

I need not even complain about the failures of those who are of the household of faith.

I need not complain about people who are not coming to the Lord.

I need not complain about false doctrines. I need not complain about divided hearts.

I need not complain about there being no love for the Lord.

I need not complain about there being no love for the Lord's Word.

I need not complain about people backsliding. I need not complain about anything.

I need to face one question truly and honestly. The question is: "Am I an intercessor? Do I intercede?" If I am an intercessor, things ought to change. Things must change. Things will change.

If I am not an intercessor, I am the one to blame. The problem is not with God. The problem is not the others. The problem is me.

My dear brother and sister, as you read this, do you see that the problem could be you?

Do not move away from it. Are you the problem? Do not leave it there. Answer, "Yes," or "No!" Do not just answer, "Yes," or "No!". Are you prepared to do something about it?

Will you begin right now?

2

THE SHORTAGE OF INTERCESSORS

Intercessors are needed because they stand in the gap between man and God, causing God to bless man or bring well deserved punishment on man. Although intercessors are so im-portant, the tragedy is that they are in short supply. God Himself has complained that they are in short supply and that there is much judgment that would have been averted had He found an intercessor. The following Scriptures speak plainly: *"Run to and fro through the streets of Jerusalem, look and take note! Search her squares to see if you can find a man, one who does justice and seeks truth; that I may pardon her"* (Jeremiah 5: 1). No such man was found! That is most sad! The Lord continued to speak:

Though they say, "As the Lord lives,"
Yet they swear falsely.
"O Lord, do not thy eyes look for truth?
Thou hast smitten them,
but they felt no anguish;
thou hast consumed them,
but they refused to take correction.
They have made their faces harder than rock;

they have refused to repent.
Then I said, 'These are only the poor,
they have no sense;
for they do not know the way of the Lord,
the law of their God.
I will go to the great,
and will speak to them;
for they know the way of the Lord,
the law of their God.
But they all alike had broken the yoke,
they had burst the bonds"
(Jeremiah 5:2-5).

All of them continued in sin; all of them refused to take correction. There was no intercessor. Therefore, the Lord promised judgment instead of mercy. The Bible says: "*Therefore a lion from the forest shall slay them, a wolf from the desert shall destroy them. A leopard is watching against their cities, every one who goes out of them shall be torn in pieces; because their transgressions are many, their apostasies are great*" (Jeremiah 5:6).

If there had been an intercessor, although their transgressions were many and their apostasies great, the Lord would have pardoned. If there had been an intercessor, although their hearts were hardened, although they knowingly broke the yoke, athough they did not know the way of the Lord, although they did not know or keep the law of their God, He would nevertheless have pardoned them.

We may even say that calamity befell the people not because they sinned, but because there was no intercessor! The judgment of God has come and is coming on the world, not because the world has sinned, but because the world has sinned and there is no intercessor. If there had been one, the Lord would have pardoned them and they would have appeared as if they had never sinned.

"*The people of the land have practised extortion and committed robbery; they have oppressed the poor and needy, and have extorted from the sojourner without redress. And I sought for a man among them who should build up the wall and stand in the breach before me for the land, that I should not destroy it; but I found none. Therefore I have poured out my indignation upon them; I have consumed them with the fire of my wrath; their way have I requited upon their heads, says the Lord God*" (Ezekiel 22:29-31).

The people of the land

1. practised extortion,
2. committed robbery,
3. oppressed the poor,
4. oppressed the needy,
5. extorted from the sojourner without redress.

The people deserved judgment because God takes a hard look at such sins committed by people who know better. No one was interceding. No one pleaded before God. No one asked for pardon. God waited in vain for someone to do something about it, but nothing was done.

The Lord, instead of punishing them as they deserved, went out of His way to seek a man among them who could intercede. He looked and looked, but it was in vain. There was no one who could intercede. Yes, there was no one interceding and there was no one qualified to intercede.

Because the Lord found no one interceding and on searching He found no one who could intercede, He poured out His indignation. His wrath was there from the moment when the people began to commit sin. However, God held it under control. He held it under control as He waited for someone to intercede. He held it under control as He sought for an intercessor. When He found out after a diligent search that there was no intercessor, He acted. He pou-

red out that which He had held under control all this time. He laboured not to pour it out, but finally, since there was no one to build up the wall and stand in the breach before Him for the land; so that He might not destroy it, He destroyed it. He did the following:
1. He poured out His indignation upon them.
2. He consumed them with the fire of His wrath.
3. He requited their way upon their heads.

If there had been an intercessor, the Lord would not have done any of these, not because the people were sinless, but because the intercessor would have prevented God from doing it. They perished because they sinned and there was no one interceding. They perished because after they had sinned, God searched in vain for someone to intercede.

The Lord continues to speak out on the shortage of intercessors as follows:

"Behold, the Lord's hand is not shortened, that it cannot save, or his ear dull, that it cannot hear; but your iniquities have made a separation between you and your God, and your sins have hid his face from you so that he doesn't hear.

For your hands are defiled with blood and your fingers with iniquity; your lips have spoken lies, and your tongue muttered wickedness.

No one enters suit justly, no one goes to law honestly; they rely on empty pleas, they speak lies, they conceive mischief and bring forth iniquity.

They hatch adders' eggs, they weave the spider's web; he who eats their eggs dies, and from one which is crushed a viper is hatched.

Their webs will not serve as clothing; men will not cover themselves with what they make.

Their works are works of iniquity, and deeds of violence are in their hands.

Their feet run to evil, and they make haste to shed innocent blood; their thoughts are thoughts of iniquity, desolation and destruction are in their highways.

The way of peace they know not, and there is no justice in their paths; they have made their roads crooked, no one who goes in them knows peace" (Isaiah 59:1-8).

That was their condition. They knew it to be their condition, and they cried out, saying:

"*Therefore justice is far from us, and righteousness does not overtake us;*

We look for light, and behold, darkness, and for brightness, but we walk in gloom.

We grope for the wall like the blind, we grope like those who have no eyes;

we stumble at noon as in the twilight, among those in full vigour we are like dead men.

We all growl like bears, we moan and moan like doves; we look for justice, but there is none;

for salvation, but it is far from us.

For our transgressions are multiplied before thee, and our sins testify against us;

for our transgressions are with us, and we know our iniquities: transgressing, and denying the Lord, and turning away from following our God, speaking oppression and revolt, conceiving and uttering from the heart lying words.

Justice is turned back, and righteousness stands afar off; for truth has fallen in the public squares, and uprightness cannot enter.

Truth is lacking, and he who departs from evil makes himself a prey" (Isaiah 59:9-15).

The sad thing is that they acknowledged their sin but they did not do anything about it. They acknowledged their sin, but they did not repent! Because that was the situation, the Bible says:

"*The Lord saw it, and it displeased him that there was no justice. He saw that there was no man, and wondered that there was no one to intervene*" (Isaiah 59:15-16). "*And he saw that there was no man, and wondered that there was no intercessor*" (Isaiah 59: 16, KJV). God does not normally wonder. However, He wondered, not because of their sin, but because there was no one to intervene; there was no one to intercede. They sinned, but things would have been different had there been an intercessor to intervene. Intercessors are people who intervene. God was not looking for many of them. He was looking for one intercessor. One would have been enough. He would have intervened and things would have been different. He wanted that one should come Forth, but none was forthcoming. Because none was forthcoming, God was compelled by divine justice to do the next thing. The Bible says:

"*Then his own arm brought victory, and his righteousness upheld him. He put on righteousness as a breastplate, and a helmet of salvation upon his head; he put on garments of vengeance for clothing, and wrapped himself in fury as a mantle. According to their deeds, so will he repay, wrath to his adversaries, requital to his enemies; to the coastlands he will render requital*"

(Isaiah 59: 16-18).

Because there was no intercessor, God stepped in. His own arm brought victory to Himself. He upheld his righteousness by punishing the people. Yes, "He put on garments of vengeance for clothing and wrapped himself in fury as a mantle." He paid the people according to their deeds.

We can clearly say that without intercessors there will be judgment! Without intercessors there must be judgment!!

We can also say that normally, intercessors will change the situation. The question is, "Where are they?" God is looking for them. When will He find them? Will the situation continue? It continued in the days of the prophet Isaiah. The Bible says:

> "*Who is this that comes from Edom, in crimsoned garments from Bozrah, he that is glorious in his apparel, marching in the greatness of his strength?*
>
> *'It is I, announcing vindication, mighty to save.'*
>
> *Why is thy apparel red, and thy garments like his that treads in the wine press?*
>
> *I have trodden the wine press alone, and from the peoples no one was with me; I trod them in my anger and trampled them in my wrath; their lifeblood is sprinkled upon my garments, and I have stained all my raiment. For the day of vengeance was in my heart, and my year of redemption has come.*
>
> *I looked, but there was no one to help; I was appalled, but there was no one to uphold; so my own arm brought me victory, and my wrath upheld me.*
>
> *I trod down the peoples in my anger, I made them drunk in my wrath, and I poured out their lifeblood on the earth*"
>
> (Isaiah 63: 1-6).

We see here the same situation as before. There was sin. The Lord wanted to show mercy if He found an intercessor. Did He find any? He did not. He looked, but there was no one to help. He was appalled; but there was no one to uphold.

Because there was no one to uphold, He trod down the people in His anger and poured out their lifeblood on the earth. Had there been an intercessor, one to help, one to uphold, things would have been different.

Had there been just one person, all the rest would have received mercy, but as it was, all suffered because there was no intercessor!

THE REALITY OF THE SHORTAGE

If it were a man who sought for intercessors but did not find them, one could console oneself by saying that the search was not thorough. However, the search was made by the God from whom nothing is hidden. He said, "*Run to and fro through the streets of Jerusalem, look and take note! Search her squares to see if you can find a man, one who does justice and seeks truth; that I may pardon her*" (Jeremiah 5: 1). "*The Lord saw it, and it displeased him that there was no justice. He saw that there was no man, and wondered that there was no one to intervene*" (Isaiah 59: 15-16). "*I looked, but there was no one to help; I was appalled, but there was no one to uphold*" (Isaiah 63:5).

The shortage is so real that God searches in vain! It is so real that God wonders! It is such that God is appalled!

DOES IT MATTER TO YOU?

Because there was no intercessor, God brought judgment. What He did then He will do today. The sinful condition of the people in the world, on the continents, in the nations, and in the cities has not changed. God has not changed. His righteous demands have not changed. He will bring judgment, unless He finds an intercessor. In fact, His judgment is imminent. If it comes, it will be devastating. Does it matter to you that He will soon act in that way? Does it not matter to you that multitudes might soon perish? Does it not matter that the grain might soon be judged? If it matters to you, will you do something about it? If you intend to do something about it, will you not start today? Tomorrow may be too late. It could be that the sins of your continent, nation, tribe, city, assembly, and family have been heaping up before God for years and that He has been waiting for a long time for an intercessor. It could be that today a point will be reached where it will be too late to intercede. While there remain a few hours before the wrath of God is poured out, will you not step into the gap? Will you not do something about it?

SELF-DESTRUCTION

It could be that you are selfish and do not care about the fate of your continent, nation, tribe, city, assembly, or family. Because you do not care, you do not want to step into the gap and intercede. Maybe you are saying, "*Let the worst come if it must.*" That is all right; it will come. However, have you realized that when God's judgment comes, it will fall on them and on you? The Lord said, "*And I sought for a man among them who should build up the wall and stand in the breach before me for the land, that I should not destroy it; but I found none. Therefore I have poured out my indignation upon them; I have consumed them with the fire of my wrath; their way have I requited upon their heads, says the Lord God*" (Ezekiel 22:30-31).

When the Lord's wrath is poured out upon them, it will be poured out upon you as well. When the Lord consumes them with the fire of His wrath, you too will be consumed. When the Lord requites their way upon their heads, your own way will be requited upon your own head. You cannot say, "I am perfect. There is no ground on which my way can be requited upon my head." If you have never sinned and have obeyed God perfectly in all things, you could think that way. If, on the other hand, you have sinned, even once, you will be in trouble. Not to intercede will turn out to be self-destruction. You had better do something about it. You had better act now! Save yourself and your people from the well-earned wrath of God.

We have seen that intercessors are in short supply. We have also seen that their absence means that judgment must come upon the people. The question then arises as to why there is such a shortage of intercessors. The reasons are obvious. We shall look at them briefly.

3

WHY IS THERE SUCH A SHORTAGE OF INTERCESSORS ?

1. INTERCESSORS MUST STAND IN GOD'S PRESENCE

The Lord said, "*I sought for a man among them who should build up the wall and stand in the breach before me for the land, that I should not destroy it*" (Ezekiel 22:30). "*You have not gone up into the breaches, or built up a wall for the house of Israel, that it might stand in battle in the day of the Lord. They have spoken falsehood and divined a lie; they say, 'Says the Lord,' when the Lord has not sent them, and yet they expect him to fulfil their word*" (Ezekiel 13:5-6).

An intercessor must stand before God. He must stay in God's presence. This requires that he knows God. He must be a person who has put on God. He must be a person who has learnt to move away from man and from things and learnt to draw near to God and live in His presence. He cannot intercede from a distance.

He can only intercede from the very presence of God. .

Moses went away into God's presence each time to intercede for the children of Israel. Of Abraham the intercessor it is said:

"*Abraham still stood before the Lord. Then Abraham drew near, and said, 'Wilt thou indeed destroy the righteous with the wicked?'*" (Genesis 18:22-23). He stood before the Lord and he drew near unto the

Lord. Without being able to stand in God's presence, without being able to draw near unto the Lord, he would not have been able to intercede.

One reason why intercessors are in such short supply is that believers who ought to intercede cannot stand in God's presence. They cannot draw near Him because of their sin that is not acknowledged, confessed, and forsaken.

The Word of the Lord says:

"Who shall ascend the hill of the Lord? And who shall stand in his holy place?

He who has clean hands and a pure heart, who does not lift up his soul to what is false, and does not swear deceitfully

(Psalm 24:3-4).

The sad reality is that there are very few believers who are pure in heart. There are very few who are truly true and practise no falsehood in thought, word, or action. Because such are few, very few, there are very few who can ascend the hill of the Lord and stand in His holy place, the place of intercession! Permit me to ask you some personal questions:

1. Are your hands clean?
2. Is your heart pure?
3. Do you not lift up your soul to that which is false?
4. Do you never utter a word or carry out an action that is false or deceitful?

If your answers to these questions satisfy the heart of God, then you may become an intercessor. If they do not, then you need to repent right now. Unless you repent and get right with God, all your praying is noise. You cannot intercede. You cannot draw near God, because your sin has created a barrier between you and Him. You can lift the barrier now through acknowledging your sin, repenting, and forsaking it.

Standing in God's presence means that you are not only prepared to acknowledge, confess, and forsake sin at once, but you are prepared to do it continuously. There will be things to confess tomorrow that cannot be confessed today, because they are not yet seen as sins or weights. Light will come in the future, and the one who is prepared to stand in God's presence must be prepared for continuous acknowledgement, confession, and forsaking of sin. How sad that there are few of God's children who are prepared for that kind of intimate walk with God!

Another thing about standing in God's presence is that those who are to stand there must deny themselves every day and take up their crosses and follow the interceding Christ. This means, first of all, that they are prepared to say, "No," and to put away every motive, thought, word, and action that the Holy Spirit forbids either through the written Word or through His indwelling. This is denying yourself. Secondly, it means that you "are prepared to do everything that the Holy Spirit either through the Word or through His indwelling, commands you to do. This is taking up your cross. Those who thus deny themselves and take up their crosses daily will continue to stand in the presence of the Lord and can continue to intercede. When anyone ceases to deny himself and to take up his cross, he also moves away from God's presence, and that makes intercession impossible for such a person.

Standing in God's presence also involves a pre-occupation with God! It means that the person sets his heart to seek Him, find Him, know Him, and love Him. Such can enter more fully into the ministry of intercession, but because such are few, intercessors are few.

Standing in God's presence is a lonely business. Only those who have learnt to seek, find, know, and love Him can stand in His presence for a long time. Others occasionally make trips into His presence, rattle off a few words, and quickly run away. Intercessors have learnt how to enter into His presence, how to tune in to Him, and how to be lost in Him. They find their greatest joy and their greatest fulfilment in His presence. Consequently, they are able to stay in His presence until the task is accomplished. Once Moses needed to labour in intercession in the presence of God for forty days. He stayed away from man and was absorbed with God for that length of time. During that period, he interceded and moved God to spare His sinning people.

2. INTERCESSORS MUST STAND

Standing in the gap before God on behalf of the people also includes standing in battle. The intercessor is up against the enemy. He meets God and intercedes before God. He also meets the enemy and fights against him. The whole wrath of Satan is vented upon intercessors. They are people who frustrate his purposes and bring his schemes to nought. He would rather have God pour out His wrath on the people. He rejoices when it happens, and his kingdom prospers as it is being done. When an intercessor rises to stand in the gap so that the wrath of God is not poured out, Satan is furious against him. Later on, we shall look more carefully into the subject of the attack of Satan on the intercessor and the way of deliverance. For now we say that the intercessor is always under attack by the enemy. These attacks destroy many who have just begun their careers in the ministry of intercession. They are discouraged and give up. Others are very violently opposed, so much that they do not even start in the ministry of intercession. That is why intercessors are in short supply. Those who succeed as intercessors are those who have learnt how to wrestle with God and wrestle against Satan. The Bible says:

"Therefore take the whole armour of God, that you may be able to withstand in the evil day, and having done all, to stand. Stand therefore, having girded your loins with truth, and having put on the breastplate of

righteousness, and having shod your feet with the equipment of the gospel of peace; besides all these, take the shield of faith, with which you can quench all the flaming darts of the evil one. And take the helmet of salvation, and the sword of the Spirit, which is the word of God. Pray at all times in the Spirit, with all prayer and supplication. To that end keep alert with all perseverance, making supplication for all the saints, and also for me, that utterance may be given me in opening my mouth boldly to proclaim the mystery of the gospel, for which I am an ambassador in chains; that I may declare it boldly, as I ought to speak"

(Ephesians 6: 13-20).

The intercessor must learn to stand against Satan and to stand before God. The two acts must take place simultaneously. With one hand he must stand before the Lord, pleading, supplicating. With the other hand he must stand against Satan, destroying and bringing to nought all his plans and all his attacks.

How many believers are prepared for that kind of ministry? How many are able to stand before God and against Satan? That is the intercessor's lot, and that explains why they are very few. Oh, that God would transform me into a more able intercessor! Oh, that you would hear His voice, obey Him, follow Him, and take your place among those who intercede. Victory could depend on you. Why not act now?

3. INTERCESSORS MUST BUILD UP THE HEDGE

When the need of intercessors is most urgent, there is often a clear violation of God's law. There is a moral breakdown. The intercessor has to build up that which is broken, at least in his own life, before he can intercede for the others.

Take, for example, the situation of a nation that is under judgment because of falsehood, corruption, and selfishness. These are broken hedges in God's moral order. The intercessor must ensure that there is no falsehood, corruption, or selfishness in his life. He must make sure that while others may be practising these things on a large scale, he is not carrying them out on a small scale or in a subtle way. He must be correct. If these evils are found in his life even to a small extent, they will disqualify him from interceding. Therefore, radical repentance and radical restitution are indispensable. This means building up the hedge. With his own hedge built up, one can intercede for God's mercy on those whose hedges are yet broken. Daniel did this. He con-fessed his own sins and then those of his people. Nehemiah did the same. Because those who are prepared to deal with sin in their lives so thoroughly are in short supply, intercessors are in short supply.

Will you let the situation continue to be so? Will you not arise and put away every idol from your heart and life? Will you not arise and put away that sin that clings so closely, abandon it completely, be restored to the Lord, and find your place among God's intercessors? You do well to act today. You do well to act now!

4. INTERCESSORS MUST PRESS ON UNTIL VICTORY IS WON

There are many believers who are prepared to be involved in minor skirmishes for the Lord. However, there are few who are prepared for sustained battle! An intercessor who is bent on winning must go out to battle and be prepared to put in all that he has and to remain at the battlefront of intercession until the Lord answers. Such are oblivious of what it will cost them. They are also oblivious of the time it will cost them. If the battle takes minutes, they will enter into it and fight through to victory. If, on the other hand, the battle takes hours, days, weeks, or years, they are prepared to press on without relenting. If it costs them one night, ten nights, or one hundred nights of sleeplessness and wrestling, if it costs them their health and all, they nevertheless go on without counting the cost. They refuse to focus on what it is costing them. Rather, they focus on the Lord and on the battle that must be won. They "see" the day of God's mercy, of God's move, of God's blessing and, by faith, they press on. The Lord in talking of some such intercessors, said:

"Upon your walls, O Jerusalem, I have set watchmen; all the day and all the night they shall never be silent. You who put the Lord in remembrance, take no rest, and give him no rest until he establishes Jerusalem and makes it a praise in the earth"

(saiah 62:6-7).

The intercessor knows that he must continue to intercede: "Until he establishes Jerusalem and makes it a praise in the earth." That is the time when his task will be finished. He, therefore, presses on night and day, taking no rest and giving God no rest, until it is done.

If many believers were prepared for such labours, there would be many intercessors. Unfortunately, most believers are at ease: They want the things that are easy and, thereby, they miss God's best.

May the Lord move by His Holy Spirit so that the situation be changed! May the saints rise up from slumber and team up with God; so that the situation is changed! May you and I act today. May the result be the raising up of a people who will say with the Lord:

"For Zion's sake I will not keep silent, and for Jerusalem's sake I will not rest, until her vindication goes forth as brightness, and her salvation as a burning torch.

The nations shall see your vindication, and all the kings your glory; and you shall be called by a new name which the mouth of the Lord will give.

You shall be a crown of beauty in the hand of the Lord, and a royal diadem in the hand of your God.

You shall no more be termed Forsaken, and your land shall no more be termed Desolate; but you shall be called My Delight is in her, and your land Married; for the Lord delights in you, and your land shall be mar-

ried. .

For as a young man marries a virgin, so shall your sons marry you, and as the bridegroom rejoices over the Bride, so shall your God rejoice over you"
(Isaiah 62: 1-5).

May this be said of the Jerusalem of Yaounde, Lagos, Cairo, London, Paris, Washington, Tokyo, et cetera. May it be said because you and I have interceded and God has moved. May it be said because you and I and many others have paid the price, moved into the gap, and interceded. May it be said that by so doing you and I have brought the tragedy of the shortage of intercessors to an end. Praise the Lord!

4

THE INTERCESSOR'S HEART : TOTAL IDENTIFICATION

It is possible to be burdened for the plight of others and pray for them. However, the matter of intercession becomes very different when the intercessor identifies himself completely with the people for whom he is interceding. Because he has chosen to identify himself with them, what happens to them will happen to him. He, therefore, labours in prayer for them with the same intensity with which he normally petitions his own cause before the Lord.

The matter of identification is shown clearly in the following narrative from the Word:

"And he said, 'What then is to be done for her?'

Gehazi answered, 'Well, she has no son, and her husband is old.'

He said, 'Call her.'

And when he had called her, she stood in the doorway.

And he said, 'At this season, when the time comes round, you shall embrace a son.'

And she said, 'No, my lord, O man of God; do not lie to your maidservant.'

But the woman conceived, and she bore a son about that time the following spring, as Elisha had said to her.

When the child had grown, he went out one day to his father among the reapers. And he said to his father, 'Oh, my head, my head!'

The father said to his servant, 'Carry him to his mother.' And when he had lifted him, and brought him to his mother, the child sat on her lap till noon, and then died. And she went up and laid him on the bed of the man of God, and shut the door upon him, and went out.

Then she called to her husband, and said, 'Send me one of the servants and one of the asses, that I may quickly go to the man of God, and come back again.'

And he said, 'Why will you go to him today? It is neither new moon nor sabbath.'

She said, 'It will be well.' Then she saddled the ass, and she said to her servant, 'Urge the beast on; do not slacken the pace for me unless I tell you.' So she set out, and came to the man of God at Mount Carmel.

When the man of God saw her coming, he said to Gehazi his servant, 'Look, yonder is the Shunammite; run at once to meet her, and say to her, Is it well with you? Is it well with your husband? Is it well with the child?'

And she answered, 'It is well.' And when she came to the mountain to the man of God, she caught hold of his feet. And Gehazi came to thrust her away.

But the man of God said, 'Let her alone, for she is in bitter distress; and the Lord has hidden it from me, and has not told me.'

Then she said, 'Did I ask my lord for a son? Did I not say, Do not deceive me?'

He said to Gehazi, 'Gird up your loins, and take my staff in your hand, and go. If you meet any one, do not salute him; and if any one salutes you, do not reply; and lay my staff upon the face of the child.'

Then the mother of the child said, 'As the Lord lives, and as you yourself live, I will not leave you.'

So he arose and followed her. Gehazi went on ahead and laid the staff upon the face of the child, but there was no sound or sign of life.

Therefore he returned to meet him, and told him, 'The child has not awaked.'

When Elisha came into the house, he saw the child lying dead on his bed. So he went in and shut the door upon the two of them, and prayed *to the Lord. Then he went up and lay upon the child, putting his mouth upon his mouth, his eyes upon his eyes, and his hands upon his hands; and as he stretched himself upon him, the flesh of the child became warm. Then he got up again, and walked once to and fro in the house, and went up, and stretched himself upon him; the child sneezed seven times, and the child opened his eyes.*

Then he summoned Gehazi and said, 'Call this Shunammite.' So he called her.

And when she came to him, he said, 'Take up your son.'

She came and fell at his feet, bowing to the ground; then she took up her son and went out"

(II Kings 4: 14-37).

As is seen in this story, the child was not brought back to life when he was touched with the prophet's staff. He only came back to life when there was total identification of the prophet with him. The Lord could have stayed in heaven and sent an angel to come and handle the problem of sin. He did not do it. He Himself came down to earth and became a man. He identified Himself with man completely. He also identified with the sin of man. He Himself became sin so that He might save sinners. The Bible says: "*For our sake he made him to be sin who knew no sin, so that in him we might become the righteousness of God*" (II Corinthians 5:21). It would have been impossible for Him to save sinners without becoming one with them. Even though He was without any personal sin, He bore the sins of all men upon Himself and by that He became the Saviour.

Many of the great intercessors of the Bible identified themselves with those for whom they interceded. We shall look at a few examples.

1. NEHEMIAH

The Bible says:

"*The words of Nehemiah the son of Hacaliah.*

Now it happened in the month of Chislev, in the twentieth year, as I was in Susa the capital, that Hanani, one of my brethren, came with certain men out of Judah; and I asked them concerning the Jews that survived, who had escaped exile, and concerning Jerusalem.

And they said to me, 'The survivors there in the province who escaped exile are in great trouble and shame; the wall of Jerusalem is broken down, and its gates are destroyed by fire.'

When I heard these words I sat down and wept, and mourned for days; and I continued fasting and praying before the God of heaven.

And I said, 'O Lord God of heaven, the great and terrible God who keeps covenant and steadfast love with those who love him and keep his commandments; let thy ear be attentive, and thy eyes open, to hear the prayer of thy servant which I now pray before thee day and night for the people of Israel thy servants, confessing the sins of the people of Israel, which we have sinned against thee.

Yea, I and my father's house have sinned.

We have acted very corruptly against thee, and have not kept the commandments, the statutes, and the ordinances which thou didst command thy servant Moses'"

(Nehemiah 1:1-7).

Nehemiah had not actually sinned. He was faithful to the Lord. However, he was a part of the people of Israel and they had sinned. He identified fully with their sin.

He said:

1. We have sinned against thee.
2. We have acted very corruptly against Thee.
3. I and my father's house have sinned.
4. We have not kept Thy

a) commandments,
b) statutes,
c) ordinances.

Do you see the words "we," "I and my father's house," et cetera? He was not just talking to the Lord about them. It was about him and them. The people of Israel had sinned, and even though he as an individual had not sinned, because his people had sinned, he considered that he had sinned and, therefore, interceded for them and for himself. He and they became as if they were inseparable in the sin and the punishment. He and they became one in repentance and the plea for pardon. Because they did not see the gravity of their sin or were unwilling to repent, he needed to repent for all of them. He put the Lord in a position in which He had to forgive all the people, if He was not going to allow him to suffer for the sins of the others! God forgave the people and granted his request.

2. DANIEL

Daniel said:

"Then I turned my face to the Lord God, seeking him by prayer and supplications with fasting and sackcloth and ashes.

I prayed to the Lord my God, and made confession, saying, "O Lord, the great and terrible God, who keepest covenant and steadfast love with those who love him and keep his com-mandments,

We have sinned and done wrong and acted wickedly and rebelled, turning aside from thy commandments and ordinances; we have not listened to thy servants the prophets, who spoke in thy name to our kings, our princes, and our fathers, and to all the people of the land.

To thee, O Lord, belongs righteousness, but to us confusion of face, as at this day, to the men of Judah, to the inhabitants of Jerusalem, and to all Israel, those that are near and those that are far away, in all lands to which thou hast driven them, because of the treachery which they have committed against thee.

To us, O Lord, belongs confusion of face, to our kings, to our princes, and to our fathers, because we have sinned against thee " (Daniel 9:3-8).

Do you see the recurrent "we"? Daniel identified himself completely with the others in their sin. He maintained a close walk with God, but as an intercessor on their behalf, he became totally identified with them in their sin, rebellion, and folly.

3. THE LORD JESUS

The Lord Jesus is the supreme Intercessor. He identified Himself fully with those for whom He was to intercede. The Bible says of Him:

"Who though he was in the form of God, did not count equality with God a thing to be grasped, but emptied himself, taking the form of a servant, being born in the likeness of men. And being found in human form he humbled himself and became obedient unto death even death on a cross"

(Philippians 2:8).

It will take the putting off of our mortal bodies and human minds to truly fathom what was involved in the incarnation. To say the least, it was awful humiliation that God should put on human flesh and actually come to earth and live like a man. However, we know that He did. Without that, He could not have become our Saviour. He not only became man. As a man, He fully identified Himself with our sin. The Bible says: *"For our sake he made him to be sin who knew no sin, so that in him we might become the righteousness of God"* (II Corinthians 5:21). In addition to identifying Himself with humanity in her sin, He also identified Himself with humanity in being separated from God because He bore our sin, and in tasting death. His identification with man was full and complete.

4. MOSES

Even though Moses did not sin when the rest of the children of Israel sinned, he nevertheless identified himself fully with them, consequently, saying to God:

"If thy presence will not go with me, do not carry us up from here. For how shall it be known that I have found favour in thy sight, I and thy people? Is it not in thy going with us, so that we are distinct, I and thy people, from all other people that are upon the face of the earth?"
(Exodus 33: 15-16).

Do you see the words that indicate identification "us," "I and thy people," and "we"? Moses was fully identified with the people for whom he was interceding. He was so identified with them that he was prepared to give away his place in the Kingdom of God for their salvation.

5. THE EXAMPLES OF THE HIGH PRIEST AND THE PRIESTS

The Lord said of Aaron the high priest:

"So Aaron shall bear the names of the sons of Israel in the breastpiece of judgment upon his heart, when he goes into the holy place, to bring them to continual remembrance before the Lord.

And in the breastpiece of judgment you shall put the Urim and Thummim, and they shall be upon Aaron's heart, when he goes in before the Lord; thus Aaron shall bear the judgment of the people of Israel upon his heart, before the Lord continually.
(Exodus 28:29-30).

The Bible again says:

"Now Moses diligently inquired about the goat of the sin offering, and behold, it was burned!

And he was angry with Eleazar and Ithamar, the sons of Aaron who were left, saying, 'Why have you not eaten the sin offering in the place of the sanctuary, since it is a thing most holy and has been given to you that you may bear the iniquity of the congregation, to make atonement for them before the Lord?'"

(Leviticus 10: 16-17).

The Bible again says:

"And you shall make a plate of pure gold, and engrave on it, like the engraving of a signet, 'Holy to the Lord.

And you shall fasten it on the turban by a lace of blue; it shall be on the front of the turban.

It shall be upon Aaron's forehead, and Aaron shall take upon himself any guilt incurred in the holy offering which the people of Israel hallow as their holy gifts; it shall always be upon his forehead, that they may be accepted before the Lord"

(Exodus 28:36-38).

We can draw the following conclusions from these passages of Scripture:

1. Aaron was to bear the names of the sons of Israel in the breastpiece of judgment upon his heart. He thus in a sense bore upon himself judgment for their sins. It is as if he took the judgment for their sins upon himself and bore it until he was able to intercede for them when he went into the holy place, i.e, God's presence (the place of intercession).

2. Aaron was to bring the people whose names he bore

continually before the Lord, pleading for mercy on their behalf.
3. The judgment of the people of Israel was to be borne on Aaron's heart. This indicates how intimately united to their judgment he was to be.
4. He was to do it continually, tirelessly, regardless of the frequency of their sin.
5. His sons who were priests were also to bear the iniquity of the congregation to make atonement for them before the Lord.
6. Aaron was to take upon himself any guilt incurred in the holy offering that the people of Israel hallowed as their gift.
7. Aaron was to bear it on his forehead always; so that they might be accepted before the Lord.

This means that when God looked at Aaron (since He always looks at the heart), what He saw first was that which distinguished Aaron as an intercessor. When man looked at Aaron (and man always looks at the forehead first), what he saw was the distinguishing marks of his ministry as an intercessor. So Aaron was inwardly and outwardly marked as an intercessor. It was his primary ministry. He stood in the gap between the people and God. He took their sacrifices and he brought them to God. He did it without ceasing. All his life was wrapped around that ministry. He laboured to walk close to God, so that he might perform it satisfactorily.

His children were involved in the same ministry. They could lose their lives for any carelessness on their part with regard to that ministry, and two of them were smitten by the Lord for carelessness in that ministry.

Aaron stood between the people and God, ministering to Him on their behalf and making atonement to Him on their behalf. That, in a sense, is what intercession is all about. I am touched by the delicate nature of that ministry. They went into God's presence for the people. He was in touch with God. He feared God. He knew that he could die if he did anything in a way that God did not want. He knew that he had no right to do anything according to his own imagination. So he heard God's voice, trembled before Him, and obeyed Him accordingly.

The thing that worries me most is that I do not know the same fear of the Lord in my heart. I do not have the same sensitivity towards Him. I labour to know His will and to do it, but I do not have the same fear that Aaron had, even though I have been in the ministry of intercession for some time. Aaron knew that any failure in obedience would lead to death. I, too, know that any disobedience will lead to some measure of death in the relationship between my God and myself, but my heart does not seem to know the same degree of fear. It is as if my heart knows some measure of hardening. Lord, have mercy on me. Touch my hardened heart and grant that it be sensitive towards You in all things. Lord, grant that Your fear should not only be in my heart; grant that it should possess my heart and my total being. Reveal Yourself to me, O Lord my God, so that I may know You better and fear You as I ought to.

THE MEASURE OF LEADERSHIP

What is the extent of a man's leadership before men? The answer can be varied, but it will include all that he can coax, deceive, draw, force, or crush to follow him wholeheartedly, half-heartedly, or in physical appearance only. This may include the limits of a nation(s) or continent(s). It may also include a denomination, groups of local churches, a local assembly, or some individuals. The people may mean much to the leader, or they may mean nothing to him. He may give himself to them, or he may give nothing to them and instead exploit and plunder them. That is the extent of a man's leadership before man. It could include millions of people or just two or three people.

What is the extent of a man's leadership before God? I believe that the extent of a man's leadership before God is determined by the number of people whose judgment and sin he carries in his heart in intercession before God. The extent of his leadership is determined by the number of people with whose sin he identifies completely, taking all their sin and the consequence of their sin upon himself and interceding for them as desperately as he would do if he himself had sinned.

If a man can take on himself the sins and judgment of one person, then he is the leader of one person. If it is ten people, then he is the leader of ten people. If it is a thousand, ten thou-sand, 1 million, or 1 billion people, then that is the extent of his leadership.

It is immediately obvious that there are many denominational leaders, local assembly leaders, et cetera, who are not leaders before God. Before God they are leading no one. They may carry very big names and organise very big programmes and even have worldwide influence before man, but before God they are nothing. Their problem is that they have never known how to be fully and completely identified with the sin, failure, and judgment of anyone and thus carried that one's sin, failure, and judgment in their hearts continually in intercession before God. They have never known heartache at the sin of anyone and restless intercession before God until the judgment that the person was meant to have has been averted by the Lord.

The person who can talk lightly about the sin of another is not that person's leader. He cannot intercede for him. The person who when he hears about the sin of another is not broken-hearted because of the damage that the sin has brought to the person, is not that one's leader. He cannot intercede for him. The person who can divulge secret information about the sin of another is not that one's leader. He cannot intercede for him.

A leader before God leads to the extent to which he can take the sins of the people on himself and bear the judgment that they deserve. Such receive the knowledge of the sin committed with deep pain and agony. They carry it in their hearts and do nothing to expose the sinful one to man. They cover his sin before man and carry it as if it were theirs, and begin to wrestle with God in intercession, until He has pardoned. Such do not raise the sin committed in a prayer meeting of two or more people, for this would be to expose the person first to man and probably secondly to God.

A true leader always has a burden. He is always bearing in his heart the judgment for the sins of the people and on his forehead any guilt incurred: He is to some extent like the Son of man, the Man of Sorrows who bore the sin and the sickness of this world upon himself and they made Him so ugly that the Bible says that there was no comeliness in Him that we should desire Him.

A true leader is ever interceding. He labours at it night and day. If he leads two people, he carries them and intercedes for them. If he leads ten, he does the same for them, and if a thousand, he does the same again. He cannot lead more people than his heart has expanded to bear before the Lord. His leadership capacity is determined, not by his administrative skills or his power to pull money out of people's pockets, but by his strength as an intercessor before God.

THE LORD COMMANDED EZEKIEL TO BEAR THE PUNISHMENT OF ISRAEL AND JUDAH

The Lord said to Ezekiel:

"Then lie upon your left side, and I will lay the punishment of the house of Israel upon you; for the number of the days that you lie upon it, you shall bear their punishment.

For I assign to you a number of days, three hundred and ninety days, equal to the number of the years of their punishment; so long shall you bear the punishment of the house of Israel.

And when you have completed these, you shall lie down a second time, but on your right side, and bear the punishment of the house of Judah; forty days I assign you, a day for each year"

(Ezekiel 4:4-6).

It was a tough task. Can you imagine Ezekiel lying down nonstop for 390 days? Can you imagine that he lay for those 390 days on one side the left side without turning and without changing sides? Do you see that bearing the sins of others is no easy task? Do you see that intercession is no easy task? Do you see that identification is no easy task? Do you see that leadership of many people calls for extreme suffering on the part of the leader? Do you see that God's call to the all-important ministry of intercession is also a call to inescapable suffering in full measure? That is one of the reasons why intercessors are in short supply. Will you receive the Lord's strength and brave it out and become one of God's victorious minority? You can begin today. The Lord is willing to aid you to pay the price. God bless you.

PART 3

Daniel The Intercessor

1

DANIEL'S QUALIFICATION TO INTERCEDE

The Bible says:

"*In the first year of Darius the son of Ahasuerus, by birth a Mede, who became king over the realm of the Chaldeans—in the first year of his reign,*

I, Daniel, perceived in the books the number of years which, according to the word of the Lord to Jeremiah the prophet, must pass before the end of the desolations of Jerusalem, namely, seventy years....

Then I turned my face to the Lord God, seeking him by prayer and supplications with fasting and sackcloth and ashes.

I prayed to the Lord my God and made confession, saying,

'O Lord, the great and terrible God, who keepest covenant and steadfast love with those who love him and keep his com-mandments, we have sinned and done wrong and acted wickedly and rebelled, turning aside from thy commandments and ordinances; we have not listened to thy servants the prophets, who spoke in thy name to our kings, our princes, and our fathers, and to all the people of the land.

'To thee, O Lord, belongs righteousness, but to us confusion of face, as at this day, to the men of Judah, to the inhabitants of Jerusalem, to all Israel, those that are near and those that are far away in all the lands to which thou hast driven them, because of the treachery which they have committed against thee.

To us, O Lord, belongs confusion of face, to our kings, to our princes, and to our fathers, because we have sinned against thee.

To the Lord our God belong mercy and forgiveness; because we have rebelled against him, and have not obeyed the voice of the Lord our God by following his laws, which he set before us by his servants the prophets.

All Israel has transgressed thy law and turned aside, refusing to obey thy voice.

And the curse and oath which are written in the law of Moses the servant of God have been poured out upon us, because we have sinned against him.

He has confirmed his words, which he spoke against us and against our rulers who ruled us, by bringing upon us a great calamity; for under the whole heaven there has not been done the like of what has been done against Jerusalem.

As it is written in the law of Moses, all this calamity has come upon us, yet we have not entreated the favour of the Lord our God, turning from our iniquities and giving heed to thy truth.

"Therefore the Lord has kept ready the calamity and has brought it upon us; for the Lord our God is righteous in all the works which he has done, and we have not obeyed his voice.

And now, O Lord our God, who didst bring thy people out of the land of Egypt with a mighty hand, and hast made thee a name, as at this day, we have sinned, we have done wickedly.

O Lord, according to all thy righteous acts, let thy anger and thy wrath turn away from thy city Jerusalem, thy holy hill; because for our sins, and for the iniquities of our fathers, Jerusalem and thy people have become a byword among all who are round about us.

Now therefore, O our God, hearken to the prayer of thy servant and to his supplications, and for thy own sake, O Lord, cause thy face to shine upon thy sanctuary, which is desolate.

O my God, incline thy ear and hear, open thy eyes and behold our desolations, and the city which is called by thy name; for we do not present our 'supplications before thee on the ground of our righteousness, but on the ground of thy great mercy.

'O Lord, hear; O Lord, forgive; O Lord, give heed and act; delay not, *for thy own sake, O my God, because thy city and thy people are called by thy name.'*

While I was speaking and praying, confessing my sin and the sin of my people Israel, and presenting my supplication before the Lord my God for the holy hill of my God; while I was speaking in prayer, the man Gabriel, whom I had seen in the vision at the first, came to me in swift flight at the time of the evening sacrifice.

He came and said to me, 'O Daniel, I have now come out to give you wisdom and understanding.

At the beginning of your supplications a word went forth, and I have come to tell it to you, for you are greatly beloved; therefore consider the word and understand the vision.

Seventy weeks of years are decreed concerning your people and your holy city, to finish the transgression, to put an end to sin, and to atone for iniquity, to bring in everlasting righteousness, to seal both vision and prophet, and to anoint a most holy place.

Know therefore and understand that from the going forth of the word to restore and build Jerusalem to the coming of an anointed one, a prince, there shall be seven weeks.

Then for sixty-two weeks it shall be built again with squares and moat, but in a troubled time.

And after the sixty-two weeks, an anointed one shall be cut off, and shall have nothing; and the people of the prince who is to come shall destroy the city and the sanctuary.

Its end shall come with a flood, and to the end there shall be war; desolations are decreed.

And he shall make a strong covenant with many for one week; and for half of the week he shall cause sacrifice and offering to cease; and upon the wing of abominations shall come one who makes desolate, until the decreed end is poured out on the desolator'"

(Daniel 9:1-27).

DANIEL'S QUALIFICATION TO INTERCEDE

Not everyone can intercede. Intercession is carried out in the very presence of God. Anyone who is going to make progress in the ministry of intercession must be popular in the courts of God. He very often will be standing in the presence of God. He must be One who can stand there and be pleasing to God.

There is a sense in which all believers can intercede. There is a sense in which all believers can come with boldness into the presence of God. The Bible says:

"*This was according to the eternal purpose which he has realized in Christ Jesus our Lord, in whom we have boldness and confidence of access through our faith in him*"

(Ephesians 3: 11-12).

"*Therefore, brethren, since we have confidence to enter the sanctuary by the blood of Christ Jesus, by the new and living way which he opened for us through the curtain, that is, through his flesh, and since we have a great priest over the house of God, let us draw near with a true heart in full assurance of faith, with our hearts sprinkled clean from an evil conscience and our bodies washed with pure water*"

(Hebrews 10:19-22).

All believers who have their hearts sprinkled clean from an evil conscience and their bodies washed with pure water can intercede.

However, there is a plane of communion with God that is opened only to those who pay a special price. Daniel was a man who walked in this higher plane. He was told, "*You are greatly beloved*" (Daniel 9:23). "*O man greatly beloved*" (Daniel 10: 19). Daniel was greatly loved by the Lord. Was this love based on some whimsical, baseless emotion on God's part? The answer is, "No." Daniel laboured and walked with God and therefore became a man greatly beloved of God. What did he do? We shall just outline below the path that he trod in order to become one who was greatly beloved of the Lord. We write out that pathway because it is open to all blood-bought children of God. Any who want to walk in it can follow the example of Daniel and, thereby, qualify for a special place in the heart of God and in the ministry of intercession.

1. He did not complain about his lot. There were justifiable reasons for complaint. First of all, he was made a eunuch. His possibility of leading a normal sexual and married life was taken away from him. He could never become a husband. He could never become a father. He was without blemish. He was handsome and he was skilful in all wisdom. He was endowed with knowledge. He was endowed with understanding and learning and he was competent to serve in the king's palace, but he was a eunuch. However, he was satisfied; he was content even in that condition. He did not ask, "Of what use has my handsomeness been to me, since I can never attract a girl and be married to her?" He accepted this condition as God's ordering for his life and was thus content. Such men are rare and they satisfy God's heart. They are beloved of God. They are greatly beloved of Him. Secondly, Daniel was carried away from home at a tender age; so that he had to serve in a foreign land. He did not become bitter and full of complaints. He accepted his captivity as a sovereign act of God and knew that only the best could come out of it; for he loved the Lord and God was working out everything in his life for His highest glory and Daniel's best interest. The Bible says: "*We know that in everything God works for good with those who love him, who are called according to his purpose*" (Romans 8:28). Daniel knew this and was content. Those who truly know this are content, regardless of what may be happening to them.

2. He refused to compromise with regard to food and drink. The Bible says: "*The king assigned them a daily portion of the rich food which the king ate, and of the wine which he drank*" (Daniel 1:5). "*But Daniel resolved that he would not defile himself with the king's rich food, or with the wine which he drank; therefore he asked the chief of the eu-*

nuchs to allow him not to defile himself" (Daniel 1: 8). Many would have said, "I am a captive. Let me do as the Babylonians do. When I go back to Jerusalem, I will return to the demands of the religion of my people." Daniel knew his God and could not part with His demand under any condition. He would not disobey God in the matter of food and drink. He could do it because he was not a worshipper of food. He was not tempted by the opportunity offered to him to eat the food that the king ate and to drink the wine that he drank. Some would have said, "What an honour! Am I not great? How many people are ever so honoured?" By feeling so elevated, they would have fallen prey to the sin of pride and compromised. Daniel did not. He did not say, "I am being prepared for great opportunities. Let me not lose them by being narrow. What is really wrong with the king's food and wine? I will eat it and still believe in God in my heart." Daniel did not. He was more anxious to satisfy the heart of God than to gain all the glory of the world. He counted his fellowship with God and his position before God of far greater value than the throne of Babylon. Therefore, he refused to compromise.

3. He was a man of faith. He asked that he and the other Hebrew youths who were selected be fed with vegetables only and be given water to drink. He further asked that after ten days their appearance was to be compared with that of those who ate the king's rich food. That was done and they appeared before the king. They who ate only vegetables and drank only water looked better than those who ate the king's rich food. Daniel had believed that God would work, and He did. By believing God he pleased God and became greatly beloved by the Lord.

4. He was a man who sought God. When the king dreamt and demanded that the magicians, the enchanters, the sorcerers, and the Chaldeans tell him the dream or die, Daniel and his brethren were involved. What did he do? The Bible says: *"Then Daniel went to his house and made the matter known to Hananiah, Mishael, and Azariah,*

his companions, and told them to seek mercy of the God of heaven concerning this mystery, so that Daniel and his companions might not perish with the rest of the wise men of Babylon. Then the mystery was revealed to Daniel in a vision of the night. Then Daniel blessed the God of heaven" (Daniel 2:17-19).

5. He was interested in others. When Daniel told the king the dream and the interpretation thereof, the king honoured him: "*The king gave Daniel high honours and many great gifts, and made him ruler over the whole province of Babylon, and chief prefect over all the wise men of Babylon*" (Daniel 2:48). Daniel was not content to be exalted alone. The Bible says, "*Daniel made request of the king, and he appointed Shadrach, Meshach, and Abednego over the affairs of the province of Babylon; but Daniel remained at the king's court*" (Daniel 2:49). Daniel, in a way, gave away his appointment to others. He was so great that he could lift others to greatness without a thought for himself. He had truly died to the self-life. Such a spirit that has truly died to self-glory is precious in God's sight and makes its possessor beloved by God! The sad thing is that it is a rare spirit in an assembly that has known something of the true move of God; there are only a few who are prepared to tread the way of death to self. Lord, make me one such man.

6. Daniel fearlessly warned King Nebuchadnezzar. The king had a dream, and Daniel interpreted it. He did not fear the king but told him the whole truth, warning him and giving counsel. The Bible says: "*This is the interpretation, O king: It is a decree of the Most High, which has come upon my lord the king, that you shall be driven from among men, and your dwelling shall be with the beasts of the field; you shall be made to eat grass like an ox, and you shall be wet with the dew of heaven, and seven times shall pass over you, till you know that the Most High rules the kingdom of men, and gives it to whom he will. And as it was commanded to leave the stump of the roots of the tree, your kingdom shall be sure for you from the time that you know that Heaven rules. Therefore, O king, let my counsel be acceptable to you; break off your sins by practising righteousness, and your iniquities by showing mercy to the oppressed, that there may perhaps be a lengthening of your tranquillity*"

(Daniel 4:24-27). Daniel had nothing to defend. He had nothing to protect. He sought no favours from the king. Only God could grant him favours. Therefore, he told the king all the truth. He took God's side and enhanced his position in God's heart.

7. He fearlessly interpreted the handwriting on the wall and proclaimed the imminent death of the king. When King Belshazzar was desecrating the holy vessels that had been taken out of the temple by Nebuchadnezzar by drinking from them, he, his wives, and his concubines, the Lord sent the fingers of a man and they wrote his doom on the wall. Daniel was called in to interpret the writing on the wall. He was promised many things in the following words: "*You shall be clothed with purple, and have a chain of gold about your neck, and shall be the third ruler in the kingdom*" (Daniel 5: 16). This was if he interpreted the handwriting. He said, "Let your gifts be for yourself, and give your reward to another; nevertheless I will read the writing to the king and make known to him the interpretation." He then exposed the king's sin of not humbling his heart but rather of lifting up himself against the Lord of heaven. He then interpreted the handwriting that spelt the king's doom. There are not many who would tell rulers the verdict of God about them. Such have to have died to self completely; for what may a ruler whose sin is exposed to him not do? The king could cause Daniel to be hanged.

8. Daniel was fearless for his life. He was concerned only for the glory of God. Daniel was blameless. The Bible says: "*It pleased Darius to set over the kingdom a hundred and twenty satraps, to be throughout the whole kingdom; and over them three presidents, of whom Daniel was one, to whom these satraps should give account, so that the king might suffer no loss. Then this Daniel became distinguished above all the other presidents and satraps, because an excellent spirit was in him; and the king planned to set him over the whole kingdom. Then the presidents and the satraps sought to find a ground for complaint against Daniel with regard to the kingdom; but they could find no ground for complaint or any fault, because he was faithful, and no error or fault was found in him. Then*

these men said, 'We shall not find any ground for complaint against this Daniel unless we find it in connection with the law of his God'" (Daniel 6:1-5). Daniel was blameless. All who seek to advance in the ministry of intercession must also make progress in the School of Blamelessness. Blessed is the man whom the world will not find any ground of complaint against except in the matter of his faith. Lord, make me into such a man. Such are greatly beloved of the Lord!

9. He was a man to be plotted against. Daniel more or less committed the crime of distinguishing himself above the others through hard work, character, and service. He caused the others to be jealous of him. He did not boast. He had received much from the Lord. The Bible says: "*As for these four youths, God gave them learning and skill in all letters and wisdom, and Daniel had understanding in all visions and dreams*" (Daniel 1: 17). He had sought the Lord and received more. He was just superior to the rest! They could not stand him. His superiority disturbed them. He was superior, yet he did not talk of his superiority or boast about it. He was humble. He was meek. He held his great gifts and abilities under control. He did not talk of his accomplishments. He did not even do what most people do—advertise the flesh under the cover of a testimony to God's glory. The plotters set a trap. The Bible says: "*Then these presidents and satraps came by agreement to the king and said to him, 'O king Darius, live for ever! All the presidents of the kingdom, the prefects and the satraps, the counsellors and the governors are agreed that the king should establish an ordinance and enforce an interdict, that whoever makes petition to any god or man for thirty days, except to you, O king, shall be cast into the den of lions. Now, O king, establish the interdict and sign the document, so that it cannot be changed, according to the law of the Medes and the Persians, which cannot be revoked.' Therefore King Darius signed the document and interdict*" (Daniel 6:6-9). It is normal that the world and the religious systems will plot against those who put their trust in the Lord and are faithful. Are they plotting against you? That may be indicative of the fact that you are on God's side.

10. Daniel accepted the punishment of the world without complaining, taking his case up with God and with God alone. Daniel could have made a petition at the onset of things to show the king that all the others were not agreed and that what was thus said was a lie. He did not seek help from man. What did he do? The Bible says: "*When Daniel knew that the document had been signed, he went to his house where he had windows in his upper chamber open toward Jerusalem; and he got down upon his knees three times a day and prayed and gave thanks before his God, as he had done previously*" (Daniel 6: 10). Daniel was a man of prayer. He prayed three times a day. He was in control. He did not fret. He did not try to save his position. He did not say, "Since a trap has been set, let me not fall into it. Let me modify things." He sought only the favour of God, and he sought only to please God. He was beyond the protection of man. He had the strength of his convictions. He went ahead as usual. His daily life satisfied the heart of God and what was a crisis to others was no crisis to him. It was just the normal life of being faithful to the Lord in everything and letting the world do or say what it wants.

Daniel was found praying and then accused and thrown into the lions' den. He was at peace while the king was restless. His philosophy of life was like that of the Apostle Paul, who said, "*I do not account my life of any value nor as precious to myself, if only I may accomplish my course and the ministry which I received from the Lord Jesus, to testify to the gospel of the grace of God*" (Acts 20:24). Daniel did not count his life of any value. He only sought to be faithful to the Lord, and he was faithful. He was calm. He was in control. He had borne witness. He had testified to the Gospel of the grace of God. He was saying to the king as his companions had said earlier:

"*Nebuchadnezzar, we have no need to answer you in this matter. If it be so, our God whom we serve is able to deliver us from the burning fiery furnace; and he will deliver us out of your hand, O king.*

But if not, be it known to you, O king, that we will not serve your gods or worship the golden image which you have set up"

(Daniel 3: 16-18).

Daniel was not hurt by the lions. He testified that his God sent His angel and shut the lions' mouths. Yes, the Lord did send an angel and the lions' mouths were shut. However, He could also have allowed Daniel to be devoured by the lions. If that had happened, it would not have made Daniel any less a man of God. God has sovereign rights. He permitted James to be killed by Herod and saved Peter from prison and later allowed him to be crucified head down. Both James and Peter were faithful when God allowed one to be killed and the other to be released. What mattered was the purpose He had for each of them there. The one who was killed was not less faithful than the one who was miraculously released from prison. God could have miraculously released both, but He did not. He could have allowed both to be killed, but He did not. He just worked out His sovereign will. Peter, who was miraculously saved that time, was not miraculously delivered the time he was crucified head down. God could have delivered him even on that occasion, but God allowed him to be killed. He is in control. He knows what He is doing. He is working according to a master plan. Each faithful one is immortal until his life's work is done. The pathway of the faithful has all been planned by the Lord, and He will lead each into it. Of the men of faith the Bible says:

"For time would fail me to tell of Gideon, Barak, Samson, Jephthah, of David and Samuel and the prophets—who through faith conquered kingdoms, enforced justice, received promises, stopped the mouths of lions, quenched raging fire, escaped the edge of the sword, won strength out of weakness, became mighty in war; put foreign armies to flight. Women received their dead by resurrection"

(Hebrews 11:32-35).

These were all people of faith. They satisfied God's heart in these ways. They had faith to see God intervene in mighty ways. We can say that they had faith to be delivered so that they could continue to live for God.

Of others the Bible says: *"Others suffered mocking and scourging, and even chains and imprisonment.*

They were stoned, they were sawn in two, they were killed with the sword; they went about in skins of sheep and goats, destitute, afflicted, ill-treated—of whom the world was not worthy— wandering over deserts and mountains, and in dens and caves of the earth"

(Hebrews 11:36-38).

These were also people of faith. They had faith to suffer and faith to die. The faith to live and the faith to die are both very precious. All who would satisfy the heart of God must receive faith and live by it, regardless of whether it is manifested in living or in dying. All that must concern the faithful is the satisfaction of the heart of God, be it by dying or by living.

So Daniel satisfied the heart of God. He built the type of relationship with God that enabled him to carry out the ministry of intercession that we shall see in the next chapter.

The ministry of intercession is not just words. It is a life lived out before God. It is a life delivered from sin and self. It is a life lived in victory. It is a life poured out to God. It is a life that seeks the glory of God and the glory of God alone. Out of such a life intercession will flow out to God from the heart through the mouth in prayer. The power of intercession will always be proportional to the quality of the relationship between the intercessor and God. Those who are deeply united to the Lord will flow forth accordingly. Those who are superficial will also flow forth accordingly. If a person who has depth in the Lord does not find the words that are necessary to communicate what is flowing forth from his heart to God, he will limit his potential. If a person who is not deep with God uses his head to gather big thoughts and ideas around and borrows the sentiments of others and tries to so intercede, he will be deceiving himself.

Every intercessor must grow in union with God. He must grow in the knowledge of God in his heart. He must also grow in exercising the mind of Christ, which he has received. In that way, his mind will help his spirit to flow forth in power and with the appropriate words. Then there will be great victory to the glory of God. Amen.

THE GOAL OF INTERCESSION

Daniel's intercession was not just the pouring out of any thoughts to God. It was well thought-out. There was a goal in mind. He was interceding so that God might do a particular thing. That thing was clear. It was such that he could have been stopped at any moment and asked, "What do you want God to do?" And he would have given a very clear answer. The purpose of Daniel's intercession was to cause God to bring the desolation of Jerusalem to an end. Sometime during the intercession he spelt that purpose clearly to God. He said, "*O Lord, according to all thy righteous acts, let thy anger and thy wrath turn away from thy city Jerusalem, thy holy hill*" (Daniel 9: 16). He again stated what he wanted God to do in the next verse: "O Lord, cause thy face to shine upon thy sanctuary which is desolate." Before anyone begins to intercede, he must ask himself very clearly, "What do I want God to do? When God hears this prayer, what will be produced?" The answer must be clear. The prayer must be specific, or else the person is wasting time. We insist that all intercession must be goal-oriented.

2

THE KNOWLEDGE OF THE ART OF INTERCESSION

INTERCESSION MUST BE BASED ON GOD'S PROMISE

Some people think they can just ask God to do anything they want and He will do it. That is foolish thinking; for God does not act in that way. God has His will and He acts according to the counsel of that will. He acts only in accordance with the counsel of that will. He says in His Word: "*I am God, and also henceforth I am he; there is none who can deliver from my hand; I work and who can hinder it?*" (Isaiah 43: 13). "*As I have planned, so shall it be, and as I have purposed, so shall it stand*" (Isaiah 14:24). "*The counsel of the Lord stands for ever, the thoughts of his heart to all generations*" (Psalm 33:1l).

Because God will accomplish all His purpose, because He will accomplish only what He has purposed, because He brings the counsel of the nations to naught and frustrates the plans of the peoples, all who want to intercede must, first of all, find out what is the mind of God about the matter concerning which they want to intercede. Daniel did this. The Bible says:

"*In the first year of Darius the son of Ahasuerus, by birth a Mede, who became king over the realm of the Chaldeans-in the first year of his reign, I, Daniel perceived in the books the number of years which, according to the word of the Lord to Jeremiah the prophet, must pass before the end of the desolations of Jerusalem, namely, seventy years"*

(Daniel 9: 1-2).

Daniel was a keen Bible student. He had read the prophecy of Jeremiah, which said:

"This whole land shall become a ruin and a waste, and these nations shall serve the king of Babylon seventy years.

Then after seventy years are completed, I will punish the king of Babylon and that nation, the land of the Chaldeans, for their iniquity, says the Lord, making the land an everlasting waste.

I will bring upon that land all the words which I have uttered against it, everything written in this book, which Jeremiah pro-phesied against all the nations"

(Jeremiah 25: 11-13).

Daniel also knew the promise of God that said:

"For thus says the Lord:

When seventy years are completed for Babylon, I will visit you, and I will fulfil to you my promise and bring you back to this place.

For I know the plans I have for you, says the Lord, plans for welfare and not for evil, to give you a future and a hope.

Then you will call upon me and come and pray to me, and I will hear you. You will seek me and find me; when you seek me with all your heart; I will be found by you, says the Lord, and I will restore your fortunes and gather you from all the nations and all the places where I have driven you, says the Lord, and I will bring you back to the place from which I sent you into exile"

(Jeremiah 29: 10-14).

So Daniel knew what God had promised. He knew that it was

time for that promise to be fulfilled. Yes, he knew that it was time for that promise to be fulfilled, for if it were not yet time, he could not have prayed in the way he did.

An important concept is now raised about the ministry of intercession and about prayer in general: Can God accomplish His will because the time for its accomplishment according to His purposes has come, even if man does not co-operate? The answer is: He can! There is nothing that He cannot do. The next question is: Will God do all that He can do regardless of whether or not man co-operates with Him? The answer is that there are some things that God has chosen in His sovereignty to do, regardless of whether or not man co-operates with Him and there are other things that He has decided in His sovereignty not to do, unless man co-operates with Him. Where He must have the co-operation of man, He has decided that He will not act unless and until man co-operates. So in those cases, if man does not co-operate, God will allow His will to be delayed or hindered. He will prefer to act as if He had failed, instead of acting independently of man. This is a very serious issue. God will allow His purpose to be delayed or to be frustrated temporarily unless man co-operates with Him! This places such a serious responsibility on man and raises man to such a high position! It means that in some matters God has decided that the final verdict is with man. In this way, God has given man limited sovereignty under His own limitless sovereignty.

The question may be asked: How can I know when I must co-operate with God for His will to be accomplished and when do I not have to co-operate? The answer is that God has not left us in the dark about what is what. When He makes a promise that demands the co-operation of man, He always states very clearly what the co-operation of man is to be.

In the promise made about restoring the children of Israel after seventy years in Babylon we see that in Jeremiah 29: 10 the promise was given. In Jeremiah 29: 11 the Lord revealed His purpose and His

good will towards His people. In Jeremiah 29: 12-13, He exposed clearly what the people were to do so that what is promised in Jeremiah 29:10-11 might be fulfilled. The people were to:
1. call upon Him,
2. come to Him,
3. pray to Him.

When they did these three things, He would hear them. He, however, made it clear that the spirit in which they would do the calling, coming, and praying was all-important. They had to seek Him in order to find Him, and to find Him they had to seek Him with all their hearts. If they called upon Him and came and prayed half-heartedly, if they sought Him with divided hearts, they would go away unrewarded. He then went on to tell them what He would do if they sought Him with all their hearts. In Jeremiah 29: 14 He said that:
1. He would be found by them.
2. He would restore their fortunes to them.
3. He would gather them from all the nations and all the places where He had driven them.
4. He would bring them back to the place from which they went into exile.

Daniel also knew other promises of God that were associated with being in exile and being brought out of exile. He knew for example, that the Lord had promised:

"But if they confess their iniquity and the iniquity of their fathers in their treachery which they committed against me, and also in walking contrary to me, so that I walked contrary to them and brought them into the land of their enemies;

if then their uncircumcised heart is humbled and they make amends for their iniquity; then I will remember my covenant with Jacob, and I will remember my covenant with Isaac and my covenant with Abraham, and I will remember the land.

"But the land shall be left by them, and enjoy its Sabbaths while it lies desolate without them; and they shall make amends for their iniquity, because they spurned my ordinances, and their soul abhorred my statutes.

Yet for all that, when they are in the land of their enemies, I will not spurn them, neither will I abhor them so as to destroy them utterly and break my covenant with them; for I am the Lord their God; but I will for their sake remember the covenant with their forefathers, whom I brought forth out of the land of Egypt in the sight of the nations, that I might be their God: I am the Lord"

(Leviticus 26:40-45).

Daniel, therefore, ensured that he prayed according to the will of God. As we shall see later, his prayer contained all that was necessary to satisfy the demands of God.

INTERCESSION MUST BE DONE BY AN INTERCESSOR OR INTERCESSORS

As we have seen, God demanded that His people call upon Him, come and pray to Him, and seek Him with their whole heart so that His promise to call off the exile after seventy years might be fulfilled. There was no way He could waive that demand; for it was integrally tied to the promise. One thing was also obvious. The Jews who were in Babylon were not all tuned to hearing God and obeying Him. In fact, if God had to wait for a day when they would all turn to Him and seek Him, that day might never come. Daniel also knew that it was in the mind of God that one person could represent the rest. He therefore knew that if he alone fulfilled the demands of

God and then interceded on behalf of the people, God would answer. As we saw in the preceding chapter, Daniel was a man whose life consistently satisfied God. He could then take the responsibility of praying on behalf of all the rest. He personified all the rest:

- His repentance represented the repentance of all.
- His close walk with God represented that of all.
- His calling upon God represented their calling upon Him.
- His coming to God and praying to Him represented their coming to Him and praying to Him.
- His seeking the Lord with all his heart represented their seeking the Lord with all their hearts.
- His humbling himself with fasting, sackcloth, and ashes rep-resented their humbling themselves with fasting, sackcloth, and ashes.

Daniel represented the entire people who were in exile. He was their intercessor. He was an intercessor before God on their behalf. His intercession covered them all.

God has always worked with many on the basis of what one person or a small group of people did. For example, all people died in Adam and all were potentially saved in the Second Adam—the Lord Jesus. The Bible says:

"For as by a man came death, by a man has come also the resurrection of the dead.

For as in Adam all die, so also in Christ shall all be made alive"
(1Corinthians 15:21-22).

INTERCESSION MUST ACTUALLY BE DONE

Too many people intend to do things but never get down to doing them. A man may be qualified before God to intercede, he may know the Bible grounds for intercession, and he may plan to intercede or desire to intercede or talk about intercession, but all this is to no avail until He actually gets down to interceding. My prayer is that you should not only read this book about intercession and be touched by its message, but that you should actually get down to the matter of intercession and intercede. It is not enough that the desire be there. The desire has to be transformed into action.

Why don't you stop for the moment and intercede for someone or some situation before you continue to read? You know enough to begin to put it into action. You could, for example, intercede for:

1. Someone who is not saved, that he be brought to a saving knowledge of the Lord. Ask that the gospel reach him. Ask that it be presented to him as clearly and as completely as possible. Ask that the Holy Spirit be mightily present to convict him of sin, righteousness, and judgment. Ask that the Holy Spirit bring him to repentance towards God. Ask that the Holy Spirit reveal the Lord Jesus to him. Ask that He hate sin, turn from it completely, and receive the Lord Jesus Christ as Saviour and Lord. Plead that it be done urgently. Plead that it be done today. Plead that it be done now, for now is the time of salvation.
2. Someone who has backslidden.
3. Someone who is being tempted severely.
4. Someone who believes but is resisting some aspect of the Word.
5. Someone who is in physical danger.
6. Someone who is sick physically or mentally.
7. A tribe without the Gospel.
8. The leaders of the nation.
9. The leaders of the people of God, et cetera.

Make it your life-style to intercede always.

3

ON THE JOB INTERCEDING

Intercession is an art. Daniel could have said to God, "Lord, You promised that after seventy years of exile You would call the exile off and restore Your people to their homeland. The seventy years have been fulfilled. Restore Your people now according to Your promise. Amen." He did not do that. He knew that he could not talk to God that way. God was not under any obligation to act. He, therefore, went about it differently.

1. HE USED PHRASES THAT WERE WORDS OF SUPPLICATION

Let us look at the words that Daniel used. He said:

1. "*O Lord*" (Daniel 9:8).
2. "*To the Lord*" (Daniel 9:9).
3. "*The Lord our God*" (Daniel 9:10).
4. "*The Lord our God*" (Daniel 9:13).
5. "*The Lord our God*" (Daniel 9:14).
6. "*O Lord our God*" (Daniel 9:15).

7. "*O Lord*" (Daniel 9: 16).
8. "*Our God*" (Daniel 9: 17).
9. "*O my God*" (Daniel 9: 18).
10. "*O Lord*" (Daniel 9: 19).
11. "*O my God*" (Daniel 9:19).

These words represented deep fellowship with God in Daniel's spirit and deep emotion God-ward in his soul. There are people who use God's name frequently in their prayers, but it is something very superficial and lacks depth and life. However, what we find here is something very different. Here the names of God express a longing, heart-longing and breaking after God. They also express desperation before God—desperation that the supplication be answered. All of Daniel was taken up in his intercession. He was caught up and caught away with God. He felt that God had to answer. He knew that God had to answer, or else he and his people would remain in captivity and Jerusalem would continue to be desolate.

2. HE ACKNOWLEDGED HIS PEOPLE'S SIN MANY TIMES

Daniel did not overlook the fact that his people had sinned. He saw it clearly. He not only saw it, he confessed it to God. He agreed with God that they had sinned. He said:

1. "*We have sinned*" (Daniel 9:5).
2. "*We have done wrong*" (Daniel 9:5).
3. "*We have acted wickedly*" (Daniel 9:5).
4. "*We have rebelled*" (Daniel 9:5).
5. "*We have turned from thy commandments*" (Daniel 9:5).
6. "*We have turned from thy ordinances*" (Daniel 9:5).

7. "*We have not listened to thy servants the prophets who spoke in thy name to our kings, our princes, and our fathers, and to all the people of the land*" (Daniel 9:6).

8. "*To us belongs confusion of face, as at this day, to the men of Judah, to the inhabitants of Jerusalem, and to all Israel, those that are near and those that are far away, in all the lands to which thou hast driven them*" (Daniel 9:7).

9. "*To us, O Lord, belongs confusion of face, to our kings, to our princes, and to our fathers*" (Daniel 9:8).

10. "*We have rebelled against thee*" (Daniel 9:9).

11. "*We have not obeyed the voice of the Lord our God*" (Daniel 9:10).

12. "*All Israel has transgressed thy law*" (Daniel 9:11).

13. "*Although all this calamity has come upon us, yet we have not entreated the favour of our Lord*" (Daniel 9:13).

14. "*We have sinned*" (Daniel 9:15).

15. "*We have done wickedly*" (Daniel 9:15).

Do you see that Daniel laboured to acknowledge their sin as fully as possible? He did not try to hide anyone's sin. He covered the whole spectrum of what they had done. He included all in the sin committed; so that he might carry the sin of all. He was not afraid or ashamed to be repetitive. For example, he said, "We have sinned" in verse 5 and again in verse 15. He said, "We have acted [done] wickedly" in verse 5 and in verse 15. He said, "We have rebelled" in verse 5 and in verse 9. He said the same thing more than once and expanded what was involved. For example, he said, "*To us belongs confusion of face, as at this day, to the men of Judah, to the inhabitants of Jerusalem, and to all Israel, those that are near and those that are far away, in all the lands to which thou hast driven them*" (Daniel 9:7). Again he said, "*To us, O Lord, belongs confusion of face, to our kings, to our princes, and to our fathers*" (Daniel 9:8).

3. HE EXALTED GOD

Daniel said of God:

1. "*O Lord, the great and terrible*" (Daniel 9:4).
2. "*To thee, O Lord, belongs righteousness*" (Daniel 9:7).
3. "*To thee, O Lord, belongs mercy*" (Daniel 9:9).
4. "*To our Lord God belongs forgiveness*" (Daniel 9:9).
5. "*The Lord is righteous in all the works which he has done*" (Daniel 9:14).
6. "*God did bring the people out of Egypt with a mighty hand*" (Daniel 9:15).
7. "*The Lord has made Himself a name*" (Daniel 9:15).

Daniel was ascribing greatness to the Lord. He was obeying the injunction of the Word, which says: "*For I will proclaim the name of the Lord. Ascribe greatness to our God*" (Deuteronomy 3:3). He was ascribing righteousness to the Lord, as it was said: "*I will fetch my knowledge from afar, and ascribe righteousness to my Maker*" (Job 36:3). He was ascribing power to the Lord, even as the psalmist commanded, saying: "*Ascribe power to God, whose majesty is over Israel, and his power in the skies*" (Psalm 68:34).

In intercession a man tries to please God. He labours to give God the honour that is due Him. It is as if the person were trying to bribe God. Actually, God cannot be bribed. It is a pity that man has to get to a position of utter need in order to give Him what He deserves praise, honour, and adoration. This ought to be the daily portion of God, given to Him daily by those who are His, and not only in circumstances of deep need. As we see, Daniel was doing here what he was doing on a daily basis. He was normally given to praise of the Lord. The Bible says: "*When Daniel knew that the document had been signed, he went to his house where he had windows in his upper chamber open toward Jerusalem; and he got down upon his knees three times a day and prayed and gave thanks before his God, as he had done previously"* (Daniel 6:10). Lord, grant that I should grow in the ministry of praising and exalting Your name daily. Lord, grant the Church to grow in the ministry of praising and exalting Your all-glorious name unceasingly. Lord, grant that we give You praise and worship, which are Your daily portions, uninhibitedly. Lord, grant each intercessor to grow in this spiritual art.

4. HE CONTRASTED GOD'S FAITHFULNESS WITH HIS PEOPLE'S UNFAITHFULNESS

Daniel was bent on exalting God and putting himself and his people where they were in the deep degradation of sin. For example, he prayed contrasting the covenant keeping God with themselves, the covenant-breaking people,

"O Lord, the great and terrible God, who keepest covenant and steadfast love with those who love him and keep his commandments,

we have sinned and done wrong and acted wickedly and re-belled, turning aside from thy commandments and ordinances"

(Daniel 9:4-5).

"To thee, O Lord, belongs righteousness, but to us confusion of face"
(Daniel 9:7).

"To us, O Lord, belongs confusion of face. ---To the Lord our God belong mercy and forgiveness"

(Daniel 9:8-9).

Such praying helps a man to see his sin and his sinful condition more clearly. It leads to deeper repentance. It leads to a deeper and dearer confession of sin and paves the way to a total abandonment of sin. The truth is that sometimes our notion of the extent of our sin is hazy until we start to confess them before the Lord. There, in His presence, His righteousness is revealed and our sin is exposed clearly. The more a person abides in the presence of God, the more his knowledge of the holiness of God will increase and the more his knowledge of his depravity will increase and the more he will confess his sin, sometimes over and over, not because of unbelief, but because of a sheer knowledge of how vile he is. There are people who always seem to be confessing sin. These people are not those who sin more than the others. It is just that they are more sincere with God and thus walk closer to Him. When they find that they have sinned and go before the Lord to confess, they may be shown the reality of the sin, not only in the act, but also in the motive. They will then see the same wrong motive being manifested in other things that do not look like sin before man but are sins before God; for everything that results from an evil motive is sin. Take, for example, a person who is given to self-exaltation. He may sacrificially give to the Lord, but the motive is to show man how he loves the Lord and sacrifices for Him. His motive is wrong and his sacrifice an abomination before the Lord. As I write this, I see too many acts in my life that are abominations before the Lord because of impure motives. Lord, have mercy upon me. Create in me a pure heart and give me right motives for everything I think, say, or do.

5. HE DID NOT TRY TO PALLIATE THEIR SIN

When Adam sinned, he did not take responsibility for his sin. Rather, he decided to blame another person—the wife God gave him. Adam was not repentant. Most people know close to nothing about repentance. When there is the tendency to explain why the sin was committed, there is no repentance in that heart. When there is the tendency to share the blame, there is no repentance. When there is the tendency to justify self, even one bit, there is no repentance. When the light of God has shone on a heart and the Holy Spirit has exposed the sin so that the individual sees it as God sees it, there will be no attempt whatsoever to justify it or to make it any less grave. David said:

"I know my transgressions, and my sin is ever before me. Against thee, thee only, have I sinned, and done that which is evil in thy sight, so that thou art justified in thy sentence and blameless in thy judgment. Behold, I was brought forth in iniquity, and in sin did my mother conceive me"

(Psalm 51:3-5).

He did not blame circumstances. He did not blame Bathsheba for being so beautiful that he could not resist. He did not explain it away by saying that he was only human. He owned up clearly and neatly. When he confessed the fact that he was brought forth in iniquity and conceived in sin, he was not trying to blame someone else. He was merely saying that everything in him was sinful; that he was all wrong!

Daniel did not pretend that they sinned ignorantly. Rather, he made it clear that they sinned deliberately. He said, "*We have not listened to thy servants the prophets, who spoke in thy name to our kings, our princes, and our fathers, and to all the people of the land*" (Daniel 9:6). He was owing up to the fact that they all knew what they ought to have done. Their sin was clearly deliberate.

He called their sin treachery committed against God (Daniel 9:7). He further said: "*We have not obeyed the voice of the Lord our God by following his laws, which he set before us by his servant the prophets*" (Daniel 9: 10). He could have tried to justify themselves by saying that they did not understand the laws. He did the opposite. He said that the laws were set before them. He was saying: "We sinned deliberately." He was owng up!

He was truly repentant. No one who intends to intercede should attempt to palliate sin. He should not say, "Lord, these people are ignorant. Their tribal customs are strong and binding. They have only recently come out of paganism. They are weak. They are only human. They are still learning. They will improve in the future," et cetera. An intercessor sees sin. He also sees the judgments of God, and he owns up all the sin and pleads for mercy.

6. HE SANCTIFIED GOD

"Daniel prayed, revealing the fact that he understood that God was perfect in punishing them. He said nothing that indicated any suggestion that God was severe. He proclaimed the Lord as the one Who keeps covenant and steadfast love with those who love Him and keep His commandments. He was saying, "Lord, You, did right to punish us. In fact, You were under obligation to punish us; so that Your holiness might be maintained." He said, "All Israel has transgressed Thy law and turned aside, refusing to obey Thy voice. And the curse and oath which are written in the law of Moses the servant of God have been poured out upon us, "because we have sinned against him" (Daniel 9: 11).

Daniel said to the Lord, "If You had not punished us, You would have been failing to confirm Your word." So he prayed, "*He has confirmed his words, which he spoke against us and against our rulers who ruled us, by bringing upon us a great calamity; for under the whole heaven there has not been done the like of what has been done against Jerusalem*" (Daniel 9:12).

Daniel even went further to state clearly that although the calamity came, they did not repent and seek God's face. They were not repentant. God was right. God was just.

In the dealings of man with God he must always sanctify God.

It is one thing to sin and be punished by God. It is another thing to try to make it seem as if God were too severe or unjust. It is worse to attribute mischief or evil motive to God. Moses was disqualified from entering the Promised Land because he did not sanctify the Lord. The Bible says: *"Because you did not believe in me, to sanctify me in the eyes of the people of Israel, therefore you shall not bring this assembly into the land which I have given them"* (Numbers 20: 12).

All intercessors must sanctify God. Without that, they will fail in a very significant way. In fact, unless they sanctify God, they can never succeed.

7. HE ACCEPTED THE PUNISHMENT AS GOD-GIVEN

Daniel did not see the Chaldeans. He did not see the enemy as the problem. He saw his people's punishment as from the Lord. He said:

"And the curse and oath which are written in the law of Moses the servant of God have been poured out upon us; because we have sinned against him.

He has confirmed his words, which he spoke against us and against our rulers who ruled us, by bringing upon us a great calamity"

(Daniel 9:11-12).

He continued: *"Therefore the Lord has kept ready the calamity and has brought it upon us"* (Daniel 9: 14).

The Lord may use one person or another, one circumstance or another, to punish His erring children, but it is the Lord doing it. To the one who knows the Lord, the problem was not the Chaldean desire for exploitation. The problem was sin and punishment for sin. For the mature, there is no second cause. There is only God to deal with. The mature do not labour to change the instrument by which punishment is being applied. They labour to remove the cause that led to the punishment. All the affairs of God's children are in His hands. He orders all. Peter understood this clearly and prayed:

"For truly in this city there were gathered together against thy holy servant Jesus, whom thou didst anoint, both Herod and Pontius Pilate, with the Gentiles and the peoples of Israel, to do whatever thy hand and thy plan had predestined to take place"

(Acts 4:27-28).

All these people were only serving the will of the Lord. Of course, they had no desire to do so. They thought they were accomplishing their will, but they were only doing whatever the hand and the plan of God had predestined to take place.

All intercessors must deal with God. They should face the issue and treat it with God. If they turn from God and try to deal with the persons or circumstances, they will be acting foolishly. When a wise believer faces any situation, he should, first of all, ask, "What is God saying?" If he does not find out what God is saying and simply moves to act, he will be acting foolishly. He may even find himself fighting against God.

8. HE OWNED THE LORD AS THEIRS

Daniel did not think that God had disinherited His people. He knew clearly that the Lord had said, "*Yet for all that, when they are in the land of their enemies, I will not spurn them, neither will I abhor them so as to destroy them utterly and break my covenant with them; for I am the Lord their God*" (Leviticus 26:44). Because he knew this, he kept insisting upon it. He said: "*The Lord our God*" (Daniel 9:9), "*The Lord our God*" (Daniel 9: 10), "*The Lord our God" (Daniel 9: 13),* "*The Lord our God*" (Daniel 9:14), "*O Lord our God*" (Daniel 9:15), and "*O our God*" (Daniel 9: 17).

The intercessor, though aware of God's hatred and anger against sin, must never forget that He loves to forgive. He must not forget the fact that even a child of God who has fallen into sin can yet be heard by the Lord and be blessed. To sin and give up completely is tragic. The believer must confess his irreversible position as a child of God, and from that position seek full restoration to the Lord.

The intercessor must not give up anyone. To do so would be to fail completely. No one is too bad to be interceded for, until he has died. Everyone who still has breath is a good subject for intercession. Is anything too hard for God?

9. HE PLEADED FOR THE LORD TO RESTORE THEM ON THE GROUNDS OF HIS GREAT MERCY

Daniel could not ask the Lord to act on the grounds of the repentance of the people because they had not repented. Exile had not changed their hearts. Outward circumstances do not change people's hearts. All real change must come from inside. It must be produced by the Holy Spirit. Daniel did not ask the Lord to pardon them on the grounds of his own repentance and his faithfulness before God. He knew that all such would not suffice. The Word of God says: "*We have all become like one who is unclean, and all our righteous deeds are like a polluted garment*" (Isaiah 64:6). He knew that his faithfulness and integrity could not provide him with a solid basis on which to seek forgiveness for himself and for others. He therefore prayed, saying, "*We do not present our supplications before thee on the ground of our righteousness, but on the ground of thy great mercy*" (Daniel 9:18b). He knew that the Lord was not only a God of mercy, but a God of great mercy, He was saying to God, "Although we have sinned greatly, Your mercy is greater than our sin. Therefore on the grounds of Your great mercy, forgive us who are totally bankrupt of righteousness."

The wonderful thing about the God whom we have come to know as the Father of our Lord and Saviour Jesus Christ is that He is very, very merciful. Without that capacity for great mercy, there would be no hope for me who write this, for I do sin against Him. I confess that my heart is deceitful and desperately wicked and that outside of His mercy and the blood shed for my pardon, there would be no hope whatsoever for me!

The angel could call Daniel beloved, and that was so. Daniel was faithful. However, he knew too well how far from perfect he was. He knew that the sins he committed any one day were enough to banish him from God's presence forever, were God to judge him outside the merits of His mercy.

10. HE HAD FURTHER GROUNDS FOR PLEADING THAT GOD WOULD ACT

Apart from God's great mercy, Daniel pleaded that God should forgive His people on the grounds of His name. He used this as follows:

1. "*According to all thy righteous acts, let thy anger and thy wrath turn away from thy city Jerusalem, thy holy hill*" (Daniel 9:16). Do you see the words "thy city" and "thy holy hill"? He was saying, "Lord, it is Yours. Have mercy because it is Your city, Your holy hill. If it belonged to another, You could perhaps leave it desolate, but, Lord, it is Yours, Your very own. So, do something, Lord."

2. "*Jerusalem thy holy hill and thy people have become a byword among all who are round about us*" (Daniel 9: 16). He was more or less saying, "Lord, Your people are involved. Your hill is involved. The people around are mocking Your hill and Your people. They are indirectly mocking You. Do something for Your city and Your people; so that You will be mocked no more!" It is like telling a father, "Your son is being mocked because his clothes are dirty. They got dirty because he disobeyed you. You can allow him to go out with

the dirty clothes that he merits because of his disobedience, but re-member that many people are saying that the son of Mr-- -- is dirty. They are mocking as if it were your fault. They are, thereby, making as if you love dirt. Because that is the case, clear your name by giving him new clothes, even though he dirtied the first set through disobedience." I think such an argument will win with any reasonable father. Moses used it with the heavenly Father because he expected it to work. It was another way of pleading, of supplicating or trying to move God to act.

3. "*Now therefore, O Lord our God, hearken to the prayer of thy servant and to his supplications, and for thy own sake, O Lord, cause thy face to shine upon thy sanctuary, which is desolate*" (Daniel 9: 17). He pleaded on the grounds that he was the Lord's servant and that he was praying and that he was supplicating. By using the words "thy servant," "prayer," and "supplications," he was labouring to move God to action. However, the stronger emphasis was on the fact that the Lord's own sanctuary was desolate. He was saying, "Lord, even if You do not want to do it because I am Your servant and I have prayed and I am supplicating, You should do it because Your sanctuary is desolate. Do it because of Your name's sake."

God is jealous of His name. He always acts to protect it from disgrace. To plead that He should do things because of His name's sake is to plead on very lofty grounds. On these grounds Daniel continued, "*O Lord, hear; O Lord, forgive; O Lord, give heed and act; delay not, for thy own sake, O my God, because thy city and thy people are called by thy name*" (Daniel 9: 19). Do you see the art of intercession at work? Do you see the note on which Daniel is trying to end it? He is doing all to leave the ball in God's court. He says, "thy city," "thy people," and "thy name," in rapid succession, and there he ends it. He wanted it to end as an affair that God had to be involved in because He was deeply involved. Daniel was not just a man of prayer. He was not a beginning intercessor. He had mastered the art. He had done a good job.

11. HE PRESSED FOR RESULTS

As Daniel interceded, it is as if he got to a climax, a point where he had to win. He was like a football player in the goal area of the opponent team. Every word was important. Every second was important. It is as if his heart was beating fast. It was now or never. He just had to win. The sentences became shorter; the pleading became most intense. Can you hear him and enter with him into his agony and struggle and a moment when all hung on the balance? Just hear him pray at the end.

> O my God, incline thy ear!
> O my God, hear!
> O my God, open thy eyes!
> O my God, behold our desolation!
> O my God, the city is called by your name!
> O Lord, hear!
> O Lord, forgive!
> O Lord, give heed!
> O Lord, act! Delay not!
> For thy own sake!
> O my God! Because of thy city!
> Thy people!
> Thy name!
> Lord, teach us to pray as Daniel did. Teach us to labour as he did.

It is obvious that he did it because he was desperate to see God move. Only desperate men can truly intercede. As far as he was concerned, God had to answer or there would be disaster. That moved him to such intensity in prayer. It moved him to supplicate desperately!

12. HE WAS BOLD

There was a point in the intercession when Daniel spoke to God as if commanding Him. The commands were:

1. "Lord, our God, hearken to the prayer of thy servant."
2. "Lord, hearken to the supplications of Your servant."
3. "O my God, incline thy ear."
4. "O my God, hear."
5. "Open thy eyes."
6. "Behold our desolation."
7. "O Lord, hear."
8. "O Lord, forgive."
9. "O Lord, give heed."
10. "O Lord, act."
11. "O Lord, delay not."

Who was he to be commanding God? Was he being rude? Was he being too familiar with God? Was he being disrespectful? I do not think so. He was in a crisis and he was in agony. God understands such language at such times. He accepts it and even likes it. He rejoices to see such boldness. He has even encouraged His own to command Him. He says, "*Thus saith the Lord, the Holy One of Israel, and his Maker: Ask me of things to come concerning my sons; and concerning the work of my hands, command ye me*"
(Isaiah 45:11, KJV).

May we learn to "command Him," and we shall please His heart.

13. HE WAS URGENT

Daniel pressed for an immediate answer. He said, "*And now, O Lord our God*" (Daniel 9: 15) and "*Now therefore, O Lord our God*" (Daniel 9: 17).

It had to be then. It is difficult to be burdened about things that could happen in the distant future. Daniel knew that the seventy years were over. He knew that if God did not answer then, His honour would be at stake. He was not foolish to say that God would certainly act, because it was time. He took the fact that it was time as a reason for great urgency. May we know such urgency as we intercede for people. Take the matter of a sinner coming to the Saviour. Could anything be more urgent? He may be young in age, but couldn't he die suddenly? Could his heart not become hardened beyond softening? Take the matter of a backslider needing to be restored. Is that not most urgent? Might he not suddenly be called to meet His God in his dreadful condition? Take the matter of the maturation of believers. Might the Lord not come at any moment? Would it not be most sad for Him to find the Bride immature, with spots, blemishes, and wrinkles? Would that satisfy His heart? Certainly not.

If the eyes of the people of God were opened, they would never know any moment of cold or lukewarm intercession. All their prayers would be hot. All their prayers would be urgent. All their prayers would be desperate. Lord, open the eyes of Your Bride. Begin with mine, O Lord.

THE PURPOSE OF INTERCESSION

The ultimate purpose of intercession must be God—His holiness, His kingdom, His will. It is good to intercede so that sinners be saved, but that is only a means to an end. The end is that the Lord might be glorified. When sinners are unsaved, they glorify the devil. When they are saved, they glorify God. It is true that if they are saved, they will escape damnation and enjoy eternal life. However, creation and all the acts of God are not meant to bring joy to man or to alleviate his agony (as the primary purpose), good as that is. The primary purpose is that God may be worshipped and adored. To that purpose all mature intercessors fix their eyes.

Daniel interceded with that purpose. He did not want God's Word to go unfulfilled. He did not want a promise of God to fall to the ground. He thought of God's glory and felt for God's glory. He pleaded for God's people, God's city, and God's hill. His intercession was truly rooted in God. He saw the need for God's holiness to be maintained, and that is why he saw the justice of God punishing His people. He also saw the need in God's Word of restoration being fulfilled, and that is why he strove for it. We bless the Lord for it. We bless the Lord for him, and we make it our purpose to learn from him and so overthrow self from the centre of our praying and enthrone God there!

DANIEL'S INTERCESSION WAS HEARD

The Bible says of Daniel:

"While I was speaking and praying, confessing my sin and the sin of my people Israel, and presenting my supplication before the Lord my God for the holy hill of my God;

While I was speaking in prayer, the man Gabriel, whom I had seen in the vision at the first, came to me in swift flight at the time of the evening sacrifice.

He came and said to me,

> '*O Daniel, I have now come out to give you wisdom and understanding.*
>
> *At the beginning of your supplications a word went forth, and I have come to tell it to you, for you are greatly beloved; therefore consider the word and understand the vision. 'Seventy weeks of years are decreed concerning your people and your holy city, to finish the transgression, to put an end to sin, and to atone for iniquity,*
>
> *"to bring in everlasting righteousness, to seal both vision and prophet, and to anoint a most holy place........"*
>
> (Daniel 9:20-24).

I do not know if Daniel was answered the first time that he prayed. We are, however, sure that he was answered. He was answered while he was still speaking. How good the Lord is! How precious the privilege to deal with Him is! He says that before we call He will answer, and He does just that!

Daniel had prayed and said, "And now ... " The Lord answered in the same manner, for Gabriel said, "I have, now come ... " Those who pray in the "now" are also answered in the "now." How we limit God by our lack of urgency!

Gabriel said, "At the beginning of your supplications, a word went forth." The word was there in God's heart. He was waiting. Immediately Daniel began to intercede, the word went forth. How long had that word been on God's heart? How long had He been waiting? How long would He have continued to wait had Daniel not started to intercede? Would the word ever have gone out if Daniel had not begun to intercede? Oh, how we limit God! Oh, how we frustrate Him by our prayerlessness! Oh, how we delay Him! Oh, how we stand in the way of some of His mightiest purposes! As I write this, my low level of intercession stabs my heart like a sword. I confess that I have hindered God, slowed down His actions, and frustrated His plans. I know for certain that many words would already have gone out from Him which have not yet gone out had I been more faithful and more urgent in the ministry of intercession. Lord, forgive me. Heal my poor intercessory life and set me all aflame not only to intercede, but to intercede as I ought. Lord, do it for me now. Lord, do it for the Bride, Your Bride now.

Daniel sought the Lord so that He might fulfil a promise concerning the seventy-year exile of his people in Babylon. The Lord granted that. However, the Lord did not stop there. He gave Daniel more. He gave him to know what was decreed by the Lord concerning his people for seventy weeks of years! He allowed him to know things that concerned:

1. finishing of the transgression,
2. putting an end to sin,
3. atonement for iniquity,
4. bringing in of everlasting righteousness,
5. the sealing of both vision and prophet,
6. the anointing of a most holy place,
7. et cetera.

In the beginning of Daniel's career in Babylon, he refused to compromise and the Lord gave him and his companions: "*learning and skill in all letters and wisdom; and Daniel had understanding in all visions and dreams*" (Daniel 1: 17). That was great. However, what he received as a bonus for his ministry as intercessor is in every way superior to what he had for not compromising.

May we not compromise and we shall be blessed. May we become trustworthy intercessors and we shall be blessed even more. May we seek the blessing as trophies and crowns to place at the feet of our Lord and Saviour; so that all our actions, life, prayer, intercession, and supplication may be in Him and for Him.

All things were created, through him and for Him" (Colossians 1: 16).

"And whenever the living creatures give glory and honour and thanks to him who is seated on the throne, who lives for ever and ever, the twenty-four elders fall down before him who is seated on the throne and worship him who lives for ever and ever;

they cast their crowns before the throne, singing, "Worthy art thou, our Lord and God , to receive glory and honour and power, for thou didst create all things, and by thy will they existed and were created"

(Revelation 4:9-11).

Amen.

PART 4

Moses The Intercessor

1

THE POWER OF INTERCESSION

We have shown that leadership is manifested by the extent to which a person can intercede for others. We have said that a person leads those for whom he intercedes. Those for whom he does not intercede he does not lead.

Moses was indeed the leader of the children of Israel. Soon after they left Egypt, they came to the wilderness of Shur. There they went for three days in the wilderness and found no water. Then they came to Marah and could not drink the water of Marah because it was bitter. The people murmured against Moses, saying, "What shall we drink?"

Moses did not talk back to the people. He heard their murmuring. He heard their question. He knew their need. He turned to the Lord. The Bible says: "*And he cried to the Lord; and the Lord showed him a tree, and he threw it into the water, and the water became sweet*" (Exodus 15:25). We can sum up what happened as follows:

1. The children of Israel had a need.
2. They complained to Moses.
3. Moses cried to God.
4. God provided an answer for the children of Israel.

An intercessor is a person who presents the needs of others to the Lord and labours with God until God provides what is needed. One thing comes out very clearly here. Moses did not try to use other methods to solve their problem, so that when all failed he turned to God. He turned to God immediately. Intercessors are people who present the problems and the needs of others to God and only to God. They do not present the problem to man, and when man has failed they then turn to God. They do not present the problem to man and to God and wait for whoever will provide the answer first. For the intercessor, God must answer or there is no answer. This means that the intercessor must believe God. He must have faith in God. Those who look to God and to man do not have faith. The Bible says: "And without faith it is impossible to please him. For whoever would draw near to God must believe that he exists and that he rewards those who seek him" (Hebrews 11:6). An intercessor must believe that God is able. He must also believe that man on his own is not able. He must decide to turn to the God who is able and not to man who is not able.

A SECOND EXAMPLE OF INTERCESSION

The Bible says:

"*All the congregation of the people of Israel moved on from the wilderness of Sin by stages, according to the commandment of the Lord, and camped at Rephidim; but there was no water for the people to drink. Therefore the people found fault with Moses, and said, 'Give us water to drink.'*

And Moses said to them, 'Why do you find fault with me?

Why do you put the Lord to the proof?'

But the people thirsted there for water, and the people murmured against Moses, and said, 'Why did you bring us up out of Egypt, to kill us and our children and our cattle with thirst?'

So Moses cried to the Lord, 'What shall I do with this people?

They are almost ready to stone me.'

And the Lord said to Moses, 'Pass on before the people, taking with you some of the elders of Israel; and take in your hand the rod with which you struck the Nile, and go. Behold, I will stand before you there on the rock at Horeb; and you shall strike the rock and water shall come out of it, that the people may drink.'

And Moses did so, in the sight of the elders of Israel"

(Exodus 17: 1-6).

We can sum up what happened as follows:
1. The children of Israel needed water.
2. They could turn to the Lord, who had supplied their need before, but they did not.
3. They found fault with Moses and asked him to give them water. They murmured against him, blamed him, and accused him.
4. Moses turned to the Lord and presented their need and the situation to God. In fact, he cried to the Lord.
5. The Lord heard him and gave him clear and detailed instructions as to what was to be done to handle the situation.
6. What God said did not look very scientific; however, Moses believed Him and obeyed the instructions accordingly.
7. God answered and the needs of the people were met.

An intercessor must be able to remain calm when others around him are losing their heads. He must not be carried away by what is carrying all the others away. He must be in control of himself. This control comes out of unshakeable faith that the Lord is in full control of all that is happening. Moses was like that.

An intercessor must know how to present the situation clearly to God. He must have a clear mind and the right wording. In presenting his case to God, he is to make as if God knows nothing about it. He must be as detailed as possible. He must present a clear, detailed report of what the situation is. It is no use for him to say, "God, You know this situation. I do not need to bother You with the details, because nothing is hidden from You. Act as You see fit." Such a person might as well never pray, because God knows all that we need! Although God knows all the details, He wants the intercessor to present them to Him. Although He knows what ought to be done, He wants man to tell Him what he (man) wants Him (God) to do.

An intercessor must have the capacity to listen to God. When requests are made to God, He will often speak back to the intercessor. He should therefore not only ask and then go away, but he should, after asking, wait before the Lord so as to hear what the Lord has to say. How sad that most of God's children do not wait before the Lord for an answer! In the case at hand, it would have been hopeless if Moses had run away from God's presence shortly after presenting the situation to the Lord and making a request. He would have received no answer, not because God was unwilling to answer, but because he did not wait for an answer. How many of the prayers of God's people today remain unanswered because His people do not wait in His presence for His answers to their requests! We suggest that every intercessor must be able to wait in the presence of God. He must be able to wait in His presence until He speaks. He should not be preoccupied with the length of time that he has spent in God's presence. He should be preoccupied with whether or not God has spoken. When an intercessor goes before the Lord, he should stay in His presence for as long as it will take him to present his needs to the Lord clearly and in detail, and for as long as it will take God to speak back to him. It may take five minutes, five hours, five days, five months, or five years. It is not a question of how long it has taken in God's presence, but if God has answered. All who have the burden to become intercessors must grow in the art of waiting on God and waiting before Him.

An intercessor must be able to remember the instructions that God has given clearly and correctly. People like me, who do not have a tape recorder for a brain, we advise to wait before God with a pen and paper; so that when the Lord Jesus speaks, His instructions will be recorded clearly and carefully. It is a most serious thing to forget what God said in answer to a prayer of intercession!

An intercessor must be obedient. God will often speak back, giving instructions as to what should be done as the intercessor's (or the other's) contribution to having the answer. Moses was told to pass on before the people, take with him some of the elders of Israel, take in his hand the rod with which he struck the Nile, and strike the rock. These were clear instructions for Moses to obey. This was Moses' contribution to the answer that was coming. These instructions, though simple, had to be obeyed. They did not originate in Moses. He did not come before God, present the problem, and suggest a solution in which he had to do the above things. We insist that intercessors must receive instructions from God and not make suggestions to God. That which has its origin in man is flesh, and the flesh can never please God.

Although the instructions were from God, they were not enough to answer the need. There was something that God had to do Himself. The Lord said to Moses, "I will stand before you there on the rock at Horeb." God was to be there personally.

Moses was a man of God. The children of Israel were in need. The rod he was carrying was the rod of God. He had interceded. If on his own he had gone and hit any rock in the wilderness, there would have been no flow of water. The water flowed because God commanded Moses to do what he did. The water flowed because God Himself was there and caused it to flow.

Miracles happen when an intercessor obeys God's instructions.

They happen because God is present to cause them to happen. They originate in God. They fit into His timing. He cannot be manipulated by man. How useless the multitudes of suggestions that many people throw at God, and how useless the gimmicks of man! How useless the carnal efforts of man to get God to perform miracles! How transient the acts of man are! How abiding the acts of God are!

Oh, that we would learn to hear God! Oh, that we would learn to listen to Him! Oh, that we would learn to carry out His instructions and wait on Him to act! How needful it is to put away our own plans, timing, and methods!

ANOTHER INCIDENT OF MOSES INTERCEDING

The Bible says:

"Then came Amalek and fought with Israel at Rephidim.

And Moses said to Joshua, 'Choose for us men, and go out, fight with Amalek; tomorrow I will stand on the top of the hill with the rod of God in my hand.'

So Joshua did as Moses told him, and fought with Amalek; and Moses, Aaron, and Hur went up on the top of the hill.

Whenever Moses held up his hand, Israel prevailed; and whenever he lowered his hand, Amalek prevailed.

But Moses' hands grew weary; so they took a stone and put it under him, and he sat upon it, and Aaron and Hur held up his hands, one on one side, and the other on the other side; so his hands were steady until the going down of the sun.

And Joshua mowed down Amalek and his people with the edge of the sword"

(Exodus 17:8-13).

This is another incident in which Moses ministered as inter-cessor. We do not have the details of the whole story. We do not have information on what transpired between Moses and God before the battle began. We can only imagine that Moses must have cried to God and presented the situation to Him. We also presume that he must have waited before God and received from God the instructions that he was carrying out. What we have in the passage is his execution of the instructions he received from God. A number of things are obvious from the passage. It will be instructive to learn from them:

1. There were two fronts on which the battle was to be fought.
2. One was on the plain with the physical enemy, and the other place was on the mountain with the spiritual enemy.
3. Moses knew that he could not tackle the two fronts by himself; that is, he could not lead the battle on the two fronts.
4. Moses knew that there was a relationship between the two fronts.
5. Moses knew that although the two fronts were related, what happened in the valley depended on what happened in the mountain, and not vice versa.
6. Moses decided that he, being the spiritual authority, was compelled to choose the more difficult battlefront, which is the front against the unseen enemy.
7. The battle was decided by what happened on the mountain and not by what happened in the plain. Moses was on the mountain as an intercessor, standing in the gap between God and the people at war. He was in the gap, lifting up his hands in prayer of intercession. He was also lifting up his hands of intercession to God against Satan. He carried out transactions with God, who is Spirit, and with Satan and his hosts, who are spirits. He was warring with the invisible. The Apostle Paul wrote: *"For we are not conten-*

ding against flesh and flood, but against the principalities, against the powers, against the world rulers of this present darkness, against the spiritual hosts of wickedness in the heavenly places" (Ephesians 6: 12).

8. The battle was decided on the mountaintop. Joshua and his men fought very fiercely and very intelligently in the valley. However, regardless of how they fought; the battle was not decided there. It was decided on the mountaintop where Moses was fighting with the "invisible Amalek." Obviously, it was Satan who moved Amalek against Israel, and it was satanic principalities, powers, evil spirits, demons, et cetera, that were moving and controlling Amalek in the battle. When Moses, the intercessor put these under control by moving God to dislocate their efforts, Joshua had a breakthrough and was winning. When Moses' hands were down, indicating that he was not interceding, the powers of darkness moving through Amalek began to gain ground.

9. The battle was won when intercession became permanent. For this permanence, Moses needed the help of Aaron and Hur.

PRAYER IS WHERE DECISIVE ACTION IS

God has called us to pray. The most important thing that anyone can do for God or for man is pray. There are physical enemies, but these physical enemies are nothing compared with the spiritual enemies that are in control of the physical enemies. If we saw things as they really are, we would pray instead of acting in the energy of the flesh. Take the matter of bringing people to Christ as an example. It is easier to find people who will give money for the campaign than people who will actually pray. It is easier to find people who will print posters and put them up than people who will pray. It is easier to train counsellors than to pray. So-called evangelists find more time to prepare their physical ap-pearances than to pray. Some evangelists who appear before crowds for hours do not know how to wait before God for even one hour. There is dependence on the publicity mechanism, and much is put into it. There is dependence on everything except on God. If there were dependence on God, the organizers and the evangelists would make prayer the priority long before the campaign, during the campaign, and long after the campaign. Then things would be different. However, things are not different. People are manipulated to decide. In a city of about 1 million people, five hundred thousand people were said to have decided for Christ in a period of three days, but after that the city continued as before, without any real evidence of God's presence, and the decisions lasted only an evening, while reports of the great things done were printed and circulated shamelessly round the world to the glory of man. The situation is like the one that persisted of old and forced the Lord to say, "*For my people have committed two evils, they have forsaken me, the fountain of living waters, and hewed out cisterns for themselves, broken cisterns, that can hold no water*" (Jeremiah 2: 13).

Any work that is not conceived, born, and executed in prayer is a broken cistern. Any campaign, crusade, convention, missionary enterprise, Gospel publishing work, teaching ministry, et cetera, et cetera, that is not conceived, born and executed in prayer, has failed before God and will eventually fail before man. What God does lasts. What He does is often done in response to the prayers of interceding people.

Even a casual observer will notice that the current brand of Christianity—be it Roman Catholic, Protestant, or Pentecostal—is largely devoid of God. There are real differences between these denominations in doctrine. There are obvious differences in outward form. However, in depth they are very similar. God is essentially absent. You can go into any of their midst in search of the manifest presence of God and find nothing. Activities abound, but God is absent. The men and women who are said to pray are just carrying out a routine exercise, be they of the rosary or in tongues. How-ever, the people who know God and who know how to call on Him on behalf of others in such a way that He feels compelled to answer, seem to have disappeared from Planet Earth, and their successors do not seem to have been born.

Oh, for an intercessor! Oh, for intercessors! Oh, for people who will cry out to God and cause Him to answer! Such men may not be eloquent evangelists, understanding pastors, gentle counsellors, known in many circles, or accepted in any religious system. Ho-wever, they will be men who have not only stopped the tragic art of hewing for themselves broken cisterns that can hold no water; they will be men who scatter all such cisterns. They will be people who know the way to the lonely hilltop, who know how to enter their rooms, close the door, and pray to the God who sees and hears in secret, pray for maybe one hour, one month, or one year. They will pray, knowing that praying is more important than preaching; they will pray knowing that prayer is more important than the sending of missionaries by human beings and human organizations. They will pray because they know that all else without prayer is not only useless but evil. They will lay hold on God and, because they will have laid hold on God, He will act and all else will change.

As we have seen, one such man will do. The following story will illustrate what we are labouring to communicate:

Brother R. Edward Miller, missionary to Argentina, related an interesting story. A revival campaign had been planned for a large South American city a few years back. Every conceivable preparation had been made to make the meeting a success. A daily radio broadcast, thousands of leaflets distributed, and newspaper publicity were all used to ensure a successful revival. On the opening night, after weeks of hard toil and labour, the revival speaker came to the big tent only to find it full ... of empty chairs. No one, even after that intense publicity, attended the opening night. As a result of this discouraging experience, Brother Miller began to earnestly seek God for the answer to successful evangelism. He was seeking a revival akin to that which the early church prayed for and received.

The early church prayed, "*Lord ... grant unto thy servants, that with all boldness they may speak thy word, by stretching forth thine hand to heal; and that signs and wonders may be done by the name of thy holy child Jesus*" (Acts 4:29-30 KJV).

After weeks of intercessory prayer (praying for eight to twenty-four hours a day) by Brother Miller, the Lord sent His angel to one of the Bible School students. The student began to speak by the word of the Lord, "God is going to perform mighty signs and wonders in Argentina for the strong man of Argentina; has been bound." From that night forth, it was evident that God was able to move in an unprecedented way in South America.

Shortly after this angelic edict, Brother Tommy Hicks came to the capital of Argentina where he arranged the campaign that is today heralded as "The largest Christian gathering in the history of Christendom." Before the campaign concluded, upwards of a quarter of a million people were turning out nightly to the great meetings in the tremendous sports arena in Buenos Aires. Wheelchairs and crutches discarded by those who were healed were carried out by the truckloads after the meetings each night.

In the same city where missionaries had laboured for several generations to gather a handful of converts, upwards of a quarter of a million professed faith in Christ in a short campaign. What made the difference? The strong man of Argentina had been bound!

Till this day, Brother Miller reports, a church can be established in any city in Argentina where they can get workers to go. Praise the Lord!

-Ralph Mahoney,
Acts 2, no 5.
September/October 1983

Generations of labours passed without any real result. One man, an intercessor, stepped in, and the situation changed. That one man paid the price. He prayed for at least eight hours every day. Some days he prayed for all twenty-four hours. He was desperate to have an answer. He poured himself out and he went on for weeks and weeks until God answered. When God answered, he stopped. Before God answered, even though he had prayed for weeks and weeks, he kept on.

Something in me tells me that God will do the same thing in any city and nation if He finds one man who will pay the price. He may have to pray for eight hours a day for weeks, then for twelve hours a day for many more weeks and months, and then for days, weeks, and perhaps months, and so on. He may have to go on for years upon years. However, one thing is certain: If he presses on, God will answer. When God answers, more will be accomplished in one day or one week or one month than for centuries at the current rate of world conquest. The one who leaves aside his current ministry as pastor, evangelist, writer, or what-not and gives himself to intercessory prayer will have done the city, the nation, the continent, and Planet Earth limitless good. He will also have done the Kingdom of God limitless good. The question that is before you and me today now is, "Will God find such a man?" I ask you as I ask myself, "Will God find such a man?"

2

THE ART OF INTERCESSION

"And he said to Moses, 'Come up to the Lord, you and Aaron, Nadab and Abihu, and seventy of the elders of Israel, and worship afar off.

"Moses alone shall come near to the Lord; but the others shall not come near, and the people shall not up with him'"

(Exodus 24: 1-2).

Then Moses and Aaron, Nadab, and Abihu and seventy of the elders of Israel went up, and they saw the God of Israel; and there was under his feet as it were a pavement of sapphire stone, like the very heaven for clearness.

And he did not lay his hand on the chief men of the people of Israel;

they beheld God, and ate and drank.

The Lord said to Moses, 'Come up to me on the mountain, and wait there; and I will give you the tables of stone, with the law and the commandment, which I have written for their instruction.'

So Moses rose with his servant Joshua, and Moses went up into the mountain of God.

And he said to the elders, 'Tarry here for us, until we come to you again; and behold, Aaron and Hur are with you; whoever has a cause, let him go to them.'

" Then Moses went up on the mountain, and the cloud covered the mountain.

The glory of the Lord settled on Mount Sinai, and the cloud covered it six days; and on the seventh day he called to Moses out of the midst of the cloud.

Now the appearance of the glory of the Lord was like a de-vouring fire on the top of the mountain in the sight of the people of Israel.

And Moses entered the cloud, and went up on the mountain. And Moses was on the mountain forty days and forty nights"

(Exodus 24:9-18).

"When the people saw that Moses delayed to come down from the mountain, the people gathered themselves together to Aaron, and said to him, 'Up, make us gods, who shall go before us; as for this Moses, the man who brought us up out of the land of Egypt, we do not know what has become of him.

And Aaron said to them, 'Take off the rings of gold which are in the ears of your wives, your sons, and your daughters, and bring them to me."

So all the people took off the rings of gold which were in their ears, and brought them to Aaron.

And he received the gold at their hand, and fashioned it with a graving tool and, made a molten calf; and the y said, 'These are your gods, O Israel, who brought you up out of the land of Egypt!'

When Aaron saw this, he built an altar before it; and Aaron made proclamation and said, 'Tomorrow shall be a feast to the Lord.

And they rose up early on the morrow, and offered burnt offerings and brought peace offerings; and the people sat down to eat and drink, and rose up to play."

(Exodus 32: 1-6).

"And the Lord said to Moses, 'Go down; for your people, whom you

brought up out of the land of Egypt, have corrupted themselves; they have turned aside quickly out of the way which I commanded them;

"they have made for themselves a molten calf, and have wor-shipped it and sacrificed to it, and said, 'These are your gods, O Israel, who brought you up out of the land of Egypt!'"

And the Lord said to Moses, 'I have seen this people, and behold, it is a stiff-necked people;

now therefore let me alone, that my wrath may burn hot against them and I may consume them; but of you I will make a great nation"

(Exodus 32:7-10).

"But Moses besought the Lord his God, and said, 'O Lord, why does thy wrath burn hot against thy people, whom thou hast brought forth out of the land of Egypt with great power and with a mighty hand?

Why should the Egyptians say, 'With evil intent did he bring them forth, to slay them in the mountains, and to consume them from the face of the earth?'"

"Turn from thy fierce wrath, and repent of this evil against thy people. Remember Abraham, Isaac, and Israel, thy servants, to whom thou didst swear by thine own self, and didst say to them, 'I will multiply your descendants as the stars of heaven, and all this land that I have promised I will give to your descendants, and they shall inherit it for ever.'"

And the Lord repented of the evil which he thought to do to his people."

(Exodus 32:11-14).

MOSES' ABSENCE

Moses the intercessor was a man of the glory. He walked with God. He spent time in God's presence. In the situation before us he had been called away into the mountain and into the cloud by the Lord. He was away, lost in God for forty days and nights without any food or water. He left the children of Israel under the leadership of Aaron and Hur.

THE GREAT SIN

The people waited in vain for Moses to come, back from the mountain. Forty days was too long a time for them. Moses was away. The Lord's glory was absent. Although the other teachers were there, they lacked God's glory. They lacked what it takes to keep people looking up to God. How sad that the people of the glory of God are so few and so rare! How sad that the multitude of leaders present know nothing or know too little of the glory of God. Oh, that the Lord would raise up some people of the glory in our midsts! Aaron was present, but he could not bring God to the people. He gave in to the people and made for them a golden calf. The people worshipped and sacrificed to it!

This was a great sin. Moses was still lost in God when this happened.

THE SIN ANNOUNCED AND THE PUNISHMENT SPELT OUT

The forty days had barely finished when God said the following to Moses:

1. "Go down."
2. "Your people whom you brought up out of the land of Egypt have corrupted themselves."
3. "They have turned aside quickly out of the way which I commanded them."
4. "They have made for themselves a molten calf and have

worshipped and sacrificed to it."
5. "They have said of it, 'These are your gods, O Israel, who brought you up out of the land of Egypt.'"
6. "I have seen this people."
7. "It is a stiff-necked people."
8. "Now therefore, let me alone that My wrath may burn hot against them, that I may consume them. I will make of you a great nation."

THE INTERCESSOR AT WORK

Immediately after Moses heard this, he must have quickly analysed things and drawn some conclusions, like the following:

1. God was serious.
2. The sin committed was of a very grave nature.
3. If God was allowed to act as promised, the following would happen: a. The people of Israel would all be destroyed; b. The honour of the Lord would be at stake before the Egyptians and all the surrounding nations, who would all say that God brought His people out of Egypt with an evil intent; c. The Lord's promises and oaths to Abraham, Isaac, and Jacob about the people and the land would collapse, and God would be seen as a liar; and d. Moses would be the starting point of a new and great nation.

So Moses saw that the action would destroy or tamper with God's glory and would lead to the destruction of the people and he would gain. If Moses had been a self-centred man, he would have rejoiced. He would have said, "What a wonderful opportunity to be promoted by God! I will become the starting point of a new nation.

The Lord has at last seen my faithfulness and is about to reward me. How wonderful! Lord, go on. Act quickly, O Lord, my God." Moses was not self-centred, so he did not act along the above lines.

If Moses had not identified himself entirely with the children of Israel, if he had been vengeful, he would have said, "These people have always rebelled against me. Recently they even wanted to stone me. They do not accept my leadership. They do not love me, and they do not want me. Let them have their due. Let them be destroyed, so that future generations will learn. Lord, act quickly. Lord, do it. Let justice be done." However, Moses was identified entirely with the children of Israel. He could not afford to have them destroyed. They did not accept him, but he accepted them. They did not love him, but he loved them. They were close to his heart.

Moses was a man of the glory. He knew God and He was united to God. He was concerned for God's honour and for God's glory. He was anxious that the nations around should say nothing evil of the Lord. He was concerned about the promise that God had made in the past. He was anxious about the oaths that He had made. The Lord was prepared to break them. Moses was caught up with what would be said of God. If the Lord broke His oaths, it would be breaking Himself. Moses then interceded.

Let us look at the way he went about it; for it is an art that all intercessors need to grow in.

First of all, the Lord had rejected the people. He said to Moses, "For your people whom you brought out of the land of Egypt ... " The Lord was saying, "These people have said that the golden calf was their god. They said that this golden calf brought them out of Egypt, since Moses, the man who brought them out of Egypt, was nowhere to be found. Since I did not bring them out of Egypt, since I am not their God, since you who brought them out were lost and would soon be found by them, they are your people."

Moses did not accept this, but he did not fight back. He just spoke to God, calling the people "thy people whom thou hast brought out of Egypt." So the people were shifted back to the Lord. Moses then added, "You brought them out with great power and with a mighty hand." He was exalting the Lord in His power and might. He was also saying to God, "The act of bringing them out of Egypt cost You Your power and might. Surely You do not want to waste these. If You destroy them, Your great power and might that were used would have been wasted."

Moses boldly asked the Lord a question: "Lord, why does thy wrath burn hot against thy people?" He was not being disrespectful. He was being bold and courageous. He was also speaking out of great intimacy. He had just been in His presence for forty days. Intercessors must be intimate with God. This will enable them to speak to God as others are not able to. It will enable them to ask God questions that others cannot ask, and even command God as others who are not intimate with Him cannot do.

Moses then went on and "preached a sermon at God." His sermon was: "Lord, do not do what You have said. These people are not mine. They are Yours. I did not bring them out of Egypt. You brought them. They have said that the calf brought them, but, Lord, You know that is a lie. Are You going to act on the basis of a lie that Your people have told? No. You will not do that. You should not destroy them. If You do, it will tamper with Your honour and not with theirs. They have no honour. The Egyptians had no problem with them. They had a problem with You. They know that it was You who brought them out. They do not know why You brought them out. If You destroy them, the Egyptians will never know the details. All they will say is that You are a bad God. They will say You are like their wicked gods. They will say that You brought them out with an evil intent to slay them in the mountain and to consume them from the face of the earth. God, that is not the picture of Yourself that You want to present, is it? Certainly not. Because that is not the picture You want to paint of Yourself, and because that is the picture that they will see of You, turn from Your fierce wrath and turn from this evil against Your people." It was a call on God to change His mind. It was a call on God to "repent." It was a command to God to "repent of this evil." This was courageous. It was boldness. But for the intimacy between God and Moses, one would easily have called it foolish boldness, but as it was, the two were very intimate, and between very intimate parties there is nothing like rudeness. There is communion.

Moses did not stop there. He pressed on. In order to press on, he knew the promises that God had made to Abraham, to Isaac, and to Israel. (Intercessors must know God's Word and God's promises. These are mighty weapons to use.) Moses then called the Lord to remember. It is as if he was saying to the Lord, "Lord, remember that Abraham was Your friend. Remember that You made a promise to him about his posterity living and occupying the land of Canaan forever. Remember that You sealed the promise with an oath. Remember that You made the same promise to his son Isaac and You repeated it to his grandson Israel. If You destroy these people, that promise will no longer be fulfilled. The God of heaven would have made Himself a liar. He would have lied to three people on separate occasions. His oath would have become useless." He might have said, "Lord, if You carry out this action and break Your oath, the principles on which the moral world holds together, i.e, Your Word, will collapse. Lord, remember and do not do it. As for me, I am not interested in being the starting point of a great nation. I have found my greatness in You. I have found my greatness in being Your servant."

THE SUCCESSFUL INTERCESSOR

The Bible says: "And the Lord repented of the evil which he thought he would do to his people." They were spared death. They were spared destruction. The honour of God as God who did not intend harm for the people that He brought out of Egypt, was assured. The promises that He made to Abraham, to Isaac, and to Jacob were safe and would be fulfilled.

Moses was successful. He had won a battle so that the glory of the Lord be established. He had won a battle so that the people of Israel should not be destroyed.

The primary purpose of the ministry of intercession is that God's glory should be maintained. It is a ministry that is primarily unto God. It is a ministry that aims at granting Him honour and praise. The intercessor seeks the glory of God. He intercedes so that God may be glorified. All other benefits of intercession, like the salvation of sinners and the provision of human needs, are secondary. May God open our eyes to see this. Amen.

3

WARFARE IN INTERCESSION

" *And Moses turned, and went down from the mountain with the two tables of the testimony in his hands, tables that were written on both sides; on one side and on the other were they written.*

And the tables were the work of God, and the writing was the writing of God, graven upon the tables.

When Joshua heard the noise of the people as they shouted, he said to Moses, "There is a noise of war in the camp."

But he said, "It is not the sound of shouting for victory, or the sound of the cry of defeat, but the sound of singing that I hear."

As soon as he came near the camp and saw the calf and the dancing, Moses' anger burned hot, and he threw the tables out of his hands and broke them at the foot of the mountain.

And he took the calf which they had made, and burnt it with fire, and ground it to powder, and scattered it upon the water, and made the people of Israel to drink it.

And Moses said to Aaron, "What did this people do to you that you have brought a great sin upon them?"

And Aaron said, "Let not the anger of my lord burn hot; you know the people that they are set on evil.

"For they said to me, 'Make us gods, who shall go before us; as for this

Moses, the man who brought us up out of the land of Egypt, we do not know what has become of him.'

"And I said to them, 'Let any who have gold take it off; so they gave it to me, and I threw it into the fire and there came out this calf.'

And when Moses saw that the people had broken loose (for Aaron had let them break loose, to their shame among their enemies) then Moses stood in the gate of the camp, and said, "Who is on the Lord's side? Come to me."

And all the sons of Levi gathered themselves together to him. And he said to them, "Thus says the Lord God of Israel, 'Put every man his sword on his side, and go to and fro from gate to gate throughout the camp, and slay every man his brother, and every man his companion, and every man his neighbour.'"

And the sons of Levi did according to the word of Moses; and there fell of the people that day about three thousand men.

And Moses said, "Today you have ordained yourselves for the service of the Lord, each one at the cost of his son and of his brother, that he may bestow a blessing upon you this day."

On the morrow Moses said to the people, "You have sinned a great sin.

"And now I will go up to the Lord, perhaps I can make atone-ment for your sin"

(Exodus 32: 15-30).

Moses had interceded on the mountain for the people of Israel, and the Lord had agreed not to destroy them. However, the Lord had not committed Himself to restoring them into His heart as His people. It is one thing not to be destroyed. It is another to be restored to one's original position.

Moses then came to the people, and when he saw the actual site of the worship of the calf, his anger waxed hot. He broke the tables on which the commandments were written and ground the golden calf, scattered it upon water, and made the people drink of it. He had pleaded that God's anger should not wax hot. However, he let his own anger wax hot. It waxed so hot that Aaron had to plead, "Let not the anger of my lord burn hot."

Moses was not perfect. He was consecrated. Intercessors are not perfect people. However, they must be consecrated people. The anger of Moses arose out of his commitment to God. He might have slipped when he burned hot with anger and forgot that he had just been pleading with God that His should not burn hot. However, Moses was in the right place. May none who are consecrated run away from interceding because they are not perfect. May they come boldly to the Lord and acknowledge that they have the treasure in earthen vessels. May they thank God, Who has put the heavenly ministry of intercession into earthen vessels like themselves so that it might be obvious that *"transcendent power belongs to God and not to us"* (II Corinthians 4:7).

THE NEED FOR FURTHER INTERCESSION

Moses had interceded. He had interceded to have God change His mind about destroying the people. He had hoped that the people would repent and come over to God's side. Aaron did not repent. He merely excused himself. Moses offered the people another opportunity of taking God's side. He asked that those who were on the Lord's side should come to him. He expected that they would all come to him. He expected them to choose God's side. However, they refused. Only the sons of Levi did. Moses then had before him a people who had sinned and would not repent. It looked like a hopeless situation. Would Moses give up on the people? Would he say, "I have tried to save them, but since they would not be saved, since they continue to choose the way of sin, let them have what they deserve." If he had said that, he would have failed. He did not fail. Rather, he saw the need for further intercession.

INTERCEDING FOR AN UNREPENTANT PEOPLE

Moses returned to the Lord to intercede for the unrepentant people of Israel. It was a big struggle. He lay before the Lord for forty days and forty nights, during which he neither ate bread nor drank water.

He said to the Lord, "*Alas, this people have sinned a great sin; they have made for themselves gods of gold. But now, if thou wilt forgive their sin—and if not, blot me, I pray thee, out of thy book which thou hast written*" (Exodus 32: 31b-32).

Moses made an all-out attempt to save the people. He was saying to the Lord, "I plead with You to pardon them. If You can pardon them because I have interceded, then, Lord, do so. If You would not pardon them on that ground, pardon them at the price of my eternal salvation. Blot my name out of Your Book of Life and pardon them. I am willing to atone for them at the cost of my eternal salvation."

Moses was really an intercessor! He was really united with the people of Israel. There was nothing that he was not prepared to give up so that the Lord might spare them. He was prepared to make the ultimate sacrifice for their salvation. The Apostle Paul had similar desires. He said:

"*I am speaking the truth in Christ.*

I am not lying! my conscience bears me witness in the Holy Spirit, that I have great sorrow and unceasing anguish in my heart.

For I could wish that I myself were accursed and cut off from Christ for the sake of my brethren, my kinsmen by race"

(Romans 9: 1-3).

That is the lot of an intercessor: great sorrow, unceasing anguish in the heart, and a desire to become nothing and even lose one's place in heaven for the sake of the salvation of those for whom he is interceding.

A real intercessor puts everything into interceding. He puts all that he has into jeopardy for those for whom he is interceding. He puts all of himself at stake for the sake of those for whom he is interceding, and he puts his place in the Kingdom of God at stake for the sake of the salvation of those for whom intercession is being made. There is no price that the intercessor is not prepared to pay. He gives all and holds nothing back!

Moses was the greatest intercessor only next to the interceding Lord Jesus. He had completed an absolute forty-day fast (no food and no water), and because the people had sinned and were at the verge of being destroyed, he decided to go and intercede for them with another fast. He knew that the battle could be long (and it actually lasted forty days and forty nights), yet he did not give up the people in order to protect his health. He was recklessly committed to the Lord and to the people. He was prepared to die physically from the long absolute fasts and spiritually from being blotted out of God's Book of Life so that the Word of the Lord might be established and the people saved.

Intercession is a most costly ministry. Those who enter into that ministry must be prepared to pay any price that it demands. It is only on those grounds that they may hope to win. It could demand any price, but God never demands a price that anyone does not have. Besides, it is not God demanding. It is the intercessor bargaining with God. He lays down all in exchange for the object of intercession.

It is only possible to intercede in this way if the intercessor knows great sorrow and unceasing anguish about the plight of a person or a people. The problem with the Church today is that she is so caught up with herself and so married to the world that she knows hardly any sorrow or anguish for the lost. She also knows no sorrow or anguish for the backslidden, the stillbirths, and the dwarfs that make up the majority of her ranks. She hardly knows any love for the Saviour who gave His all that He might purchase a Bride for Himself in splendour—without spot, without wrinkle, without blemish. If she loved the Lord, she would labour and sacrifice everything to ensure that the Lord Jesus had His heart's desire. But because she does not love, she hardly does a thing and sacrifices nothing! Oh, that a new day would dawn upon the Church! Oh, that intercessors would be raised! Oh, that in-tercessors would carry out the type of ministry that would cause God to raise other intercessors! Oh, for men and women whose one purpose for living would be to take no rest and give God no rest until He raises intercessors!

By bargaining that, if necessary, God should pardon the people and send him to hell, Moses had put down his "trump card." He hoped that it would work, but it did not. The fact that the people, after having sinned, were not prepared to repent and take God's side was too much for God to take lightly. It was too much for Him to take even at the price of Moses' perdition. In addition, the Lord was not interested in Moses perishing.

The Bible says: "*But the Lord said to Moses, 'Whoever has sinned against me, him will I blot out of my book*'" (Exodus 32:33). The Lord was saying to Moses, "Intercession now is useless. There is no need to intercede. You cannot do anything for these people. They will have the punishment that they deserve. It is the one who has sinned that will perish, and perish he must"

INTERCEDING LN AN APPARENTLY HOPELESS SITUATION

There are situations when God does say that intercession will not help. He says:

"*Though Moses and Samuel stood before me, yet my heart would not turn towards this people.*

Send them out of My sight, and let them go!

And when they ask you, 'Where shall we go?' you shall say to them, 'Thus says the Lord: 'Those who are for pestilence, to pestilence, and those who are for the sword, to the sword; those who are for famine, to famine, and those who are for captivity, to captivity.'

I will appoint over them four kinds of destroyers, says the Lord; the sword to slay, the dogs to tear, and the birds of the air and the beasts of the earth to devour and destroy. And I will make them a horror to all the kingdoms of the earth because of what Manasseh the son of Hezekiah, king of Judah, did in Jerusalem."

(Jeremiah 15: 1-4).

Speaking in the same terms, the Lord said to Ezekiel: "Son of man, when a land sins against me by acting faithlessly, and I stretch out my hand against it, and break its staff of bread and send famine upon it, and cut off from it man and beast, even if these three men, Noah, Daniel, and Job, were in it, they would deliver but their own lives by their righteousness, says the Lord God.

If I cause wild beasts to pass through the land, and they ravage it, and it be made desolate, so that no man may pass through because of the beasts; even if these three man were in it, as I live," says the Lord God, "they would deliver neither sons nor daughters; they alone would be delivered, but the land would be desolate.

"Or if I bring a sword upon that land, and say; let a sword go through the land; and I cut off from it man and beast; though these three men were in it, as I live,"says the Lord God, they would deliver neither sons nor daughters, but they alone would be delivered. Or if I send a pestilence into that land, and pour out my wrath upon it with blood, to cut off from it man and beast; even if Noah, Daniel, and Job were in it, as I live, says the Lord God, they would deliver neither son nor daughter; 'they would deliver but their own lives by their righteousness. 'For thus says the Lord God: 'How much more when I send upon Jerusalem my four sore acts of judgment, sword, famine, evil beasts, and pestilence, to cut off from it man and beast !"

(Ezekiel 14:13-21).

In situations like the ones above, most intercessors would have said, "It is a lost cause. There is no use interceding. God will never change His mind. Judgment and doom must come." Moses was faced with a similar situation. He had staked his life on it, but God did not change His mind. What was he to do? The situation was apparently hopeless. The glory of the Lord was at stake, for a disinherited Israel meant loss of honour for God and destruction for the people. Moses did not accept that the Lord should lose His glory. Therefore, he continued to wrestle as if against hope.

As if to assure Moses that it was useless interceding, He sent a plague upon the people because of their sin. In addition, He said something that was worse.

AN ISRAEL UNACCOMPANIED BY THE LORD

The glory of Israel lay in the fact that the Lord was their God and that He walked in the midst of them. Without their being so specially related to the Lord, their glory would be no more.

The Lord then said to Moses, "Since you were anxious that the Egyptians would say that I brought these people out of Egypt with an evil intent to destroy them in the wilderness, I will not destroy them so the Egyptians will have nothing to say. Also, I made a promise to Abraham, to Isaac and to Israel. I will keep that promise. The people will enter the Promised Land. There is only one thing that will be different. That thing is that I will not come with them. I will send an angel to go with them."

The Lord said to Moses, "*But now go, lead the people to the place of which I have spoken to you; behold my angel shall go before you. Nevertheless, in the day when I visit, I will visit their sin upon them*"

(Exodus 32:34).

The Lord continued to speak to Moses, "*Depart, go up hence, you and the people whom you have brought up out of the land of Egypt, to the land of which I swore to Abraham, Isaac and Jacob, saying, 'To your descendants I will give it.'*

And I will send an angel before you, and I will drive out the Canaanites, the Amorites, the Hittites, the Perizzites, the Hivites, and the Jebusites.

Go up to a land flowing with milk and honey; but I will not go up among you, lest I consume you in the way, for you are a stiff-necked people"

(Exodus 33: 1-3).

The Lord did not only say it to Moses. He commanded Moses to say to the people, "*You are a stiff-necked people; if for a single moment I should go up among you, I would consume you*" (Exodus 33:5).

The Lord was offering everything—total victory over His enemy without His presence, total occupation of the land without His presence, total abundance in the land without His presence! Many of God's children would have accepted what the Lord was offering. How many today are dissatisfied because of the absence of His presence? Is it not true that for a vast majority of the Church what they desire is success in the ministry, spiritual gifts, programmes being maintained and finished, plans being maintained and fulfilled, large meetings, large numbers, huge financial budgets being met, many decisions, the Bible read many times, many hours of prayer, many days or weeks of fasting, et cetera, even if these things are accomplished without the Lord's full presence? Is it not true that most people desire the gifts and are content with the gifts even if they do not know any intimate fellowship with the Giver? How many gladly carry out their routine "quiet times" and enjoy analysing the Scriptures and saying their prayers and even having answers to the prayers, yet not knowing fellowship and union with God?

How many would find all these things empty, vain, and useless unless the presence and the glory of the Lord was manifest?

Moses was one of those who would not accept success without the Lord. He would not be led by an angel instead of being led by the Lord. He would not become the leader of the people who had been led thus far and no farther by the Lord.

THE PERSISTENT INTERCESSOR

The Lord had said to Moses, "It is better that I do not come with you and the people; for if I come even for a single moment, I would consume them." Moses could have said, "This is dangerous. I must not press further, for if the Lord comes, the people will be destroyed." He did not say that. He rather said, "It is better for the Lord to come with us and we be destroyed by Him than to succeed without Him." He truly knew God. He truly loved God. He truly loved God's people.

Where are Moses' counterparts in the Church today? Where are those who would say to God, "I prefer to fail utterly and remain in the centre of Your will than to compromise one bit and have all of the world at my feet"? Are there some who can still say to Him, "Your presence is worth everything. Give me Yourself and if in addition to Yourself You give me nothing else, my heart would know bliss"? Where are those who will disdain all gifts, all successes, all triumphs that lack the manifest presence of God?

Because Moses knew that all success without God was utter failure, he continued to intercede. He was back to the art of intercession. He made as if he had not heard what the Lord had said about sending an angel with him. He therefore asked the Lord a question, saying:

"*See, thou sayest to me, 'Bring up this people; but thou hast not let me know whom thou wilt send with me. Yet thou hast said, 'I know you by name, and you have also found favour in my sight.' Now therefore, I pray thee, if I have found favour in thy sight, show me now thy ways, that I may know thee and find favour in thy sight. Consider too that this nation is thy people"*

(Exodus 33: 12-13).

Moses was not lying when he asked whom the Lord would send with him. He was not lying when he said that the Lord had not told him. He was just interceding. Intercession is a spiritual battle. It has rules that are peculiar to it that only make sense in it, rules that when applied elsewhere will be found faulty or evil and false. God knows these rules and those who will make progress in the ministry of intercession must learn the art and the rules.

As Moses continued to intercede, he changed the tactics. He decided to "play it cool" as regards the children of Israel and take up his own affairs with God, yet the goal of it all was to have God accept the children of Israel.

Moses said to God, "You have told me to bring up this people. You have not let me know whom You will send with me, Lord. You cannot leave me in this ignorance, because You had said to me, 'I know you by name, and you have found favour in My sight.' If indeed You know me by name as You said and if I have found favour in Your sight, show me now Your ways, that I may know Thee and find favour in Thy sight." Moses was concentrating on himself and his relationship with God. He knew the word that God had spoken about him. He knew that as one who had found favour in God's sight it was normal that God would:

1. delight to show him His ways,
2. gladly enable him to know Him more, and so
3. enable him to find more favour in His sight.

Moses thus asked that which the Lord would gladly do. Having asked that, he added something else, acting as if it was not important, even though it was the very centre of things. He said to God, "If I have found favour in thy sight, show me now thy ways that I may know thee and find favour in thy sight. Consider too that this nation is thy people."

These words, "Consider too that this nation is thy people," were the very heart of the matter, but the art of intercession made him say them as an addition. He was saying, "Lord, after You have considered me, consider this people also. Let the fact that You consider them be as a result of the fact that You have considered me. Let it be a part of Your favour towards me."

The Lord heard Moses and answered, "*My presence will go with you, and I will give you rest*" (Exodus 33: 14). The Lord made as if He did not hear the second part of Moses' request. He said nothing about it but went ahead to assure Moses that His presence would go with him.

Moses had won a major battle. The Lord's presence was with him and not a mere angel. That was good, but what of the Lord's presence coming with the people? God had said nothing about that. The battle was not fully won. No intercessor is satisfied with, partial" victory. He decides from the beginning what he wants, and he presses on until it is received in full. We can say that what Moses received for himself was a bonus. He had gone into God's presence not to seek God for himself nor to seek blessings for himself. He had gone to intercede for the children of Israel, and he did not lose sight of his goal. He did not allow the secondary issues to cause him to forget the central one. So he pressed on with God. He was not being ungrateful. He was being goal-directed. He was being single of heart!.

Moses then interceded, saying:

"*If thy presence will not go with me, do not carry us up from here.*

For how shall it be known that I have found favour in thy sight, I and thy people? Is it not in thy going with us, so that we are distinct, I and thy people, from all other people that are upon the face of the earth?"

(Exodus 33: 15-16).

Do you see what Moses was doing? He said "me" but soon turned to "us." He said, "How shall it be known that I have found favour in thy sight, I and thy people?" Do you see the "I and thy people"? He asked a question and he began to answer God, telling Him what He should do. He was saying, "Lord, show that I have found favour in Thy sight by going with us so that we are distinct, I and thy people."

"We," "us," and "I and thy people" are the words of a man who has found favour before God and who is capitalizing on that favour so that others may find favour. May we find favour before Him so that because of the favour He delights to show us, others may receive His favour and be restored.

I see here the possibility of a wife obtaining favour for her husband and vice versa. I see the possibility of a brother obtaining favour for a brother, a brother for a sister, a son for a father, a father for a son, a man for his nation, and a leader for those he is leading!

4

THE BURDEN AND THE GLORY

"*And he said to him, 'If thy presence will not go with me, do not carry us up from here.*

For how shall it be known that I have found favour in thy sight, I and thy people?

Is it not in thy going with us, so that we are distinct, I and thy people, from all other people that are upon the face of the earth?

And the Lord said to Moses, 'This very thing that you have spoken I will do; for you have found favour in my sight, and I know you by name.

Moses said, 'I pray thee, show me thy glory.

And he said, 'I will make all my goodness pass before you, and will proclaim before you my name 'The Lord'; and I will be gracious to whom I will be gracious, and will show mercy on whom I will show mercy.

But he said, 'You cannot see my face; for man shall not see me and live.

And the Lord said, 'Behold, there is a place by me where you shall stand upon the rock; and while my glory passes by I will put you in a cleft of the rock, and I will cover you with my hand until I have passed by; then I will take away my hand and you shall see my back; but my face shall not be seen.'"

"*The Lord said to Moses, 'Cut two tables of stone like the first; and I will write upon the tables the words that were on the first tables, which you broke.*

Be ready in the morning, and come up in the morning to Mount Sinai, and present yourself there to me on the top of the mountain.

No man shall come up with you, and let no man be seen throughout all the mountain;

Let no flocks or herds feed before that mountain. So Moses cut two tables of stone like the first;

And he rose early in the morning and went up on Mount Sinai, as the Lord had commanded him, and took in his hand two tables of stone.

And the Lord descended in the cloud and stood with him there, and proclaimed the name of the Lord.

The Lord passed before him, and proclaimed, 'The Lord, the Lord, a God merciful and gracious, slow to anger, and abounding in steadfast love and faithfulness, keeping steadfast love for thousands, forgiving iniquity and transgression and sin, but who will by no means clear the guilty, visiting the iniquity of the fathers upon the children and the children's children, to the third and fourth generation.

And Moses made haste to bow his head toward the earth, and worshipped.

And he said, "If now I have found favour in thy sight, O Lord, let the Lord, I pray thee, go in the midst of us, although it is a stiff-necked people; and pardon our iniquity and our sin, and take us for thy inheritance."

And he said, "Behold, I make a covenant.

Before all your people I will do marvels, such as have not been wrought in all the earth or in any nation; and all the people among whom you are shall see the work of the Lord; for it is a terrible thing that I will do with you.

Observe what I command you this day.

Behold, I will drive out before you the Amorites, the Ca-naanites, the Hittites, the Perizzites, the Hivites, and the Jebusites.

Take heed to yourself, lest you make a covenant with the inhabitants of the land whither you go, lest it become a snare in the midst of you.

You shall tear down their altars, and break their pillars, and cut down their Asherim (for you shall worship no other god, for the Lord, whose name is Jealous, is a jealous God), lest you make a covenant with the inha-

bitants of the land, and when they play the harlot after their gods and sacrifice to their gods and one invites you, you eat of his sacrifice, and you take of their daughters for your sons, and their daughters play the harlot after their gods and make your sons play the harlot after their gods"

(Exodus 33: 15-23; 34: 1-16).

In the preceding chapter, we saw that Moses had won a major battle. He had wrestled with God until it was settled that God's presence would go with him and not an angel. He still had a major problem as to whether God's presence was coming with him as an individual or was coming with him and coming with the people of God. The question was: "Had God accepted the people of Israel back into His heart? Was He going to be once more their God in that deep and intimate way?"

Moses then said to God, "Lord, You have said that Your presence will come with me and You will give me rest. That is wonderful. However, I am not alone. I am with Your people. I cannot accept that offer if it is made to me alone. In fact, as it is I refuse it. You can do something about it. You can decide to come with us, me and Your people. That will make us distinct from all the people that are upon the face of the earth."

Moses knew God. Moses was related to God. They were intimate. Moses was bold and he was honest. His commitment to his people was without the slightest doubt. He had been prepared to sacrifice even his place in eternal life for them. Now he was saying to God, "If You will not come with me, me and Your people, do not carry us from here. If You are not coming with us, let this be the end. I will forget the Promised Land. It is best that it ends here, for any move without You coming with me and without You coming with these people, is a tragic one." That is intercession! That is an intercessor at work! Intercession includes the holy boldness to command God, the humble courage to present ultimatums to Him. It includes something that for lack of better words I will call "putting God in a fix." This level of intercession is therefore open to those who have made history with God; these people know God's heart and dwell in it.

The Lord answered Moses, "This very thing that You have spoken I will do, for you have found favour in My sight and I know you by name." Moses had thus won another major battle. The Lord was coming with him and with them. They would be distinct from all the other people upon the earth. We can say that Moses was 80 percent successful. He had only one more problem, and it was whether the Lord would take the people of Israel as

His and be their God in that intimate way.

A BREAK LN THE BATTLE

It can be understood that this was the greatest battle Moses ever fought and it was not a battle with Satan, but with God. He came prepared to win or perish. He came denying everything of the flesh in an absolute fast (no food and no water), and he came prepared to wrestle until it was over. He must have said to himself, "If it takes one week to be through, I will wrestle through. If, on the other hand, two, three, six, eight, twenty, or fifty weeks are needed to win the battle, I will put them in." He forgot about his health. He did not say, "I will make sure that it does not exceed forty days so that I do not die because of the fast." His heart was given to winning and not to precautions. Real intercessors are reckless people. They damn all consequences.

Because the battle had been so fierce, Moses decided to have a break and move to something that was not in the realm of intercession. He decided to let the Lord "cool off" for some time. He then turned to something that was personal and said to God, "I pray thee, show me thy glory." It seemed like a small request, but it was indeed big, very big.

THE GLORY OF THE LORD

There are various manifestations of the Lord for example, Moses saw something of the glory of the Lord when the Lord spoke to him, as He did often. Moses saw something of the glory of the Lord in His power exhibited in Egypt, at the Red Sea, and in the wilderness. He saw something of the glory of the Lord when he spent forty days in God's presence in order to be shown God's model of the tabernacle that he was to build. He saw something of the glory of God when he, Aaron, Nadab, Abihu, and seventy of the elders of Israel went up the mountain at the call of God and all saw the God of Israel.

However, Moses knew that there was more. What he saw made him desire more. He was not desiring to see God's power. He had seen much of that. He just wanted to see the glory of God. He knew that he could not see the glory of God by any activity of his own. One way was open to him—the way of asking—and he used it. It was not a right, and so he spoke differently: "I pray thee, show me thy glory." What big asking! What an unsatisfied heart! Someone could have said, "Moses, what is wrong with you?

You know God more than any other person on earth, and you are not satisfied!"

HOLY DISSATISFACTION

It is a wonderful thing to enter into the fullness of the Lord and know deep satisfaction in Him. It is wonderful to be fulfilled in the Lord. Those who have no longing because they are satisfied are a blessed people. However, I am afraid that satisfaction is the lot of those who have made some progress in the seeking after God but have stopped somewhere before entering into all of the fullness. Those who enter into the fullness know that it is the fullness of being satisfied in Him, "but also fullness that makes them want Him more, so that they burn for Him after they have " known His fullness more than they burned after Him in their initial search for fullness. The words of the Psalmist express the desire of those who have made much progress and have passed from being satisfied in the Lord to the plane of holy dissatisfaction:

"As a hart longs for flowing streams, so longs my soul for thee O God.

My soul thirsts for God, for the living God. When shall I come and behold the face of God?"

(Psalm 42: 1-2).

"O God, thou art my God, I seek thee, my soul thirsts for thee; my flesh faints for thee, as in a dry and weary land where no water is.

So I have looked upon thee in the sanctuary, beholding thy power and glory. Because thy steadfast love is better than life, my lips will praise thee.

So will I bless thee as long as I live; I will lift up my hands and call on thy name"

(Psalm 63: 1-4).

This experience of knowing God and being fulfilled in Him yet burning after Him is the lot of those who have really matured, not only in walking in the ways of God, but in walking with God. The tragedy is that such saints are in very short supply in our day. It is sad but true to say that some saints know the salvation of God and His work in sanctification, are consecrated to Him, and serve Him faithfully. Such are considered God's choicest servants, and they are indeed, for most believers cannot be described in these terms. However, it can equally be said that most of these faithful servants of God are content to know something of the faithfulness and the power of God but do not know God. They know His acts, but they do not know Him. They have never "seen" Him. They have never been shown His glory. They faithfully ask and receive things from Him, but they have never asked that He show Himself to them. Because they are satisfied with His acts and His gifts, He leaves them at the level where they have chosen to be. They do not know His glory. They have taken His gifts for His glory. They are dissatisfied when His power is not manifest, but they are not dissatisfied because they have never seen Him.

It is true that in the age to come all who are His will see Him.

It is also true that in the current age those who seek Him, ask Him and pay a price before Him are allowed to have a foretaste of what shall be common in the age to come. That foretaste affects the quality of their lives and service significantly, for who can see the Lord and His glory and ever be the same?

My prayer to the Lord is that the Holy Spirit will raise up in our day in His Church some who are no longer satisfied to see only God's acts, but burn to see Him. This will bring a needed dimension to the pilgrim Body of Christ. Lord, do it quickly.

THE GOD OF ABUNDANCE

Moses had a need. He needed to see the Lord's glory. He presented his need to God. It was now up to God to do something about it. The Lord agreed to grant Moses' request. He said to Moses, "I will make all My goodness pass before you, and will proclaim before you, My name 'The Lord,' and I will be gracious to whom I will be gracious and will show mercy on whom I will show mercy."

Is it not wonderful that God immediately agreed to show His glory to Moses? Is it not wonderful that He decided to do more than Moses asked for? The Lord promised:

1. To make all His goodness pass before Moses. It was not

to be some of His goodness but all of His goodness.
2. To proclaim before Moses His name "The Lord." This is most wonderful. How could God condescend to honour Moses so exceedingly? Can you imagine God passing before a man and proclaiming His name to man? Normally, it should be the lesser proclaiming the name of the greater, but how wonderful our God is. He decided to take a lowly position in order to reach out to His seeking servant. Glory be to His holy name!
3. To expose something of His character permanently to Moses.

He decided to make all His goodness pass before Moses and proclaim His name and His character, saying, "I will be gracious to whom I will be gracious and will show mercy on whom I will show mercy." He was saying to Moses, " I will show you all My goodness, proclaim My name to you, and let you forever know that I am gracious and merciful." I find in this an encouragement to Moses from the Lord that Moses could count on Him to be gracious to the children of Israel and to show mercy on them.

Moses asked for one thing and received three. Is that not characteristic of the God we have come to know as the Father of our Lord and Saviour Jesus Christ? The Bible says: "*Give, and it will be given to you; good measure, pressed down, shaken together, running over, will be put into your lap*" (Luke 6:38).

How sad that we do not ask! How sad that we do not ask for big things! How sad that we have not learnt to deal with Him who does far more abundantly than we ask or think! How sad that we have not learnt to deal with the One who commands us, saying. "*Ask of me, and I will make the nations your heritage, and the ends of the earth your possession. You shall break them with a rod of iron, and dash them in pieces like a potter's vessel*" (Psalm 2:8-9)

May we repent and begin not only to intercede for others, but also to pray for ourselves. Then we shall be giving Him an opportunity to display His abundance, and we shall be rich in Him.

SOLVING GOD'S PROBLEMS FOR HIM?

Very often God's children out of carnal zeal decide to solve God's problems for Him. Often they even disobey God in an attempt to help Him. They make as if God is weak and unable and has got Himself into a mess out of which He must be helped. This is the reason for the compromises of believers who are otherwise consecrated to God.

The Lord had told Moses that He would cause all of His goodness to pass before him. There was a problem involved with this. Moses knew it. It was a problem that arose from a promise made by God. Should Moses try to solve it? Should he say, "Lord, I am sorry, this is going to cause You a problem. I withdraw my request. Let us see how things can be rearranged"? He kept quiet.

When problems or requests are made to God, those who make them must leave things with Him and only act at His commands. They must not offer help that is not called for. God has not left man to initiate things. Rather, He has willed that His should receive instructions from Him and obey them.

God realized that there was a problem associated with His showing His glory to Moses. He said, "You cannot see My face, for man shall not see me and live." So the problem was stated. However, it was God's problem and not that of Moses. Therefore, Moses kept quiet.

God found an answer. He said, "Behold, there is a place by Me where you shall stand upon the rock, and while My glory passes by I will put you in a cleft of the rock and I will cover you with My hand until I have passed by; then I will take away My hand, and you shall see My back, but My face shall not be seen."

That was God's solution. It was an excellent solution and it worked well. What God does is always excellent.

A PLACE BY ME, A PLACE UPON THE ROCK

It is good to make big requests to God. It is good to ask Him to do good things. A question then arises as to what should, be done after the request has been made and God is "working at the answer." I think that the one who has asked should stand on the rock-the rock that is Christ. He should believe God to act. Even if the answer does not come quickly, he should stand on the rock. He should not be moved by the suggestions that come from man or from demons. He must be fully assured that God will act, and he must wait on Him.

The second thing is that the position where the asking believer should wait is a place by the Lord. The closest intimacy between the asking believer and the supplying God is of importance. Such intimacy must be entered into and maintained from the moment of initial waiting on God to hear Him, then at the next moment of asking and through the period of waiting. It must also be maintained during the period that follows the reception of what was asked. "There must never be a time in a believer's life when he allows that intimacy to be broken. It must be jealously guarded.

So the one who will succeed in the school of prayer will know how to stand constantly on the rock and how to stand at the place by the heart of the Lord!

AN ADDED BLESSING

It is surprising that after Moses broke the two tables of stone on which the law was written he did not bother to ask God about their replacement. He seemed too preoccupied with the destiny of his people to bother about them.

Or could it be that he was afraid or ashamed to speak to God about them, since he had acted in anger and failed to seek the Lord about the matter? It would seem that the issue was on his heart, even though he said nothing about it.

God saw what was in his heart, and while handling Moses' demand to see His glory, He decided to give Moses another thing that he did not ask. He said to Moses, "*Cut two tables of stone like the first; and I will write upon the tables the words that were on the first tables, which you broke. Be ready in the morning, and come up in the morning, to Mount Sinai, and present yourself there to Me on the top of the mountain. No man shall come up with you, and let no man be seen throughout all the mountain; let no flocks or herds feed before that mountain.' So Moses cut two tables of stone like the first; and he arose early in the morning and went up on Mount Sinai, as the Lord had commanded him, and took in his hand two tables of stone*" (Exodus 34: 1-4).

What a gracious God our Father is! How tender is His care! He answers us when we ask. He gives us in excess of what we ask, and when we are afraid to present our requests to Him, He goes ahead and answers them. Personally, I find this a great encouragement. I find it also a great challenge. I will increasingly bring all that is in my heart to Him. I will bring to Him the things about which I am sure. I will also bring to Him the things that are in my heart but confuse me. I will bring my victories to Him, and I will bring my failures to Him. I will bring my all to Him and let Him have all and supply me everything as well as lead me in everything. Glory be to His name!

THE GLORY

All is now ready. Moses has cut the two tables and has moved to the top of the mountain. His heart is on fire. He will soon see the glory of the Lord. Then the glorious moment arrives. The Lord descends in the cloud and stands with him there and proclaims, "The Lord, the Lord, a God merciful and gracious, slow to anger and abounding in steadfast love and faithfulness, keeping steadfast love for thousands ... " Moses was standing in the cleft, and all the goodness of the Lord passed before him. He saw all the goodness of God. He heard the proclamation and in the proclamation God was saying more and offering more to him than He had promised.

Moses was overwhelmed. He made haste to bow his head towards the earth. He worshipped. It had happened. It was awe-inspiring. The marks of it would remain on him forever. They would cause permanent awe of the Eternal God to be upon him. He would never be the same. He had seen God. He had heard God and he had been shown the character of God. He would deal with God differently for the rest of his life.

The event did not last long. It did not need to be long. It does not take long to change the course of a life, provided the power at work is from above. Paul saw the light from heaven and heard a few words from the Lord, and the course of his life was changed permanently and radically. All who meet God are changed. All who see God are changed.

THE GLORY AND THE INTERCESSOR

Moses had seen the glory of God. He had bowed and worshipped. He was still overwhelmed. However, he did not forget that his asking to see the glory of the Lord was just a break in his battle as an intercessor. He could not afford the luxury of bathing for too long in what he had seen. He immediately took up the arms of intercession and said to the heavenly Father, "If now I have found favour in thy sight, 0 Lord, let the Lord, I pray thee, go in the midst of us, although it is a stiff-necked people, and pardon our iniquity and our sin, and take us for thy inheritance."

Do you hear the groanings of the intercessor? Do you see the language that is being used? He says: "O Lord," "Let the Lord," and "1 pray thee."

Do you see the total identification of the intercessor? He now identified fully with them and with their sin. He says to the Lord, "Go in the midst of us," "We are a stiff-necked people," "Pardon our iniquity," "Pardon our sin," and "Take us for Your inheritance."

The Lord had just let Moses see His glory because he found favour in His sight. As if to put that aside, Moses asked that if he had found favour in God's sight, God should do the things outlined above to them. He did not give any room for God to separate him from the people of Israel. Moses seemed to put all that in the past and say to God, "If I have found favour in Thy sight, pardon us and take us for Thy inheritance."

PARDONING AN UNREPENTANT PEOPLE

It is normal to expect that God in His graciousness will pardon a repentant people. Moses had with him a people who were prone to sin. He had with him people who even after they had sinned refused to take God's side. He had before him and with him people who did not have any merit whatsoever so that he could ask for, the Lord's pardon on that account. He could not promise that they would do better. He could give no assurance to God that they had learnt their lesson. From the human part it was a very hopeless situation. Most intercessors would have given up.

Moses, however, did not give up. He had one trump card, and he used it. God had said to him that he had found favour in His sight. On the basis of that favour, God had allowed all His goodness to pass before him. Moses more or less said, "God, if I have found favour in Your sight, that favour was most unmerited. I do not deserve to have seen what You let me see of You today. If that favour still remains, I beg You to pardon us (Your people and me) even though we are stiff-necked and unrepentant. Do not only pardon us. Take us for Your inheritance."

If God answered this request of Moses, then Moses would have achieved the purpose of his intercession 100 percent. He would have succeeded in persuading God to go with the people of Israel in the place of an angel. He would have succeeded in having God pardon the people, become their God, and make them His people, as was the case before the tragic sin. He would have succeeded to have God do it on grounds that would not change, not depending on what the people did but on the unchanging grounds of His favour. .

I see in this a wonderful hope for all intercessors. It simply means that no intercessor can come against a situation in which there are no grounds to intercede. No people and no situations are beyond intercession. The grounds of God's favour are limitless.

This also calls for Faith and those who have no Faith cannot make progress in the school of intercession. Believing that God will have mercy on a rebellious people while they remain in their rebellion requires much faith. Moses had such faith. Each intercessor should ask and receive such Faith from the Lord. It is a basic need.

THE VICTORIOUS INTERCESSOR

Was Moses successful in his last plea to God? God did not answer simply, but what He said shows clearly that Moses' request was granted. He said to him, "*Behold, I make a covenant. Before all your people I will do marvels, such as have not been wrought in all the earth or in any nation; and all the people among whom you are shall see the work of the Lord; for it is a terrible thing that I will do with you. 'Observe what I command you this day. Behold, I will drive out before you the Amorites, the Canaanites, the Hittites, the Perizzites, the Hivites, and the Jebusites*" (Exodus 34:10-11).

Do you see that it is the Lord Himself who was to do marvels? He was surely going to do it from their midst. They were to see the work of the Lord and not the work of the Lord's angel. He was making a covenant with them, and they were not to make covenants with others. He was their exclusive God, and they were His exclusive people. All was settled. Moses had won. The Lord had taken back His people and further said to them:

"*All that opens the womb is mine*"

(Exodus 34: 19).

"*Three times in the year shall all your males appear before the Lord God, the God of Israel. For I will cast out nations before you, and enlarge your borders; neither shall any man desire your land, when you go up to appear before the Lord your God three times in the year*"

(Exodus 34:23-24).

Those words, "The Lord God, the God of Israel, the Lord your God," are very heartwarming and echo clearly the fact that Moses had succeeded in all the purpose of his intercession.

May the Lord be glorified that a man like him walked on earth and did business with God. May we labour to know God as he did and commit ourselves to the ministry of intercession as he did. May we not only commit ourselves to the ministry of intercession, may we actually intercede, and may we know the depth of intercession that he knew and the extent of victory that was his. This will bring glory to the Lord. To Him be glory, honour, majesty, power, and dominion. Amen.

5

THE PERSISTENT INTERCESSOR

"*The Lord said to Moses, 'Send men to spy out the land of Canaan, which I give to the people of Israel; from each tribe of their fathers shall you send a man, every one a leader among them.*

So Moses sent them from the wilderness of Paran, according to the command of the Lord, all of them men who were heads of the people of Israel"

(Numbers 13:1-3).

"*Moses sent them to spy out the land of Canaan, and said to them,*

'Go up into the Negeb yonder, and go up into the hill country, And see what the land is, and whether the people who dwell in it are strong or weak, whether they are few or many, and whether the land that they dwell in is good or bad, and whether the cities that they dwell in are camps or strongholds, and whether the land is rich or poor, and whether there is wood in it or not.

Be of good courage, and bring some of the fruit of the land'"

(Numbers 13: 17-20)

"*So they went up and spied out the land from the wilderness of Zin to Rehob, near the entrance of Hamath.*

"*They went up into the Negeb, and came to Hebron; and Ahiman, Sheshai, and Talmai, the descendants of Anak, were there. (Hebron was built seven years before Zoan in Egypt.)*

And they came to the Valley of Eshcol, and cut down from there a branch with a single cluster of grapes, and they carried it on a pole between two of them; they brought also some pomegranates and figs"

(Numbers 13:21-23).

"*At the end of forty days they returned from spying out the land.*

And they came to Moses and Aaron and to all the congregation of the people of Israel in the wilderness of Paran, at Kadesh; they brought back word to them and to all the congregation, and showed them the fruit of the land.

And they told him, 'We came to the land to which you sent us; it flows with milk and honey, and this is its fruit.

Yet the people who dwell in the land are strong and the cities are fortified and very large; and besides we saw the descendants of Anak there.

The Amalekites dwell in the land of the Negeb; the Hittites, the Jebusites, and the Amorites dwell in the hill country; and the Canaanites dwell by the sea, and along the Jordan" (Numbers 13:25-29).

"*But Caleb quietened the people before Moses, and said, 'Let us go up at once, and occupy it; for we are well able to overcome it.'*

Then the men who had gone up with him said, 'We are not able to go up against the people; for they are stronger than we.'

So they brought to the people of Israel an evil report of the land which they spied out, saying, "The land, through which we have gone, to spy it out, is a land that devours its inhabitants; and all the people that we saw in it are men of great stature.

And there we saw the Nephilim (the sons of Anak, who come from the Nephilim); and we seemed to ourselves like grasshoppers,

and so we seemed to them" (Numbers 13:30-33).

"*Then all the congregation raised a loud cry; and the people wept that night.*

And all the people of Israel murmured against Moses and Aaron; the whole congregation said to them, 'Would that we had died in the land of Egypt!

Or would that we had died in this wilderness!

Why does the Lord bring us into this land, to fall by the sword?

Our wives and our little ones will become a prey; would it not be better for us to go back to Egypt?' And they said to one another, 'Let us choose a captain, and go back to Egypt.'

Then Moses and Aaron fell on their faces before all the as-sembly of the congregation of the people of Israel.

And Joshua the son of Nun and Caleb the son of Jephunneh, who were among those who had spied out the land, rent their clothes, and said to all the congregation of the people of Israel, 'The land, which we passed through to spy it out, is an exceedingly good land.

If the Lord delights in us, he will bring us into this land and give it to us, a land which flows with milk and honey. Only, do not rebel against the Lord; and do not fear the people of the land, for they are bread for us; their protection is removed from them, and the Lord is with us; do not fear them.'

But all the congregation said to stone them with stones"

(Numbers 14: 1-10)

Then the glory of the Lord appeared at the tent of meeting to all the people of Israel.

And the Lord said to Moses, "*How long will this people despise me? And how long will they not believe in me, in spite of all the signs which I have wrought among them?*

I will strike them with the pestilence and disinherit them, and I will make of you a nation greater and mightier than they"

(Numbers 14:10-12).

"But Moses said to the Lord,

Then the Egyptians will hear of it, for thou didst bring up this people in thy might from among them, and they will tell the inhabitants of this land. They have heard that thou, O Lord, art in the midst of this people; for thou O Lord, art seen face to face, and thy cloud stands over them and thou goest before them, in a pillar of cloud by day and in a pillar of fire by night. Now if thou dost kill this people as one man, then the nations who have heard thy fame will say,

'Because the Lord was not able to bring this people into the land which he swore to give them, therefore he has slain them in the wilderness.'

'And now, I pray thee, let the power of the Lord be great as thou hast promised, saying,

"The Lord is slow to anger, and abounding in steadfast love, forgiving iniquity and transgression, but he will by no means clear the guilty, visiting the iniquity of fathers upon children, upon the third and upon the fourth generation.'

Pardon the iniquity of this people, I pray thee, according to the greatness of thy steadfast love, and according as thou hast forgiven this people, from Egypt even until now.'

Then the Lord said,

'I have pardoned according to your word; but truly, as I live, and as all the earth shall be filled with the glory of the Lord, none of the men who have seen my glory and my signs which I wrought in Egypt and in the wilderness, and yet have put me to the proof these ten times and have not hearkened to my voice, shall see the land which I swore to give to their fathers; and none of those who despised me shall see it.

But my servant Caleb, because he has a different spirit and has followed me fully, I will bring into the land into which he went, and his descendants shall possess it.

Now, since the Amalekites and the Canaanites dwell in the valleys, turn tomorrow and set out for the wilderness by the way to the Red Sea"

(Numbers 14:13-25).

THE SIN OF THE CHILDREN OF ISRAEL

It is sad that the children of Israel were always sinning against God. It is also sad to know that they always committed the sins that were most offensive to the Lord. Earlier on, it was the sin of idolatry. In the case at hand it was the tragic sin of unbelief. The Lord had said to Moses, "Send men to spy the land of Canaan which I give to the people of Israel." From that statement alone it was obvious that God's position on the matter was settled. He was going to give them the land. The type and numbers of people who were there did not matter; the type of cities and defences did not matter. All that mattered was that God had promised them the land and He would surely give it to them. The land was flowing with milk and honey. That is what God said. Could it be any less? The matter of sending out the spies was just a test to see if the people believed Him. When He had restored them after their last great sin, He had said to them:

"Behold, I make a covenant. Before all your people I will do marvels, such as have not been wrought in all the earth or in any nation; and all the people among whom you are shall see the work of the Lord; for it is a terrible thing that I will do with you.

"Observe what I command you this day. Behold, I will drive out before you the Amorites, the Canaanites, the Hittites, the Perizzites, the Hivites, and the Jebusites"

(Exodus 34:10-11).

With such promises it was obvious that God had committed Himself to getting rid of the enemy regardless of how strong he was. If they had believed God, they would have reported, "We came to the land to which You sent us; it flows with milk and honey, and this is its fruit. Let us go up at once and occupy it, for we are well able to overcome it."

If they had believed God they would not have added, "Yet the people who dwell in the land are strong and the cities fortified and very large, and besides, we saw the descendants of Anak there. The Amalekites dwell in the land of the Negeb; the Hittites, the Jebusites, and the Amorites dwell in the hill country; the Canaanites dwell by the sea and along the Jordan." This report sounds very factual. However, the undertone was that victory was not possible. They were more or less saying that the land was too secure for any penetration. They did not speak forthrightly of the impossibility of victory, but they let the audience understand it. There is a faithlessness that is well construed in the presentation of clear, logical, and negative facts that destroy by impressing upon the heart the fact that all is lost even though those final words may not be said. In the case of the children of Israel, the spies were quietly saying, "Forget it. It will never work. It is an impossible project."

When Joshua and Caleb presented God's position on the matter, the position of the doubters was challenged. It was then that they came out with full force to try to win the people to unbelief. They exaggerated everything and they presented it in such a way that it left no doubt about what was in their hearts. They said:

"The land, through which we have gone, to spy it out, is a land that devours its inhabitants; and all the people that we saw in it are men of great stature.

And there we saw the Nephilim (the sons of Anak, who come from the Nephilim); and we seemed to ourselves like grasshoppers, and so we seemed to them."

(Numbers 13:32-33).

The evil intent of this report is obvious. They said that the land devoured its inhabitants, but it did not devour the men of great stature that they saw there and it did not devour them who had moved through it to spy it. Earlier on they had given a report of all the peoples who dwelt there. How could they dwell in a land that devoured its inhabitants? They saw themselves as grasshoppers before the sons of Anak and therefore thought the sons of Anak saw them as so. This had no root in realty but in the unbelief in their hearts.

BY FAITH OR BY SIGHT

These spies walked by sight. They saw what was around. They used their senses to analyse the situation and they took a decision as to what was possible and what was impossible. Those who walk by sight measure the possibility of victory by:

1. what is seen,
2. what is heard,
3. what is felt,
4. what is analysed.

None who walk according to the results obtained from these natural senses can please God, because they are walking by sight. They are not walking by faith, and without walking by faith it is impossible to please God. In fact, all that is by sight is a sin before God, for it is that which comes from faith that means something to Him.

Those who walk by faith ask only one question, and it is, "What does God say? What does His Word say? What is His position in this matter?" When what God or His word says or wants is achieved, the position of the one who is walking by faith is settled permanently.

Joshua and Caleb walked by faith. They knew what God's mind about the matter was. They knew that it was God's will to give them the land. They knew that God would accomplish His purpose. They took God's position. They made it theirs and they proclaimed it. They said something like the following: "God has promised to give us the land. He will give us the land whether or not there are giants in it. He will give us the land regardless of the strength of the enemy. He will give us the land regardless of the extent of the fortification of their cities." *They were speaking the language of the God who said, "As I have planned, so shall it be, and as I have purposed, so shall it stand"* (Isaiah 14:24). *"For the Lord of hosts has purposed, and who will annul it? His hand is stretched out, and who will turn it back?"* (Isaiah 14:27). *Yes, they were speaking the language of the God who had said, "Behold, I will drive out before you the Amorites, the Canaanites, the Hittites, the Perizzites, the Hivites, and the Jebusites"* (Exodus 34: 11).

Thus speaking the language of God from the heart, they proclaimed, "They are bread for us; their protection is removed from them, and the Lord is with us." This is the language of faith. It is not a simplistic escape from facts. It is faith. It is taking God's position from the heart and speaking it with the lips. It is faith and confession and they insisted on immediate action.

The children of Israel listened to doubters and people of faith, both of whom had been to spy out the land. They chose who to believe depending not on what they had heard but on what was in their hearts. The reality is that man's response to facts is not governed by the facts themselves but by what is in his heart. In their hearts was an unwillingness to take God's position, to move in God's direction, and to accomplish his will. In their hearts was Egypt. They walked towards the Promised Land, but their hearts were in Egypt! Their reaction was dependent on where their hearts were, and that is why the y decided: "*Let us choose a captain, and go back to Egypt*" (Numbers 14:4). They spoke out:

"*Would that we had died in the land of Egypt! Or would that we had died in this wilderness!*

Why does the Lord bring us into this land, to fall by the sword?

Our wives and our little ones will become a prey; would it not be better for us to go back to Egypt?"

(Numbers 14:2-3).

They did not only think evil; they spoke it and they wanted to act. They wanted to go back to Egypt, and they wanted to stone the men of faith who had gone with them and then taken God's position.

GOD'S REACTION

There is a time for man to think, speak, and act, but sooner or later God does step in. In the case at hand the Bible says:

"Then the glory of the Lord appeared at the tent of meeting to all the people of Israel.

And the Lord said to Moses, "How long will this people despise me? And how long will they not believe in me, in spite of all the signs which I have wrought among them?

"*I will strike them with the pestilence and disinherit them, and I will make of you a nation greater and mightier than they*"

(Numbers 14:10-12).

God cannot tolerate sin in general, but more specifically, He cannot stand the sin of idolatry and unbelief. The children of Israel had committed the sin of idolatry before, and they were following it with the sin of unbelief. God could stand it no more.

It is interesting to compare the way that God reacted this time to the way that He reacted in the preceding incident. In the preceding incident He said to Moses, "*Now therefore let me alone, that my wrath may bum hot against them; but of you; but of you I will make a great nation*" (Exodus 32: 10). It is as if God was saying to Moses, "If you stand in the way by way of intercession, I will not be able to do it. Please stand out of the way; do not intercede, so that I may do it." So in God's mind the situation depended on Moses. God also said that He would make a great nation out of Moses.

In this incident, God made His judgements at once: "I will strike them with the pestilence and disinherit them, and I will make of you a nation greater and mightier than they." There was no indication that Moses could do anything about it. The Lord spelt out how His anger was to be manifested:

1. His people were to be stricken with pestilence.
2. They were to be disinherited.
3. A greater and mightier nation was to be made out of Moses.

As can be seen, God was more vexed than before,. He gave no room for Moses to intercede. He spelt out that He would disinherit them, and He offered not only to make a great nation of Moses, as He had offered before, but to make out of him a greater and mightier nation. So Moses had more to gain if he allowed God to do what He had in mind.

THE PERSISTENT INTERCESSOR

There is a rule that "once an intercessor always an intercessor for life." We shall see this in the example of our Lord Jesus, who interceded on earth and who lived to intercede for His own from the throne.

Moses had interceded before for these people. He had put everything at stake for the sake of saving them. They had not been loyal to God. They had not been loyal to him. If he had not been an intercessor, he would have said: "I saw them through last time at great cost. Since they choose to stray and would neither regard God nor me, let them reap the consequences of their sin. Let God's will be done. Would it not serve God's purpose better that there is a greater and mightier nation to bear His name? God has not even left any room for me to do something this time. Let things be as He has said."

THE WILL OF GOD THAT MUST BE DONE

We have said that the intercessor must take sides with God, His Word, and His will. We want to make it clear that we are talking about taking sides with God's original and perfect will and not taking sides with God's permissive will or reactions.

What is the difference between the two? Let us try to illustrate.

The perfect will of God was that the children of Israel might enter and settle in the Promised Land, conquer all the tribes therein, and possess the land:

"From the river of Egypt to the great river, the river Euphrates, the land of the Kenites, Kenizzites, the Kadmonites, the Hittites, the Perizzites, the Rephaim,

The Amorites, the Canaanites, the Girgashites and the Jebu-sites"

(Genesis 15: 18-20).

This promise was made to Abraham and his descendants.

We can therefore say that any departure from this original position is not God's perfect will. It is His permissive will. It is His reaction to the failure of those who were meant to cooperate with Him in the fulfillment of His perfect will.

The new development of a greater and mightier nation out of Moses was, therefore, not God's perfect will but God's reaction, God's permissive will, and that is not what an intercessor commits himself to. He commits himself to God's perfect will.

We can draw another example from the realm of sickness and disease. God's perfect will is that all His may enjoy perfect health. He sometimes in His permissive will (as a reaction) allows His to become sick or diseased. How does one react? Does one say, "Lord, may Your permissive will that this person be sick be established?" No! One prays for healing. Praying for healing is an acknowledgment that not all that God allows is His perfect will and that not all His reactions are in accordance with His eternal purpose.

Ananias and his wife were stricken dead. God did it or allowed it to be done. However, God's perfect will for them was not premature death. His perfect will for them was that they grow and mature in the church and serve Him. However, when they chose the way of sin and were thereby bringing far-reaching contamination to the young church, He reacted to this (in His permissive will) by removing them at once.

There are many abnormalities today that are carried out by man in the name of the Lord and His Church. There are many groups, organizations, denominations, et cetera, that call themselves churches. Of course they are not. They were conceived after the thoughts and plans of man, and they function, but not according to God's pattern. God allows them to continue and may even allow sinners to be saved there out of His great love, but they do not represent His will. Someone who is committed to the expression of God's will on earth cannot do anything but pray off all such things as part of his cry to God, "Thy will be done on' earth as it is in heaven."

In praying for a nation one may find that the nation has been judged. He could say, "God has judged this nation. What else can I do? May His will be done." The question is: Which will? Is it His perfect will or His permissive will? If His perfect will is that a nation be judged, then an intercessor dare not Intercede. If, on the other hand, God's promise of judgment is His reaction, then there is room to intercede regardless of how great the sin has been or the imminence of the judgment promised.

THE INTERCESSOR'S FAITH

Without faith it is impossible for anyone to become an intercessor. Such a one who would Intercede must:

1. Seek God's perfect will
2. Know God's perfect will
3. Commit all that he is and all that he has to God's perfect will
4. Know what God wants or has done as a reaction.
5. Stand in the gap to ensure that that which God wants to do as a reaction is either not started or not continued.
6. Labour to ensure that the perfect will of God is done.

In order to do this the person must not only believe that God's will is the best but that it can be done. Take, for example, how it is impossible for anyone to pray for the perfection of the Bride of Christ who did not believe that Christ will one day have a Bride for Himself in splendour without spot, without blemish, and without wrinkle. He cannot really become an intercessor unless he believes the Scriptures that say:

"May the God of peace himself sanctify you wholly; and may your spirit and soul and body be kept sound and blameless at the coming of our Lord Jesus Christ

He who calls you is faithful, and he will do it"

(I Thessalonians 5:23-24)

God has promised and He is faithful. He will do it. If anyone looks at the Lord and at His Word, he will echo, "He will do it." If anyone looks at the church (which is looking by sight) he will be forced to say, "It is not possible. It will not happen. Let me pray for some of the believers, but I cannot pray for all believers to be sound and blameless in spirit, soul, and body"

An intercessor must look to God and only to God. He will look at man initially to see how hopeless the situation is, but he must believe that God will change it. He must pray, looking unto the Lord.

He must pray 'and not analyse the ways that are open to God to do it, for such analysis is on the human plane. God's ways are far higher and far too numerous for anyone to comprehend. The possibilities open to Him are limitless. All intercessors must know that and pray to the One who works the counsel of His will according to His good pleasure and according to His limitless ways.

MOSES' COMMITMENT TO GOD'S PERFECT WILL

Moses knew how serious the situation was. He also knew what God's perfect will was. He was fully aware of God's offer to him of a new start of a greater and' mightier nation. He made his choice; he made the choice that all true intercessors make. He chose God's perfect will and sought God's glory and honour and not his. He knew what he was losing. He knew what God would gain. He preferred God gaining by having His perfect will done, to any honour that could come to him. He was indeed a man of God, a true servant of God. He therefore decided not to have things go as God intended by reaction. He decided to ensure that things were returned to the original position where the children of Israel were spared and restored and would enter the Promised Land. He decided to intercede for them again. He knew how fierce the battle had been previously. He knew that it cost him fort y days of labour without food and without water. He knew how hard it had been to convince God then. He knew that God was angrier now than He had been then; he knew that in the other incident God had allowed him the possibility of interceding. He knew that there were no such offers this time. However, with all these odds against him he decided to take up the mighty weapon of intercession and go to war.

THE PERSISTENT INTERCESSOR AT WORK

It has been rightly said that prayer is the hardest work this side of heaven. We want to add that intercession is the hardest work on earth. When Moses decided to intercede for the children of Israel, he was opting to do the hardest work on earth on their behalf. He went to work.

He started straightaway with the job. There were no preliminaries. His arguments were very different from those of the last time. His main thrust this time was that God should complete what He had started to do.

He said to God that the Egyptians would hear of it. He was saying to God, "Your enemies will hear of it." Then he added, "You brought up this people in Your might from among them. In addition, they will tell the inhabitants of this land." He was saying to God, "Lord, the reputation You made in Egypt will be destroyed if You destroy the people. It will not only be destroyed amongst the Egyptians. It will be destroyed among the occupants of the Promised Land, for the Egyptians will spread the news of Your lost fame."

He further said, "Lord, the nations have heard of Your intimate companionship of them by day and by night. They have heard of what You have done so far. If You do Dot complete it, they will say, 'Because the Lord was not able to bring this people into the land that He swore to give them, therefore He has slain them in the wilderness.' "

Moses was saying, "Lord, the people will not see that it was a problem with the people. They all know that what has happened all this time has not been because of them, but because of You.

Your power has been very great, and that is known. If they died here in the wilderness, they would die because of their sin, but it would appear to the people that they died because of Your powerlessness. So, Lord, do not carry out any action that will paint a false impression of You. Let the picture of Your greatness and might that has been stamped in the minds of these people remain, for it is true."

Moses then turned to what had transpired between God and himself during the last period during which he was shut up with the Lord to intercede for Israel. During that period the Lord had revealed Himself to Moses and allowed all His goodness to pass before Moses and had proclaimed to Moses:

"*The Lord, the Lord, a God merciful and gracious, slow to anger and abounding in steadfast love and faithfulness, keeping steadfast love for thousands, forgiving iniquity and transgression and sin, but who will by no means clear the guilty, visiting, the iniquity of the fathers upon the children and the children's children, to the third and fourth generation*"

(Exodus 34:6-7).

In this revelation, the Lord had said the following about Himself:

1. He is merciful.
2. He is gracious.
3. He is slow to anger.
4. He abounds in steadfast love.
5. He abounds in steadfast faithfulness.
6. He keeps steadfast love for thousands.
7. He forgives iniquity.
8. He forgives transgression.
9. He forgives sin.
10. He will by no means clear the guilty.
11. He visits the iniquity of the fathers upon the children and the children's children to the third and fourth generations.

Moses then used what God thus said as fresh grounds for intercession. He was saying to God, "Let things be now as You said." Moses put it in the following words: "The Lord is slow to anger and abounding in steadfast love, forgiving iniquity, and transgression, but He will by no means clear the guilty, visiting the iniquity of the fathers upon the children upon the third and upon the fourth generations." The portion of what God said about Himself that Moses quoted back to Him is:

1. "The Lord is slow to anger."
2. "The Lord is abounding in .steadfast love."
3. "The Lord forgives iniquity."
4. "The Lord forgives transgression."
5. "The Lord will by no means clear the guilty."
6. "The Lord visits the iniquity of the fathers upon the children and upon the third and the fourth generations."

Then Moses pleaded, "*Pardon the iniquity of this people, I pray thee, according to the greatness of thy steadfast love, and according as thou hast forgiven this people, from Egypt even until now*" (Numbers 14:19).

THE RESPONSE OF GOD TO THE INTERCESSOR

One of the great encouragements that an intercessor must know is that he is dealing with a God who has agreed to hear and answer prayer. Moses was dealing with such a God. We have the privilege of dealing with Him.

"*The Lord said to Moses, 'I have pardoned, according to your word;*

"*But truly, as I live, and as all the earth shall be filled with the glory of the Lord, none of the men who have seen my glory and my signs which I wrought in Egypt and in the wilderness, and yet have put me to the proof these ten times and have not hearkened to my voice, shall see the land which I swore to give to their fathers;*

and none of those who despised me shall see it.

But my servant Caleb, because he has a different spirit and has followed me fully, I will bring into the land into which he went, and his descendants shall possess it.

Now, since the Amalekites and the Canaanites dwell in the valleys, turn tomorrow and set out for the wilderness by the way of the Red Sea.

And the Lord said to Moses and to Aaron, 'How long shall this wicked congregation murmur against me?

I have heard the murmurings of the people of Israel, which they murmur against me.

Say to them, 'As I live,' says the Lord,

'What you have said in my hearing I will do to you: Your dead bodies shall fall in this wilderness;

and of all your number, numbered from twenty years old and upward, who have murmured against me,

not one shall come into the land where I swore that I would make you dwell, except Caleb the son of Jephunneh and Joshua the son of Nun.

'But your little ones, whom you said would become a prey, I will bring in, and they shall know the land which you have despised.

But as for you, your dead bodies shall fall in this wilderness. And your children shall be shepherds in the wilderness forty years, and shall suffer for your faithlessness, until the last of your dead bodies lies in the wickedness.

According to the number of the days in which you spied out the land, forty days, for every day a year, you shall bear your iniquity, forty years, and you shall know my displeasure.'

I the Lord have spoken;

Surely this will I do to all this wicked congregation that are gathered together against me: in this wilderness they shall come to a full end, and there they shall die."

And the men whom Moses sent to spy out the land, and who returned and made all the congregation to murmur against him by bringing up an evil report against the land, the men who brought up an evil report of the land, died by plague before the Lord.

But Joshua the son of Nun and Caleb the son of Jephunneh remained alive, of those men who went to spy out the land.

And Moses told these words to all the people of Israel, and the people mourned greatly"

(Numbers 14:20-39).

The preceding passage is very pregnant with instruction. It is also very heavy. It would have been instructive to just study it, but we shall not. We shall concentrate on those areas that deal with intercession and intercessors.

"I Have Pardoned According to Your Word"

We have said earlier that the intercessor stands in a decisive position. He is sovereign next only to the God of heaven. Why is that so? It is so because God does things according to what the intercessor says. It is as if God has decided to change roles with the intercessor so that He receives orders from the intercessor and executes them.

"According to Moses' Word"

It is immediately obvious that Moses did not put the same amount of work into interceding for Israel this time as he did in the previous battle. The mighty wrestlings with God characteristic of the former intercession were absent. There was no fasting. There was no lying before God for fort y days. There was no risking everything for the people he led. He just pleaded and left it there. However, Moses had real weight before God and God heard him.

Looking at the art of intercession, it would seem to me that

Moses played a loser's game. God said eleven things about Himself when He revealed Himself to Moses. Nine of them were about His love, mercy, and forgiveness and two of them on His judgement. When Moses was using what God said about Himself in his intercession, he quoted only six of the eleven attributes and of the six he included the two on God's judgements. This to me is very sad. It was failure at the very art of intercession. If he were playing the game according to the rules, he would have quoted• the nine attributes of His love, mercy, and forgiveness and on these pressed on God to act accordingly. He would have made as if he did not know that God had also promised to judge. He would have left it with God to remind him that He, the Lord, judges. It is not the intercessor's duty to remind God that He judges;

At some point, an intercessor is like someone in court. He must listen carefully and answer carefully. The wrong "revelations" or the wrong arguments or statements could alter everything. It is foolish of the counsel for the defence to quote and expose those parts of the law that will help or rein force the judge's condemnation of the accused. In fact, people must weigh every word that is used in intercession very carefully. They must also weigh every word that they ever allow to go forth out of their mouths. It is instructive to remember that the Lord said to the children of Israel, "What you have said in My hearing I will do to you." Oh, how frightful is the thought! Everything we ever say is said in God's hearing. What if He did to us as we have said in His hearing? What if He did to others as we have said in His hearing?

Moses' word in intercession was: "Lord, have mercy. Forgive. Be consistent with Your nature. You are slow to anger. You abound in steadfast love. You forgive iniquity and transgression. You do not clear the guilty. You visit the iniquity of the fathers upon the children upon the third and fourth generations. Lord, that is Your nature. Act accordingly."

The Lord pardoned according to Moses' word. This meant that:

1. He was slow to anger and did not destroy His people then.
2. He was slow to anger and allowed them to slowly die one after another in the course of forty years.
3. He abounded in steadfast love and mercy so that he only destroyed those who were twenty or older when they left Egypt.
4. He does not clear the guilty, and that is why He did not spare the ten spies who gave the evil report but they died immediately of a plague before Him.
5. He visits the iniquity of the fathers upon the children, and that is why He punished the whole congregation by making them wander in the wilderness for fort y years. Their children who had not sinned were nevertheless punished because of the sins of their parents, God having said, "Your children shall be shepherds in the wilderness fort y years and shall suffer for your faithlessness."

So Moses chose some .grounds. and asked God to work on them and He did. He was faithful to His word, but what Moses got out of the intercession left rnuch to be desired.

Earlier on, when the children of Israel had made the golden calf, Moses had interceded. The consequence of that far-reaching intercession was such that:

1. The glory of God was rnaintained, and His purposes stood.
2. Moses the intercessor was honoured, receiving everything that he asked.
3. The people of Israel who sinned and did not even repent were not punished.
4. There was deep reconciliation between the people and their God, and God took them back into His bosom.

This time things were different. The consequences of the intercession were:

1. God's glory was maintained. The people of Egypt could not corn plain, since all the congregation did not perish in one day, although they were systernatically eliminated.
2. Moses the intercessor was successful in that he received all that he asked.
3. The people of Israel who sinned were eliminated. Some were eliminated in one go and others slowly through the years.
4. There was no reconciliation between the people and the Lord.

The following words were spoken by the Lord after the intercessor had been given what he asked for: "How long shall this wicked congregation murmur against me?"; "What you have said in my hearing I will do to you"; "Your dead bodies shall fall in this wilderness"; "Your children shall be shepherds in the wilderness forty years and shall suffer for your faith-lessness, until the last of your dead bodies lies in the wilder-ness"; and "You shall know my displeasure."

Moses' victory this time was twofold. In some ways, it was not a very successful intercession.

GROUNDS OF UNFAILING INTERCESSION

It would be good to spell out the grounds that can be used for unfailing intercession. In other words, we want to define clearly what grounds an intercessor should stand on in order to always succeed.

I think that the intercessor who stands on the grounds of God's love, God's mercy, and God's grace stands on grounds that need never fail. God's love is limitless, and so is His grace and mercy.

On these grounds an intercessor can ask for the pardon and the restoration of the vilest criminal. He can tell God, "Yes, Lord, this man has committed the most horrible sin. He deserves death. In fact, Your law demands that he should die, but Lord, because of Your love, forgive and restore him." There is no one's sin that can ever mount above and beyond the love, mercy, and grace of God.

A person who becomes an intercessor for many people must come on these grounds, and he will succeed. It is good to intercede on the basis of the promises of God, but very many promises of God have conditions that must be fulfilled by man for their accomplishment, and most people do not fulfil these conditions. There are, however, some unconditional promises, those in which the responsibility for fulfillment lies solely with God. The intercessor must study the Word thoroughly, know such promises, and use them. I think of the promises that God made to Jacob at the very beginning of their relationship. He said to him:

"I am the Lord, the God of Abraham your father and the God of Isaac; the land on which you lie I will give you and to your descendants; and your descendants shall be like the dust of the earth, and you shall spread abroad to the west and to the east and to the north and to the south; and by you and your descendants shall all the families of the earth bless themselves.

Behold, I am with you and will keep you wherever you go, and will bring you back to this land; for I will not leave you until I have done that of which I have spoken to you"

(Genesis 28:13-15).

Everything was dependent on God. Nothing was dependent on Jacob. In fact, Jacob was asked to do nothing. Everything was done for him as the Lord promised. A careful study of the life of Jacob shows that God never blamed Jacob for anything he did, yet He brought him to reach great heights of spiritual maturity through the working of the cross in his life.

I also think of what is sometimes referred to as the new covenant. In it the Lord said,

"Therefore say to the house of Israel, 'Thus says the Lord God; It is not for your sake, O house of Israel, that I am about to act, but for the sake of my holy name, which you have profaned among the nations to which you came.

And I will vindicate the holiness of my great name, which has been profaned among the nations, and which you have profaned among them; and the nations will know that I am the Lord, says the Lord God, when through you I vindicate my holiness before their eyes.

For I will take you from the nations, and gather you from all the countries, and bring you into your own land.

I will sprinkle clean water upon you, and you shall be clean from all your uncleannesses, and from all your idols I will cleanse you.

A new heart I will give you, and a new spirit I will put within you; and I will take out of your flesh the heart of stone and give you a heart of flesh.

And I will put my spirit within you, and cause you to walk in my statutes and be careful to observe my ordinances.

You shall dwell in the land which I gave to your fathers; and you shall be my people, and I will be your God.

And I will deliver you from all your uncleannesses; and I will summon the grain and make it abundant and lay no famine upon you.

I will make the fruit of the tree and the increase of the field abundant, that you may never again suffer the disgrace of famine among the nations. Then you will remember your evil ways, and your deeds that were not good; and you will loathe yourselves for your iniquities and your abominable deeds.

It is not for your sake that I will act, says the Lord God; let that be known to you.

Be ashamed and confounded for your ways, O house of Israel.

Thus says the Lord God: "On the day that I cleanse you from all your iniquities, I will cause the cities to be inhabited, and the waste places shall

be rebuilt.

And the land that was desolate shall be tilled, instead of being the desolation that it was in the sight of all who passed by.

And they will say, 'This land that was desolate has become like the garden of Eden; and the waste and desolate and ruined cities are now inhabited and fortified.'

Then the nations that are left round about you shall know that I, the Lord, have rebuilt the ruined places, and replanted that which was desolate; I, the Lord, have spoken, and I will do it"

(Ezekiel 36:22-36).

What wonderful promises! How far-reaching! How sure and certain!

They are sure and certain because they begin in God and they end in God. They are 100 percent God's doing. There is no way in which they can fail. There is no way in which God can opt out of any part of them. There is nothing that man can do to hinder, retard, or frustrate God about their fulfilment. They are to be carried out independently of what man is. In fact, they will be carried out on people who deserve nothing of the kind. That is God's mercy, love, and grace, and it is wonderful. These are the promises that an intercessor can use unfailingly.

FORTY YEARS OF WANDERING AND ONE GENERATION AS CORPSES LN THE WILDERNESS

In the original purpose of God (His perfect will) the generation that left Egypt was to enter into the Promised Land and inherit it. The journey was intended to last a short period. Because they sinned, God reacted (bringing in His permissive will). The way He put it is very telling: *"Now, since the Amalekites and the Canaanites dwell in the valleys, turn tomorrow and set out for the wilderness by the way to the Red Sea"* (Numbers 14:25).

In God's original plan, although these nations were where they were, the children of Israel were to go and see God destroy them and see the Promised Land safely in their hands. Since they saw the nations and not God, the Lord commanded them to move in the direction that avoided them. That direction was a backward move and gave room for the forty years of punishment and judgment.

Why did this happen? We can say clearly that it was because of the people's sin. We can also say that it is because Moses the intercessor stopped short of complete victory in a battle of intercession. He did not appeal to God's love, grace, and mercy. He did not plead for that generation that would perish in the desert. He did not wrestle with God about the fact that His purposes would be hindered for forty years. He did not plead with God about those who were righteous, like Joshua and Caleb, who would be forced to wander for forty years. He did not plead the cause of their children who did not participate actively in their sin and who would be forced to wander as shepherds in the wilderness for forty years. He did not plead for mercy on the spies who gave the wicked report.

He spoke once and God answered. He did not speak back again.

He did not argue. He did not insist. He let God have His way. He surrendered to God's permissive will, and then it happened as it did.

My prayer for myself is that I should never stop short of perfect victory. My prayer for you is that you should never stop short of perfect victory. I made a new commitment of myself to the perfect will of God and to wrestle until it is brought to pass. I separate myself from all that has to do with settling for His permissive will. I will pray for myself, and I will intercede for others that in my life and in theirs, God's perfect will be done. Will you not do the same?

We thank God for Moses, and we learn from him to make progress in the school of intercession. And we give all the glory to Jesus. Amen.

PART 5

Two other old testament intercessors

1

ABRAHAM'S MINISTRY OF INTERCESSION

Then the men set out from there, and they looked toward Sodom; and Abraham went with them to set them on their way.

"The Lord said, "Shall I hide from Abraham what I am about to do, seeing that Abraham shall become a great and mighty nation, and all the nations of the earth shall bless themselves by him?

No, for I have chosen him, that he may charge his children and his household after him to keep the way of the Lord by doing righteousness and justice; so that the Lord may bring to Abraham what he has promised him."

Then the Lord said, "Because the outcry against Sodom and Gomorrah is great and their sin is very grave, I will go down to see whether they have done altogether according to the outcry which has come to me; and if not, I will know."

So the men turned from there, and went toward Sodom; but Abraham still stood before the Lord.

Then Abraham drew near, and said, "Wilt thou indeed destroy the righteous with the wicked? Suppose there are fifty righteous within the city; wilt thou then destroy the place and not spare it for the fifty righteous who are in it? Far be it from thee to do such a thing, to slay the righteous with the wicked, so that the righteous fare as the wicked! Far be that from thee! Shall not the Judge of all the earth do right?"

And the Lord said, "*If I find at Sodom fifty righteous in the city, I will spare the whole place for their sake.*"

Abraham answered, 'Behold, I have taken upon myself to speak to the Lord, I who am but dust and ashes.

'Suppose five of the fifty righteous are lacking? Wilt thou destroy the whole city for lack of five?'

And he said, 'I will not destroy it if I find forty-five there." Again he spoke to him, and said, "Suppose forty are found there.'

He answered, 'For the sake of forty I will not do it.'

Then he said, 'Oh let not the Lord be angry, and I will speak.

Suppose thirty are found there.'

He answered, 'I will not do it, if I find thirty there.'

He said, 'Behold, I haven taken upon myself to speak to the Lord. Suppose twenty are found there.'

He answered, 'For the sake of twenty I will not destroy it." Then he said, "Oh let not the Lord be angry, and I will speak again but this once. Suppose ten are found there.'

He answered, 'For the sake of ten I will not destroy it.'

And the Lord went his way, when he had finished speaking to Abraham; and Abraham returned to his place"

(Genesis 18: 16-33).

Then the men said to Lot, 'Have you anyone else here? Sons-in-law, sons, daughters, or any one you have in the city, bring them out of the place; for we are about to destroy this place, because the outcry against its people has become great before the Lord, and the Lord has sent us to destroy it.'

So Lot went out and said to his sons-in-law, who were to marry his daughters, "*Up, get out of this place; for the Lord is about to destroy the city."*

But he seemed to his sons-in-law to be jesting.

When morning dawned, the angels urged Lot, saying, 'Arise, take your wife and your two daughters who are here, lest you be consumed in the punishment of the city.'

But he lingered; so the men seized him and his wife and his two daughters by the hand, the Lord being merciful to him, and they brought him forth and set him outside the city"

(Genesis 19:12-16).

"Then the Lord rained on Sodom and Gomorrah brimstone and fire from the Lord out of heaven;

And he overthrew those cities, and all the valley, and all the inhabitants of the cities, and what grew on the ground.

But Lot's wife behind him looked back, and she became a pillar of salt.

And Abraham went early in the morning to the place where he had stood before the Lord;

and he looked down toward Sodom and Gomorrah and toward all the land of the valley, and beheld, and lo, the smoke of the land went up like the smoke of a furnace.

So it was that, when God destroyed the cities of the valley,

God remembered Abraham, and sent Lot out of the midst of the overthrow, when he overthrew the cities in which Lot dwelt" (Genesis 19:24-29).

ABRAHAM—INTERCESSOR

It is encouraging to know that Abraham did not just pray for Sodom and Gomorrah, but that he had a personal standing with God from which to intercede. What type of man was he? What was the quality of his relationship with the Lord?

The Bible shows that Abraham was a man who knew God. From the time when contact was first entered into between the two, at the first call of God to him to go to the land of Canaan, to the time of his ministry as an intercessor, a very deep relationship had built up. It included a lot of personal revelation of God to Abraham, the making of covenants between the two, the blessing of Abraham by God, and the trial, strengthening, and blessing of Abraham's faith. The relationship was such that God dined at Abraham's.

The relation was such that God felt compelled to tell Abraham what He was about to do. He asked Himself a question, "Shall I hide from Abraham what I am about to do?" He then went ahead to show forth why He could not hide from Abraham what He was about to do. The reasons are revealing of God's opinion of Abraham:

1. He was to become a great nation.
2. He was to become a mighty nation.
3. All the nations of the earth were to bless themselves by him.

In addition to those reasons, the Lord said, "I have chosen him that he may charge his children and that he may charge his household after him to keep the way of the Lord by doing righteousness and justice so that the Lord may bring to Abraham what he has promised."

Abraham was the type of man who could be moved by God to do things that enabled God to fulfil what He had promised. When the Lord finds a man who can co-operate with Him by character and service; so that what He has promised to him might be done without a violation of any of His principles, He has found a co-worker. Abraham was such a man.

God was compelled to reveal what He was about to do to Abraham. There were many people on Planet Earth then. However, God felt no constraint to tell any of all the rest, what was in His heart.

He was not obliged to them. They did not oblige Him by their character and service. May we, too, who are called by Him become by constant obedience, great men before Him; so that He will be compelled to reveal His secrets to us. That will give us grounds, special grounds, of approach before Him.

Abraham was trusted to charge his children and his household after him to keep the way of the Lord by doing righteousness and justice. This means that Abraham himself kept the way of the Lord and, thereby, set an example which the Lord knew that his children after him would follow. When God finds a man whose example in keeping the way of the Lord is such that his children after him will be compelled to follow the example because it is glaring and in following that glaring example be what God meant them to be, God has found a great man, and He will not hide the things in His heart from him.

The question is: Where are such men in the Church today? Where are the husbands who, with a good conscience, can say to God, "Lord, I have lived my entire life as a husband and father before You in total righteousness, justice, and truth; so that it is a glaring example to my wife, children, and all"? Where are those who can say, "Lord, I have been a good prophet, priest, and king in my home and have set the proper example; my children and those who live with me will follow suit"? May the Lord be exalted for each of such men in the Church. May all other men in the Church wake up from slumber and be what they ought to be; so that God be not frustrated for want of someone with whom He can share the things that He wants to do.

KNOWLEDGE OF GOD'S PLANS AND INTERCESSION

It is possible to look around and deduce the general needs of a person, a family, a city, a nation, a continent, or a planet and pray about him or it and receive answers from God. This is good and all God's children ought to do it. In fact, the Bible commands us to do that. The apostle Paul commands:

"First of all, then, I urge that supplications, prayers, intercessions, and thanksgivings be made for all men, for kings and all who are in high positions, that we may lead a quiet and peaceable life, godly and respectful in every way.

This is good, and it is acceptable in the sight of God our Saviour, who desires all men to be saved and to come to the knowledge of the truth"

(1Timothy 2: 1-4).

This is a general call to prayer, including supplication, intercession and thanksgiving, and it has as its goal the living in peace of people and the salvation of the lost. We say again that all believers should obey these verses. No one needs anything more in addition to the fact that he is a believer to so pray.

However, the intercessor, the definite intercessor, is not someone who is just praying generally. He is a person who has received a revelation from the Lord. God has shown him something that is in His heart. God has shown him something that He wants to do. God has shown him and he has seen it and out of that has been born a burden that cannot be removed easily except by intercession.

God may reveal that He intends to do something special in the Church—for example, pour out the Holy Spirit in a most unusual way that will lead to the sanctification of the saints and the setting of them aflame for God and the conversion of the lost. The one who receives such a revelation from the Lord will at the same time or afterwards, upon asking in prayer, receive the Lord's burden about the coming move of God. He will then, out of the revelation and burden, pray and pray and take no rest until it comes to pass as God intended. Of course, there will be attacks on the revelation and there will be the need for a close fellowship with the Lord so that neither the burden nor the goal is lost. However, in each case there will be a revelation followed or accompanied by a burden. The revelation will have a clear goal in view. Yes, what God wants to do in each case is always clear to Him and He can show it clearly to anyone to whom He wants to show it.

God may also reveal to someone or to some people about someone:

"He is a chosen instrument of mine to carry my name before the Gentiles and kings and the sons of Israel; for I will show him how much he must suffer for the sake of my name"
(Acts 9: 15-16).

That revelation about a servant of the Lord will or may lead to a permanent burden on some heart or hearts to see this purpose of God accomplished. Such a heart or such hearts may then turn all their focus to interceding for that person and the things that happen in the fulfilment of the call of God on his life. They may put in all their lives as intercessors, withdrawing from all else and being oblivious of all else as they pray for eight, twelve, or sixteen hours, or perhaps a lifetime for one person. They have received a revelation, and they have responded in the ministry of intercession. They are intercessors indeed. Such will become totally loyal to God and to the person for whom they are interceding. Such will ignore his weaknesses or blame themselves for the presence of those weaknesses in the man; for would God not have taken them away if they had prayed more intently and pressed on in prayer until God's purpose had been accomplished in his life? They may receive direction from the person as to how to pray; but most of the time they will receive direction, topics, and commands from heaven on how to pray; for only God knows the full array of the devil's plans against him and the depth of his inward suffering, which he might not want to share with anyone but which needs to be taken up in storming prayer.

As another example, God may decree judgment upon a certain person, place, or ministry, et cetera. As said previously, it needs revelation for any specific burdens in intercession. When the revelation as to what God wants to do is received, it will lead to a burden and then to producing "a man in the gap".

If God intends to bring revival upon His people in a certain place in maybe twenty years' time, He will reveal this to one of His servants, who will begin to pray in accordance with what God has shown him. He will carry a burden that results from the revelation. He will keep at it. He will call other believers to pray. They may pray for an hour or two each week, but he will pray without ceasing. They will present thoughts and arguments to God, but he will present sighs, tears, and groans. They may become tired and be taken up by other preoccupations, but how can he give up? How can another thing settle on his heart? How can another aspect of the work capture his heart when the heart has not been released from its previous imprisonment? And so, he keeps on and on, praying and crying and yielding and waiting until what God said He would do happens. God often does not tell anyone from the beginning how long it will take.

When it had been revealed to Simeon that he would not taste death until he had seen the Lord's Christ, he waited and interceded, and then it happened. Then he walked into the temple when the Lord was being initiated into the things of the temple, took the child up in his arms, blessed God, and asked for permission to depart from this world.

Anna had probably received the same revelation. She had lived with her husband for seven years from her virginity, and as a widow till she was eighty-four. She did not depart from the temple, worshipping with fasting and prayer night and day. And coming up at that very hour she gave thanks to God, and spoke of him to all who were looking for the redemption of Jerusalem" (Luke 2:36-37). Then she withdrew and was soon in heaven! She had received a revelation. It had led to a burden. The burden had led to action, and the action had contributed to the accomplishment of the revelation.

In our day we try to recruit people to pray. This is not bad. There is even encouragement from the Word to that end. However, we shall never produce real intercessors that way. For real intercessors we must turn to God. We must exert ourselves before Him, and we must ask and receive them from Him. This is because one of the indispensable qualifications is that God has shown a person what He intends to do. Only He can do that. A man can tell another what God wants to do, but that will lead to head-knowledge and to human activity. When God reveals what He wants to do, it is heart-knowledge, and it results or should result in spiritual knowledge, and a work of God.

Because God decided to show Abraham what He intended to do, it was in a way God's invitation to him to intercede. It shows that somewhere in the heart of God there was an unwillingness to destroy Sodom and Gomorrah. He wanted someone who would cause Him to go back on the demands of His justice. He hoped that Abraham would do that. Is that not consistent with His nature? I find that it is. Did he not say to Jonah, "*Should not I pity Nineveh, that great city, in which there are more than a hundred and twenty thousand persons who do not know their right hand from their left, and also much cattle?*" (Jonah 4: 11).

So, although God did not directly ask Abraham to intercede, we feel certain that He wanted him to do so.

Intercession is born in the heart of God, for only the heart of God knows the depths of unchanging compassion. It is then imparted into the heart of man, who prays back to God, and then He hearkens.

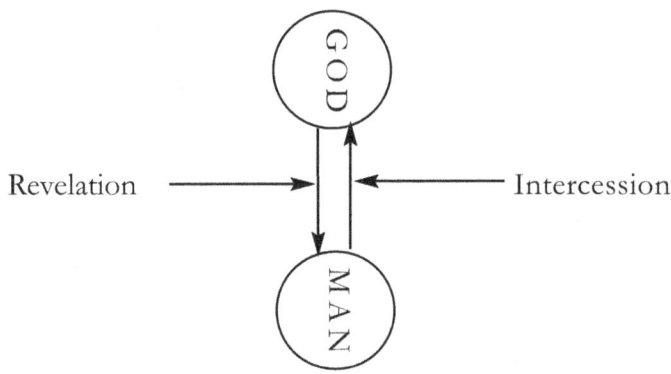

The Origin of Intercession and the Relationship between Intercession and Revelation

Although intercession is born in the heart of God, not all that is in His heart for which He wants intercession is ever interceded for. There are two main reasons for this. The first is the shortage of people to whom He can reveal what He wants to do. The second reason is that even when He does find those who are qualified to receive the things He has to reveal, not all of them act as they ought. They allow the enemy to steal some of what has been revealed, interfere with the burden, and weaken the intercessor in a way that reduces his effectiveness significantly. This is most sad.

ABRAHAM: POSITION AND ART OF INTERCESSION

When the people went towards Sodom to assess the condition of things there, the Bible says that Abraham still "stood before the Lord." He could not go away. He had to speak to Him. There was a burden in Abraham's heart. He was before the Lord. All of him was opened to the Lord. There was transparency. God saw everything in his heart and life, and it raised no barrier.

All intercessors must be pure and transparent. Those who harbour sin are disqualified from the ministry of intercession, for God must turn His back to the noise called intercession that comes from the lips of the unsanctified.

Abraham did not only stand before the Lord. He drew near. The result was that there was deepest intimacy between him and the Lord. Yes, that is the position from which to intercede. It was more or less a "tête-à-tête."

Abraham started very well. He said something that opened the door to the intercession. It seemed to have fallen from the air, but it was appropriate. He said "Wilt thou indeed destroy the righteous with the wicked?" He knew that God could not. It was the beginning of the battle, and he was anxious to start by a clean victory. Also, that statement about destroying the wicked and the righteous was not only introductory, it was definitive of the grounds on which he was to intercede. Thus his line of action was settled. As is obvious, he maintained that line of argument from start to finish.

Each intercessor must choose the grounds on which he will labour. They should be carefully chosen; so that they will lead to victory. He should not choose a basis that will cause him not to fight through to the end: He should not choose grounds that he will find himself compelled to change. Each intercessor ought to work out things quietly according to the revelation of God and be sure that from the start to finish he can win on scriptural grounds. As we said earlier, every statement, phrase, and word has to advance his cause. He ought to work out any objections that God might raise and see clearly how he will convince Him on the basis of Scripture and the reality of the situation at hand. I want to confess that I did not know much of this before I started writing this book. I only knew how to ask God for mercy; I never knew the rules that lead to victory. I have spoken and written on the intercession of Abraham for years without seeing this and without practising it. I thank God that I now see.

After Abraham asked God if He would indeed destroy the righteous with the wicked, he did not wait for an answer. He immediately pressed in his next question, "Suppose there are fifty righteous within the city, wilt thou then destroy the place and not spare it for the fifty righteous who are in it?"

Why was he pressing in that way? I think that even Abraham, knowing how many people lived in those cities, knew that only fifty righteous people was too few. That is why he immediately tried to have the request to spare the city if fifty righteous were found in it, tied to the fact that God should not destroy the righteous with the wicked. Abraham knew that asking God to spare the cities because of fifty righteous people was asking for too much. Therefore, he did not leave it like that. He added something to support, strengthen, and buttress the request. What he added was a small sermon preached to God. Intercessors who are mature and very intimate with God, are the ones who can preach sermons to Him. They possess a certain kind of "holy audacity" that stems from the depth of their relationship. God recognizes and accepts it gladly. Of course, it would be madness for others who have no history with Him to throw words at Him. In their case, that would be madness.

Abraham's sermon was: "Far be it from thee to do such a thing; to slay the righteous with the wicked, so that the righteous fare as the wicked! Far be that from thee! Shall not the Judge of all the earth do right?" In my opinion, that sermon preached by Abraham to the Lord Almighty is one of the most powerful sermons in all of Scripture. It is pregnant with a knowledge of God, His nature, and His attributes. It is sound in doctrine. Its delivery is forceful, under a deep sense of burden, and the delivery is eloquent and the time perfect. It also came from the right person, and it was addressed to the Judge of all the earth. It exalted God, it counselled Him, and it rebuked Him. It was full of pleading, and it was full of authority.

It came from a trembling man who had, as it were, received boldness from above, revelation from above, authority from above, and anointing from above. It came clearly, powerfully, and simply. The purpose was obvious.

That sermon produced the desired results and established the basis on which the intercessor was to press on and press forth. The Lord answered, much to the relief of Abraham, "If I find in Sodom fifty righteous in the city, I will spare the whole place for their sake."

Abraham was now sure that things could work along those lines: The city could be spared on the basis of the presence of some righteous people. He was fully aware now that the promise that the righteous should not be destroyed with the wicked was acceptable before God. He now felt that he could move ahead. He, however, did not become presumptuous. He knew the fear of God in his inward being. Also, he had just won the initial battle. The entire situation was still critical. He then spoke out to the Lord, acknowledging his unworthiness, yet at the same time pressing his point through. He said, "Behold, I have taken upon myself to speak to the Lord, I who am but dust and ashes. Suppose five of the fifty are lacking? Wilt thou destroy the whole city for lack of five?" He had moved in the direction of the number that had to be present and won. He moved next in a different direction. He moved in the direction of what would be lacking. In this way, he appeared to be dealing with a small number. He was saying, "God, if five were lacking, would Thou on that basis destroy the city?" He felt sure that he could convince God not to destroy the place on the basis of only five righteous people less who were there. He knew how to deal with God in the battle of intercession. He was moving surely and certainly ahead. When God answered, "I will not destroy it if I find forty-five there," He was saying to Abraham, "I understand the game you are playing, and I accept it. You have moved from fifty to forty-five. I accept it. Feel free to continue."

Again, Abraham spoke to the Lord, "Suppose forty are found

there?"

God answered, "For the sake of forty I will not do it."

Abraham again spoke. "Oh let not the Lord be angry, and I will speak. Suppose thirty are found there." He feared that the Lord might be angry with him.

Actually, the Lord was not angry. The Lord was pleased with him, for He answered him, saying, "I will not do it if I find thirty there."

What a wide door God had opened to Abraham! How willing God was prepared to hear him!!

WHY THE SLOW BATTLE?

Abraham had arrived at the point in the battle where he got the Lord to be willing to spare Sodom in its entirety if thirty righteous people were there. Someone may ask why he did not start at fifty and descend at once to thirty. The answer is that that would have been contrary to the rules and he would have lost the battle. The rules are learnt in the school of intercession. Those who have been students there do receive lessons from the Lord Jesus through His Holy Spirit and directly from the Holy Spirit. God the Son and God the Holy Spirit know that no one can rush in the ministry of intercession. The grounds are very "slippery," and those who want to rush through fail completely. Advanced students are prepared to go slowly, taking days, weeks, months, and even years to win, rather than rushing through to failure. Advanced and advancing students know that intercession is the art of penetrating into the heart of God, and no one can just rush through in one go. Another thing is that although intercession is the fiercest battle that one can ever be engaged in, it is a battle in the presence of God, it is a battle fought in the very heart of God, and who, after entering there, wants to rush away too soon? Finally, I want to say that each true intercessor, although having boldness before the Lord, never ceases to carry a certain amount of fear. It is the fear that he could fail, that God could say, "No," and his cause would crumble. This fear (and it is right that it should be there) is the possession of those who have been delivered from natural confidence and have come to know God as "The fear of Israel." Intercession is mountaintop battling, and the higher anyone climbs the slower and less presumptive his steps become, and the more the time it takes to prepare the ground for the next step. It is for this reason that some intercessors get to a point with God when they remain in His presence for hours, days, and perhaps weeks without saying a word. They are preparing for the next step, whereas for those who have abundant superficiality, their words are many and frequent.

A FATAL MISTAKE

The next statement from the lips of Abraham the intercessor got God to promise to save the city if twenty were found there. He had made so much progress. Things were working exceedingly well.

Then suddenly he said to God, "Oh, let not the Lord be angry, and I will speak again but this once. Suppose ten are found there?"

The Lord answered, "For the sake of ten I will not destroy it."

And it was settled. The Lord was going to look in Sodom, and if He found ten righteous people there, He would spare it. The Lord went, found only Lot and his two daughters, and destroyed the city and the inhabitants.

The question that I find extremely hard to answer is: "Why did Abraham decide that he was going to speak but this once? Why did he stop there? Why did he 'crash-land' the plane of his intercession?

Why did he not ask that the Lord should spare the city if five righteous were found there?" I feel persuaded that the Lord, who never said, "No," to him at any moment during that intercession•, would have agreed to spare the entire city if He found five.

Having obtained favour on condition of five righteous being present, he would then have asked God if He would destroy the city if one was missing from the five. He would have asked, "Lord, will You destroy the city and the inhabitants because of one righteous person who is absent?"

The Lord would have accepted saving the city if He found four righteous people in it. In a similar way, Abraham could have pressed on until he got the Lord to promise that He would spare the place if He found one righteous man there.

As can be seen, the righteousness of even Lot was questionable. He was prepared to give his two daughters to the men of Sodom in exchange for his guests. He was also unwilling to leave Sodom. He lingered on and it needed a special act of being seized and brought out of Sodom to get him to safety. Thus, in a sense, there was not one truly righteous man in Sodom. So on that basis the place could have still been destroyed. When Abraham got to one person, and knowing how worldly-minded his nephew was, he ought to have been warned in his heart that he might not be in spiritual order. He could then have again asked, "Shall not the Judge of all the earth do right?" Then he would have asked God if it was in accordance with divine justice to punish the people of Sodom before the other sinners of the world. He could have argued that if He destroyed them, they would all perish and go to hell, whereas if He gave them some time, some of them would perhaps believe and be saved. He would have asked the Lord, "You do not delight in the death of the wicked. How then can You allow these wicked ones to perish in their wickedness?" He could have argued and asked God if He was not jealous that the devil would enter into immediate, permanent, and eternal possession of these people. Using such arguments and refusing to relent, he would have pressed on the Lord to change His mind about the destruction of Sodom, and the Lord would have heard him and spared her, even though her iniquity was exceedingly great. He would then have won a total battle, but as it was, he fell short of victory.

Sodom and the neighbouring cities were destroyed because they sinned. Sodom and the neighbouring cities were also destroyed because Abraham, the intercessor, failed to fight and battle his way through to victory.

We do not only need intercessors. We need intercessors who win mighty victories for God.

Was God glad that Abraham failed and He therefore destroyed Sodom? I think not. He was disappointed. How glad He would have been had Abraham won the battle and "forced" Him to gladly do that which was His perfect will—spare Sodom! Every intercessor who wins brings special joy to God, for he gives Him an opportunity not to allow His permissive will (which is judgment) to become functional, but to enforce His perfect will (which is love, grace, and mercy).

WHY DID ABRAHAM FAIL?

It is very difficult to understand why Abraham ended his intercession as he did. He knew God intimately. He was rightly related to Him. To the extent that he went, he handled the art of intercession with outstanding mastery. What was the reason for his sudden surrender? It would be good to know the reason so as never to fall into the same error. There are a number of possibilities, and I am going to speculate prayerfully.

One reason could be that Abraham had battled for so long with God to get to the point where he got that by the time he got there he was so tired and just rushed things on to an end. Many authors end books badly, and the last chapters are hardly ever as thorough as the initial ones. If that is the reason, then it was a very poor performance. God did not move while Abraham was speaking. God only moved away when he stopped asking. It was Abraham and not God who determined the length of the conversation. The wonderful thing is that it is never God who tells men, "I am tired of listening. Let Me go." If God is prepared to be patient, ought not each intercessor learn patience, too? If Abraham was tired, what of the art of pressing on even when one is tired? Did Gideon and the three hundred overcomers not continue to pursue the enemy, even though they were faint from fighting and, in that way, established the victory? Are the watchmen of the city not charged to take no rest and give God no rest until He moves and makes Jerusalem a praise in all the earth? All those who hold the Lord in remembrance are similarly called to wrestle. What soldier is ever congratulated who did not press on against the enemy to the last ounce of his energy? In our day the goddess of ease is worshipped. Few there are who know to spend night after night in fierce battle. Few there are who know how to suspend sleep, rest, and tiredness and move on into God's supernatural power, and abide in it until the battle is won.

It was at this supernatural plane that Moses carried out some of his transactions with God. When God called him to the mountain for the task of showing him the blueprint of the tabernacle, eating and drinking were suspended for forty days and forty nights. He thus carried out a forty-day fast without food and without water. Normally, he ought to have died, but God did something that made his physical body become temporarily supernatural. Again, when the children of Israel sinned by making the golden calf, he went back into God's presence and lay before Him for forty days and forty nights. He was so taken up with interceding that he did not think of his body. God thought about it and again made it supernatural for some time until the battle was won. If the abject of intercession becomes so important to us that we are so caught up with seeking God's hand and God's mercy, then we can trust Him to take care of our mortal bodies, and He will. May it never happen that because you were exhausted you stopped interceding and because you stopped an individual, a family, a city, or a nation perished. In order that it never happens, you should begin to train for it. Take a prayer retreat of three hours, six hours, twelve hours, thirty-six hours, forty-eight hours, et cetera, and labour with God, praying without stopping, praying without a break, and praying without sleep. If you train gradually, you will be able to bring your body under control systhematically, and in the day of battle you will be able to win.

The other possibility is that Abraham really believed that his nephew had been effective and that there were at least ten righteous people in Sodom. If that is the case, he miscalculated. He walked by presumption and not by faith, and then reaped the results of such a move. May we learn not to walk according to our sight and thoughts as we intercede, but walk by the Spirit, and we shall be guided rightly.

The last possibility is that the devil attacked Abraham as he wrestled in intercession. The devil knew that Abraham's victory would mean great loss for him. Possibly then he attacked and caused the ruin; so that Sodom might be destroyed immediately and the people there become his forever. In fact, this to me is the most probable explanation of what happened. Satan's fiercest weapons are arrayed against intercessors. If they are left unprotected, what may he not do? The bodyguards of worldly rulers are the most competent men, and they labour at it unceasingly. Unfortunately, the Church does little to protect her mighty men. How many people give all of themselves to protect through prayer those who are the men at the forefront of God's battles? An in-tercessor is a premier prince of God. How many of God's captains make up his bodyguards? Are there even recruits guarding him in prayer?

When a priest went in to offer incense there were whole multitudes who stood outside praying until he came out safely. The same ought to be the case for the intercessor. If it were so, the intercessor would fight without interruption and win the battle, and it could change individuals, cities, nations, and continents.

UNMOVED BY FAILURE?

We find that Abraham returned to his place after he had finished talking with God. The Bible says that he went in the morning to the place where he had stood before the Lord and he looked down toward Sodom and Gomorrah and toward all the land of the valley, and beheld and lo, the smoke of the land went . up like the smoke of a furnace. That was proof to him that he had failed. The evidence was right there. There was no way that he could run away from it. It could be that the Lord told him that Lot and his daughters were safe.

What was Abraham's reaction? He had pleaded for the sparing of the people in Sodom. They were destroyed. He had not prevailed. He had stopped short of victory. Was he heartbroken? I do not think so. The way that he handled the intercession showed that his real concern was not that the sinners of Sodom and Gomorrah should not perish, but that God should not destroy the righteous. To Abraham, Lot and those who were Lot's were the righteous. Lot and his were safe and it would seem that the destruction of the rest did not bother Abraham. Therefore, he could look at the city under judgment and not weep and cry.

Normally, an intercessor will be so welded to the people for whom he is interceding that if they perished, he would feel like perishing with them. To be so taken up with an individual, family, city, nation, or continent is not something that can happen because an individual merely wants it. It cannot be the result of the ambition of a man or woman who wants to call himself by the name "intercessor for a continent." It is the result of God seeking a man, finding a man, revealing a need to a man, putting a burden on the man, setting the man aside to intercede, and sustaining the man while he intercedes.

When that happens, the heart of the intercessor is united to the Lord and to the object of intercession in such a way that if he fails to see God's victory though intercession, he is ruined.

Lord, raise such people in Your Church and receive the glory for their labours. Amen.

NEHEMIAH'S INTERCESSION: THE CONSEQUENCE OF INTERCESSION

The words of Nehemiah the son of Hacaliah,

"Now it happened in the month of Chislev, in the twentieth year, as I was in Suza the capital, that Hanani, one of my brethren, came with certain men out of Judah; and I asked them concerning the Jews that survived, who had escaped exile, and concerning Jerusalem. And they said to me, 'The survivors there in the province who escaped exile are in great trouble and shame; the wall of Jerusalem is broken down, and its gates are destroyed by fire.'

When I heard these words I sat down and wept, and mourned for days; and I continued fasting and praying before the God of heaven. And I said, 'O Lord God of heaven, the great and terrible God who keeps covenant and steadfast love with those who love him and keep his commandments; let thy ear be attentive, and thy eyes open, to hear the prayer of thy servant which I now pray before thee day and night for the people of Israel thy servants, confessing the sins of the people of Israel, which we have sinned against thee. Yea, I and my father's house have sinned. We have acted very corruptly against thee, and have not kept the commandments, the statutes and the ordinances which thou didst command thy servant Moses. Remember the word which thou didst command thy servant Moses, saying, "If you are unfaithful, I will scatter you among the peoples; but if you return to me and keep my commandments and do them, though your dispersed be under the farthest skies, I will gather them thence and bring them to the place which I have chosen, to make my name dwell there." They are thy servants and thy people, whom thou hast redeemed by thy great power and by thy strong hand. O Lord, let thy ear be attentive to the prayer of thy servants, and to the prayer of thy servants who delight to fear thy name; and give success to thy servant today, and grant him mercy in the sight of this man.'

Now I was cupbearer to the king. In the month of Nisan, in the twentieth year of King Artaxerxes, when wine was before him, I took up the wine and gave it to the king. Now I had not been sad in his presence. And the king said to me, 'Why is your face sad, seeing you are not sick? This is nothing else but sadness of the heart.' Then I was very much afraid. I said to the king, 'Let the king live for ever! Why should not my face be sad, when the city, the place of my fathers' sepulchres, lies waste, and its gates have been destroyed by fire?" Then the king said to me, 'For what do you make request?' So I prayed to the God of heaven. And I said to the king, 'If it pleases the king, and if your servant has found favour in your sight, that you send me to Judah, to the city of my fathers' sepulchres, that I may rebuild it.' And the king said to me (the queen sitting beside him), 'How long will you be gone, and when will you return?' So it pleased the king to send me; and I set him a time"

(Nehemiah 1:1-11; 2:1-7).

2

NEHEMIAH'S MINISTRY OF INTERCESSION

NEHEMIAH—AN EXILE (ALLEN)

Nehemiah was in Suza, the capital of Persia. He was an alien. He had been taken there because of war. Although he was well placed in the palace of Suza and was faithfully serving the king in his very presence, Nehemiah's heart remained that of an exile. What are the characteristics of an alien? Below are some of them:

1. He loves the Lord, the King of his true homeland, with all of his spirit, soul, and body.
2. The only things that give him joy and real satisfaction are the things of his true homeland.
3. The things of the country of exile have no power to make him happy or sad.
4. He is burdened only for the prosperity of his homeland.
5. The prosperity of the country in which he is exiled does not bother him. He will, however, see to it that all that can be acquired in the country of his exile is acquired and transferred to his homeland. He will carry out the transfer as soon as possible, since he knows that he may not be able to take money or property along.

6. He makes no permanent investments in the country in which he is exiled.
7. He keeps nothing in the country of exile that is useful and needed in his homeland.
8. He is totally unmoved and undisturbed by appointments, promotions, and demotions in the country of exile.
9. He is not moved in the least whether or not he is appointed, promoted, or demoted by the authorities of the country in which he is exiled.
10. He is not ashamed of his identity as an alien, and would not want to be mistaken for a citizen of the country of exile.
11. He lives with one great expectation—the day of the termination of his exile and his return to the homeland.
12. He bothers about how much of the goods and monies of the country of exile have been transferred to his homeland ahead of time. He is fully aware that he will not be able to take anything with him when the time comes to leave the country in which he has been in exile. He knows that untransferred wealth is not really his, because it could be lost at any time.
13. He labours at all the duties that are given to him in the country in which he is an exile. He does all of them in an exemplary way, not to impress the men of the country in which he is exiled, but to impress the King of his true homeland.

Because of Nehemiah's condition as an exile, his heart was ever open towards Jerusalem. It was then that he received one of his brethren who came with certain men out of Judah. Because his heart was bound not to what was happening in Suza but to what was happening in Jerusalem, Nehemiah inquired concerning:

1. the Jews who had survived,
2. the Jews who had escaped exile,
3. Jerusalem.

He asked concerning specific issues. There were many things that he could have asked questions about, but he did not. Too many people do not know how to sift the essential from the nonessential. There is no sense of priority. When the Lord sent the twelve out He ensured that they did not get entangled with the nonessentials of speech and property. The Bible says:

"*And he called to him the twelve, and began to send them out two by two, and gave them authority over the unclean spirits.*

He charged them to take nothing for their journey except a staff; no bread, no bag, no money in their belt; but to wear sandals and not put on two tunics"

(Mark 6:7-9).

Nehemiah asked questions that are goal-directed. May the Lord help us to become goal-directed in all we say and do. May we be delivered from the nonessentials of speech, dress, and action.

Intercessors are men and women of destiny. May they be pre-occupied with God's musts. Nehemiah was like that. Lord, make me like that.

Nehemiah got straight answers to the straight questions that he asked, namely:

1. The survivors who had escaped exile were in great trouble and shame.
2. The wall of Jerusalem was broken down.
3. The gates of the wall of Jerusalem were destroyed by fire.

Nehemiah thus obtained information that was clear and exact.

THE IMPACT OF THE INFORMATION ON NEHEMIAH

How a man receives and reacts to information is dependent on what is in his heart. It is dependent on whether the information concerns something that is central in his heart or not. Nehemiah received the information. The survivors and Jerusalem were paramount in his heart. They were doing very badly. Because he was so identified with the people and the city, he felt deep agony. It was as if he had begun to do badly himself. He sat down and wept. Things were going well in Suza, but he could not rejoice while things were going badly for the Jews in Jerusalem and the city itself.

Nehemiah not only wept. He mourned for days. He declared a personal fast and, with the fast on, he went into intercession. The facts had been revealed to him, and they resulted in a burden. He, therefore, was truly qualified to intercede.

NEHEMIAH'S INTERCESSION

Nehemiah was before the God of heaven. He prayed to the God of heaven. He was not praying to man; he was not praying to any system or structure. He was not praying to himself. He was not praying to God from a distance. He was very near the Lord. There were no barriers between God and himself. He had not taken advantage of his being away from Jerusalem to indulge in sin. He was in exile, but the Lord was not left in Jerusalem. Because he knew the Lord and loved Him, he lived his whole life as an exile in the very presence of God. His knowledge, loyalty, and commitment to God were deep and thorough.

He exalted the Lord. He worshipped Him, praying, "O Lord God of heaven, the great and terrible God who keeps covenants and steadfast love with those who love him and keep his commandments." Intercession, like all praying, should begin with praise, thanksgiving, and adoration. Praise befits the Lord and, because the Lord dwells in the praise of His children, those who come to Him, regardless of their problem, should minister to Him by praise before they present their requests. There are too many who only know how to present problems to God. They do not have time to bring anything to Him. They ought to bring Him praise; for has He not said, "He who brings thanksgiving as his sacrifice honours me" (Psalm 50:23)? Is it not wise to minister to His needs before we present ours to Him? Is it not wise to demonstrate the fact that although we have needs that concern His Kingdom to intercede about, our priority makes the King come before the Kingdom? Oh, how many have made the work of the Kingdom the goal! How sad that the King is not first in the hearts of many who serve His purposes!

It is the purpose of God that He should reign supreme in our hearts and receive preeminence in all things. Anyone who worships the work of the Lord instead of the Lord, is an idolater. Anyone who enthrones the service of the Lord in his heart is an idolater. Anyone who puts intercession before praise, thanksgiving, and worship, has made a sad error.

Nehemiah put God first. He put the King before the Kingdom. May we do the same. He pleaded with God to listen. He said, "Let thy ear be attentive. Let thy eyes be open to hear the prayer of thy servant which I now pray before thee day and night."

Nehemiah declared clearly for whom the prayer was being made- "for the people of Israel, thy servants." He was not praying vaguely. He was not praying for everybody. He was making his prayer for the people of Israel. In humility he added that the people of Israel were the Lord's servants. He was saying, "Lord, they are not just the people of Israel. They are a people linked to You. They are Your servants. Lord, because they are Your servants, take an interest in them."

Nehemiah was bent on success. He was not just throwing a few words at God. He was praying night and day. The burden on him was such that he bore it always, night and day and, consequently, he bore it before the Lord night and day. There was nothing of a man carrying out a religious formality. There was nothing of someone just trying to be involved. His whole being was taken up. He was giving God no rest. He was taking no rest. He was pouring himself out to the only One who could help him, and he was doing it night and day.

He prayed in full assurance that there was no help possible outside the Lord. There is a sense in which no one can truly turn to God for help if he can obtain help elsewhere. Real intercessors know how useless the arm of flesh is. They know that only God can' solve their problems, and they turn to Him without reservation. They share the experience of the Psalmist, who wrote:

"For God alone my soul waits in silence; from him comes my salvation.

He only is my rock and my salvation, my fortress; I shall not be greatly moved"

(Psalms 62:1-2).

All intercessors turn desperately to God, They cling to Him. He is everything to them. Because they trust Him absolutely and trust only Him, He never leaves them unaided.

Nehemiah identified himself fully and completely with the sins of the people of Israel for whom he was interceding. He put it as follows:

1. "We have sinned against thee."
2. "I and my father's house have sinned."
3. "We have acted very corruptly against thee,"
4. "We have not kept thy commandments."
5. "We have not kept thy statutes."

6. "We have not kept thy ordinances."
7. "We have not kept all these even though you did command us to keep them."

Nehemiah did not say anything to make their sins less than they were. He did not try to:
1. excuse them on the basis of ignorance,
2. excuse them on the basis of weaknesses,
3. excuse them on the basis of the fact that Moses died long ago and there was none to remind them.

He let the guilt fall squarely on the people.

Nehemiah sanctified the Lord. He showed and owned up to the fact that the fault was 100% percent that of the people of Israel, and that the Lord was righteous. He owned up to the fact that the sin was committed against the Lord. It was not against man or against any nation. It was against God.

Nehemiah had earlier on chosen the basis on which he was going to intercede. In fact, he chose it early, for he said, 'O Lord God of heaven, the great and terrible God who keeps covenants and steadfast love." He chose to base his intercession on "the God Who keeps covenants." Having established that basis in the beginning, he clung to it.

He built and developed his pleading with God on that basis. He, therefore, asked God to remember the word that He had commanded in the past to His servant Moses. Of course, there were many—commandments given to Moses. He knew them and, consequently, he chose that which was best for the situation at hand. As we have said before, an intercessor must know God, man, and the Word of God as thoroughly as possible. Without this threefold knowledge, he will surely fail.

What was Nehemiah calling on God to remember? He was calling on Him to remember that He had said:

1. If they were unfaithful, He would scatter them among the people.
2. If while being scattered among the people they returned to Him and kept His commandments, then
3. Though they were dispersed to the farthest skies, He would gather them thence and bring them to the place He had chosen to make His name dwell there.

Nehemiah then argued that they had been unfaithful and the Lord had scattered them, they, being scattered, had repented and returned to Him, and they were keeping His commandments.

He further argued that he was not alone. He was one of the repentant ones, but there were others. He said, "Let thy ear be attentive to the prayer of thy servant. Let thy ear be attentive to the prayers thy servants." He and the other servants delighted to fear God's name. The fact that they delighted to fear His name was evidence of their repentance.

He nowhere said that all those who went into exile had turned to the Lord and were delighting in the fear of Him. He, however, stated that there were some and he was one of them. He, as one of those who had repented, was standing in the gap on behalf of those who had repented, and they were representative of all the exiles.

He then pleaded that God would grant him favour before the king; so that he might be allowed to go and execute the plan of restoration that was in his heart.

THE CONSEQUENCE OF THE INTERCESSION

God showed Nehemiah what needed to be done in order to take care of the Jews who had survived exile and were in bad shape and also what needed to be done about the wall and the gates of Jerusalem. It would seem that when Nehemiah got the news about what was happening in Jerusalem, he was burdened by the feeling that something ought to be done. His burden led to his intercession. In the course of the intercession God showed him what needed to be done and who needed to do it. It could be that the revelation was progressive and thus it guided the way Nehemiah interceded. That is obvious from the fact that at the end of his intercession he was already asking for success and for favour in the sight of the king of Suza.

We can say the following about Nehemiah's intercession.

1. The children of Israel sinned.
2. God sent them into exile as punishment.
3. One of them, Nehemiah, walked close to the Lord and was burdened for Jerusalem and for the exiles.
4. He obtained information about the poor condition of the survivors and the broken wall and gates of Jerusalem.
5. He began to Intercede night and day to the Lord for the survivors and for the wall of Jerusalem and the gates.
6. In the course of his intercession, the Lord revealed to Nehemiah what needed to be done for the survivors and for the wall and the gates.
7. He continued to intercede and God showed him that it was he who had to do something about the survivors and the wall and gates.
8. He continued to pray that God would give him success by touching the heart of the king of Suza.
9. The burden gripped his heart even after the intercession; so that the king noticed the grief on his heart.

10. The king asked and was told things as they were, and permission and help were sought for the journey.
11. Permission was granted and the intercessor became involved in God's plan of restoration and rebuilding.
12. The work of restoration and rebuilding was completed.

Many people think that prayer is easy. As we have said, it is the hardest thing on earth. Intercession is the most difficult part of the hardest thing on earth. However, it is possible to think of intercession as something that saves people from involvement with the battles of life. That was not the case for Nehemiah. He was comfortably serving in the immediate presence of the king in Suza. His job was easy. When the wine was brought before the king, Nehemiah would take it up and give it to him. Could any job be easier? Could any job be freer of risk?

However, Nehemiah dared to intercede. From that time on life was never the same for him. First of all, there was the sorrow, the agony, the fasting, the intercession night and day. Then there was the requesting of the king, followed by the journey to Jerusalem. Then there was the task of building up a team. Then there were the enemies to fight against, so hard that there was constant battle. Then there was the sacrifice of all that he had to provide for the people. All was conflict, but there came a day when the wall was completed and the gates built and the gatekeepers, the singers, and the Levites appointed. But that was only a part of the burden.

Nehemiah pursued the work of reformation—reestablishing temple worship, leading the people in worship and the restoration of the Sabbath and all the other aspects of holy living that had been lost or neglected. He summed it up in the following words:

> Thus I cleansed them from everything foreign, and I established the duties of the priests and Levites, each in his work; and I provi-

ded for the wood offering, at appointed times, and for the first fruits" (Nehemiah 13:30-31).

Intercession had led him into practical and spiritual work. Intercession had brought his ease to an end, taken him from the comforts of a royal court, and placed him in the front line of building, battling, and spiritual restoration.

There is a sense in which he remained an intercessor until the work was complete. That which started in Suza continued in Jerusalem. There is a sense in which he remained an intercessor, for did he not always have to plead with God that the people might walk in His ways? Did he not always have to plead with God; that the enemy might not break in and destroy the wall and the gates again? I believe he did. Intercessors never stop interceding.

INTERCESSORS, BEWARE!

If the Lord calls you to become an intercessor for a city, it may be, first of all, a call away from man and a call to God in the loneliness of spiritual warfare in intercession, followed by your being thrown into a public and perhaps a greatly resisted ministry of preaching the Gospel, saving souls, and building up the church of the Lord, God's way. It may be a call first into silence before Him and then into battling before man that may lead to great persecution and even death. Unless you are prepared for the latter, forget about the former.

Moses did not stay on the mountaintop interceding. He interceded for some time in deep agony, but he who "went up" also had to "go down" to the children of Israel and lead them into the Promised Land even though it meant that along the way he was disqualified and was not allowed into the Promised Land.

Great revelations carry with them responsibilities. To Mary it was said:

"Behold, this child is set for the fall and rising of many in Israel, and for a sign that is spoken against (and a sword will pierce through your own soul also),
that thoughts out of many hearts may be revealed"
(Luke 2:34-35).

It was good that Mary was blessed. It was also good to know that her Son was given for the fall and rising of many in Israel. However, it was also a must that a sword pierce her own soul. That is a divine law.

It was good for her son that He be set for the fall and rising of many in Israel, but it was indispensable that He be a sign that is spoken against. That indeed is God's law, for those who will be exalted by the Lord will also be exalted to great sacrifices, great 'sufferings, and great unpopularity. There is no way out of it.

It could be that you aspire to become an intercessor for an individual, a family, a town or city, a nation or nations, a continent, or a planet. You do well to so aspire. However, bear in mind that the price you will have to pay will be proportional to the consequence of that individual, family, town or city, nation or nations, continent, or planet before God.

Intercession for an individual whose ministry has consequence in an assembly in a village is not the same as intercession for an individual whose ministry spans continents. Intercession for an individual who is doing "surface" work is not the same as intercession for a man who is deeply involved in the overthrow of principalities and powers on a worldwide scale. Intercession and the price that has to be pa id are proportional to the consequence of that person or work before God and before the devil.

Do not aspire beyond your willingness to pay the price. Do not step into a battle for which you are ill-equipped. Do not exalt yourself to intercede for a nation when you do not have the weight before God to intercede for a small town or a division. If you want to kill a very big viper with a small stick, you may end up being killed. Consequently, start at the level of your faith and your willingness to pay the price and move up steadily. God bless you.

PART 6

Two new testament intercessors

1

THE APOSTLE PAUL'S MINISTRY AS AN INTERCESSOR: UNCEASING ACTIVITY

" *For this reason, because I have heard of your faith in the Lord Jesus and your love toward all the saints, I do not cease to give thanks for you,*

remembering you in my prayers, that the God of our Lord Jesus Christ, the Father of glory, may give you a spirit of wisdom and of revelation in the knowledge of him,

having the eyes of your hearts enlightened, that you may know what is the hope to which he has called you, what are the riches of his glorious inheritance in the saints, and what is the immeasurable greatness of his power in us who believe,

according to the working of his great might which he accom-plished in Christ when he raised him from the dead and made him sit at his right hand in the heavenly places, far above all rule and authority and power and dominion, and above every name that is named, not only in this age but also in that which is to come; and he has put all things under his feet and has made him the head over all things for the church, which is his body, the fullness of him who fills all in all"

(Ephesians 1: 15-23).

"*For this reason I bow my knees before the Father, from whom every family in heaven and on earth is named, that according to the riches of his glory he may grant you to be strengthened with might through his Spi-*

rit in the inner man, and that Christ may dwell in your hearts through faith; that you, being rooted and grounded in love, may have power to comprehend with all the saints what is the breadth and length and height and depth, and to know the love of Christ which surpasses knowledge, that you may be filled with all the fullness of God. Now to him who by the power at work within us is able to do far more abundantly than all that we ask or think, to him be glory in the church and in Christ Jesus to all generations, for ever and ever. Amen"

(Ephesians 3: 14-20).

"And so, from the day we heard of it, we have not ceased to pray for you, asking that you may be filled with the knowledge of his will in all spiritual wisdom and understanding, to lead a life worthy of the Lord, fully pleasing to him, bearing fruit in every good work and increasing in the knowledge of God. May you be strengthened with all power, according to his glorious might, for all endurance and patience with joy, giving thanks to the Father, who has qualified us to share in the inheritance of the saints in light"

(Colossians 1:9-12).

"For I want you to know how greatly I strive for you, and for those at Laodicea, and for all who have not seen my face, that their hearts may be encouraged as they are knit together in love, to have all the riches of assured understanding and the knowledge of God's mystery, of Christ, in whom are hid all the treasures of wisdom and knowledge"

(Colossians 2:1-3).

PAUL: A MAN RIGHT WITH GOD

We have said that it is imperative that the intercessor be right with God. He should be right with God all the time. He should live a life that constantly satisfies the Lord. Was Paul such a man? I believe we can trust his testimony about himself. He said:

> "*This is how one should regard us, as servants of Christ and stewards of the mysteries of God. Moreover it is required of stewards that they be found trustworthy. But with me it is a very small thing that I should be judged by you or by any human court. I do not even judge myself. I am not aware of anything against myself, but I am not thereby acquitted. It is the Lord who judges me.*"

(1 Corinthians 4: 1-4).

> "*Now concerning the unmarried, I have no command of the Lord, but I give my opinion as one who by the Lord's mercy is trustworthy*"

(1 Corinthians 7:25).

> "*Brethren, I have lived before God in all good conscience up to this day*"

(Acts 23:1).

> "*In Christ Jesus, then, I have reason to be proud of my work for God.*
>
> *For I will not venture to speak of anything except what Christ has wrought through me to win obedience from the Gentiles, by word and deed, by the power of signs and wonders, by the power of the Holy Spirit, so that from Jerusalem and as far round as Illyricum I have fully preached the gospel of Christ, thus making it my ambition to preach the gospel, not where Christ has already been named, lest I build on another man's foundation, but as it is written,*
>
> *'They shall see who have never been told of him, and they shall understand who have never heard of him*"

(Romans 15: 17-21).

He was not only rightly related to God; he had deep personal experiences with God. He testified as follows:

> *"I know a man in Christ who fourteen years ago was caught up to the third heaven—whether in the body or out of the body I do not know, God knows.*
>
> *And I know that this man was caught up into Paradise—whether in the body or out of the body I do not know, God knows—and he heard things that cannot be told, which man may not utter.*
>
> *On behalf of this man I will boast, but on my own behalf I will not boast, except of my weaknesses.*
>
> *Though if I wish to boast, I shall not be a fool, for I shall be speaking the truth.*
>
> *But I refrain from it, so that no one may think more of me than he sees in me or hears from me.*
>
> *And to keep me from being too elated by the abundance of revelations, a thorn was given me in the flesh, a messenger of Satan, to harass me, to keep me from being too elated"*
>
> (II Corinthians 12:2-7).

He not only had deep experiences with the Lord; he suffered very much for the Lord and for the Gospel. He testified about his sufferings as follows:

> *"Are they servants of Christ? I am a better one—I am talking like a madman—with far greater labours, far more imprisonments, with countless beatings, and often near death. Five times I have received at the hands of the Jews the forty lashes less one. Three times I have been beaten with rods; once I was stoned. Three times I have been shipwrecked; a night and a day I have been adrift at sea; on frequent journeys, in danger from rivers, danger from robbers, danger from my own people, danger from Gentiles, danger in the city, danger in the wilderness, danger at sea, danger from false brethren; in toil and hardship, through many a sleepless night, in hunger and thirst, often without food, in cold and exposure. And apart from other things, there is the daily pressure upon me of my anxiety for all the churches.*

Who is weak, and I am not weak? Who is made to fall, and I am not indignant?"

(IICorinthians 11:23-29).

So the apostle Paul walked closely to the Lord. He had deep experiences with the Lord and suffered much for the Lord. He was in every way qualified to intercede.

PAUL: BURDENED FOR THE PEOPLE OF GOD

We have already shown that it is impossible to intercede without a burden. The greater the burden, the greater the intercession. The question is: Was the apostle Paul a man with a burden? If so, what was his burden? His testimony speaks dearly. He said:

"And, apart from other things, there is the daily pressure upon me of my anxiety for all the churches"

(II Corinthians 11:28).

"My little children with whom I am again in travail until Christ be formed in you!"

(Galatians 4: 19).

"Him we proclaim, warning every man and teaching every man in all wisdom, that we may present every man mature in Christ. For this I toil, striving with all the energy which he mightily inspires within me"

(Colossians I :28-29).

"For I want you to know how greatly I strive for you, and for those at Laodicea, and for all who have not seen my face,

that their hearts may be encouraged as they are knit together in love, to have all the riches of assured understanding and the knowledge of God's mystery,

of Christ, in whom are hid all the treasures of wisdom and knowledge"

(Colossians 2: 1-3).

Paul was burdened that Christ might be fully formed in the believers; he was burdened that each believer might be presented mature in Christ. He was anxious that all believers attain the unit y of the faith and the knowledge of the Son of God, to mature manhood, to the measure of the stature of the fullness of Christ.

PAUL: A MAN WITH A GOAL FOR THE BELIEVERS

Paul's ministry was goal-directed. Everything he did was goal-directed. For the lost he had one goal, and it was to bring them to the Lord Jesus. That goal resulted in a crushing burden. He said:

"I am speaking the truth in Christ, I am not lying;

My conscience bears me witness in the Holy Spirit, that I have great sorrow and unceasing anguish in my heart.

For I could wish that I myself were accursed and cut off from Christ for the sake of my brethren, my kinsmen by race"

(Romans 9: 1-3).

That burden led to intercession for their salvation and the intercession led to evangelistic action.

He wrote to the Romans:

"For God is my witness, whom I serve with my spirit in the gospel of his Son,

that without ceasing I mention you always in my prayers, asking that somehow by God's will I may now at last succeed in coming to you.

For I long to see you, that I may impart to you some spiritual gift to strengthen you, that is,

that we may be mutually encouraged by each other's faith, both yours and mine.

I want you to know, brethren, that I have often intended to come to you (but thus far have been prevented), in order that I may reap some harvest among you as well as among the rest of the Gentiles.

I am under obligation both to Greeks and to barbarians, both to the wise and to the foolish:

So I am eager to preach the gospel to you also who are in Rome"

(Romans 1:9-15).

He wanted to go to Rome so as to evangelize the lost and to build up the saints. Both tasks were burdens to him. His goal was clear. He soaked it in prayer and yearned to carry out practical action.

We can deduce the following:

GOAL → BURDEN → INTERCESSION → ACTION

The goal will influence the burden, the intercession, and the action. The intercession will determine whether or not the goal will be accomplished. The action will succeed to the extent to which it was interceded for. The burden will influence the depth of intercession, for great burden will lead to great intercession, and where there is no burden there can be no real intercession.

PAUL PLACED PRIMARY IMPORTANCE ON INTERCESSION

Paul placed premium value on intercession. This was manifested in two ways:

1. He interceded.
2. He invited others to intercede.

1. He Interceded

To the Ephesians Paul wrote: Without ceasing I mention you always in my prayers.

To the Ephesians he wrote:

"*I do not cease to give thanks for you, remembering you in my prayers ...*"

(Ephesians 1:16).

"*For this reason I bow my knees before the Father ... that according to the riches of his glory he may grant you....*"

(Ephesians 3:14-16).

To the Colossians he wrote:

"*We always thank God, the Father of our Lord Jesus Christ, when we pray for you*"

(Colossians 1:3).

"*And so, from the day we heard of it, we have not ceased to pray for you ...*"

(Colossians 1:9).

"For I want you to know how greatly I strive for you, and for those at Laodicea, and for all who have not seen my face"

(Colossians 2: 1).

To the Thessalonians he wrote: *"We give thanks to God always for you all, constantly mentioning you in our prayers"*

(1 Thessalonians 1:2).

Paul was always interceding for the churches. He interceded without ceasing. He made mention of them always in his prayers. He bowed his knees before the Father on their behalf. Intercession to him was mighty warfare. His ministry in this domain was great striving. It was war. He mentioned them in prayer, and he warred on their behalf in prayer. His prayers were labours, toils, conflicts, mighty wrestles, et cetera. He knew God's will for them, and he laboured so that that will should come to pass. He knew the enemy's plans against them and so laboured so that those plans might be destroyed.

The apostle described his ministry as toiling and striving with all the energy that the Lord mightily inspired in him (Colossians 1:29). These strivings and toilings were predominantly in intercession. There were obstacles caused by the devil, the world, and the flesh to the maturation of the saints. Those obstacles had to be broken in prayer. That part of Paul's intercession was destructive warfare. He pulled down all that the enemy had built up and all that the enemy was building up. He took no rest because the enemy took no rest. He interceded always because the enemy was always at work. He watched in prayer always because the enemy was always at work. He watched in prayer always, because the enemy was always prowling around like a roaring lion, seeking someone to destroy.

The apostle interceded for all of them. In intercessory prayer he built a protective wall around each saint, so that the fiery darts of the enemy might not get at him. He also built a wall around each church and around all the churches; so that they might be kept from all the attacks of the wicked one.

The apostle knew very clearly that the devil would attack anyone he could attack. He knew that he would destroy anyone he could destroy. He knew that the believers were sometimes careless and ignorant and that if he did not build a wall around them, they would be destroyed. This knowledge led to mighty warfare, not only in destroying that which the enemy had built, but also in building a protective wall around the saints, so as to make future attacks difficult or impossible.

In dealing with the enemy on their behalf, Paul did two main things:

1. He destroyed that which the enemy had done.
2. He built protective walls in prayer around each saint and each assembly to check the future moves of Satan. The devil understands this kind of warfare clearly. He once said to God, "Does Job fear God for naught? Hast thou not put a hedge about him and his house and all that he has, on every side?" (Job 1:9-10.) The protective hedge put by the Lord made Satan's penetration impossible. The intercessor for the saints has the crucial responsibility to put a hedge in prayer around each saint and each group of saints. Without this there could be excessive losses owing to satanic attacks.

We shall look at the other aspect of the apostle's intercession later on. Suffice it for the moment to say that the intercessor on behalf of the church and the saints not only carries out a destructive and protective work; he also does a building work.

2. He Invited Others to Intercede

To the Romans Paul wrote:

"I appeal to you, brethren, by our Lord Jesus Christ and by the love of the Spirit, to strive together with me in your prayers to God on my behalf, that I may be delivered from the unbelievers in Judea, and that my service for Jerusalem may be acceptable to the saints, so that by God's will I may come to you with joy and be refreshed in your company"

(Romans 15:30-32).

He wanted them to intercede. The intercession was to be striving in prayer on his behalf, so that three things might happen. First of all, he might be delivered from the unbelievers in Judea. Secondly, his services for Jerusalem might be acceptable to the saints. Thirdly, by God's will he might come to them with joy and be refreshed by their company. The apostle did not take anything for granted. He knew that safety only lay in bringing everything to God in prayer.

Paul was striving in prayer. However, he did not consider that enough. He valued individual prayer. He also knew that the Word of the Lord had said, *"Five of you shall chase a hundred and a hundred of you shall chase ten thousand"* (Leviticus 26:8). He did not say, "*I am the apostle; I have prayed. I have striven in prayer. God always hears me. The Bible says that I can chase one thousand of my enemies*" (Joshua 23:10). I can do without the prayers of others." He instead pleaded and begged them to pray for him. He knew the power of the enemy, and he knew the greater power of God that was released when many believers prayed.

To the Corinthians Paul wrote: "*You also must help us by prayer, so that many will give thanks on our behalf for the blessing granted us in answer to many prayers*" (II Corinthians 1: 11). He considered their intercession a help. He also considered it a must. He saw the value not just of prayer but of many prayers. He kept an eye on the quality. He also kept an eye on the quantity. He knew that his success depended on their many prayers. He was humble enough to express his need so openly. He did not advertise for funds. He advertised for prayers!

To the Ephesians he wrote: "*Pray at all times in the Spirit, with all prayer and supplication. To that end keep alert with all perseverance, making supplication for all the saints, and also for me, that utterance may be given me in opening my mouth boldly to proclaim the mystery of the gospel, for which I am an ambassador in chains; that I may declare it boldly, as I ought to speak*" (Ephesians 6: 18). He was commanding the Ephesians to do the following:

1. Pray at all times.
2. Pray in the Spirit.
3. Pray all prayers praise, petition, intercession, et cetera.
4. Supplicate.
5. Keep alert in prayer, watching to see any attacks of Satan and destroy them.
6. Persevere in prayer.
7. Intercede for all the saints.
8. Intercede for him that utterance might be given him in opening his mouth, that boldness might be given him to proclaim the mystery of the Gospel, and that he might declare it boldly, as he should.

To the Colossians he wrote:

"*Continue steadfastly in prayer, being watchful in it with thanksgiving;*

and pray for us also, that God may open to us a door for the word, to declare the mystery of Christ, on account of which I am in prison,

that I may make it clear, as I ought to speak"

(Colossians 4:2-4).

He urged them to continue:
1. steadfastly in prayer,
2. watchfully in prayer,
3. with thanksgiving in prayer.

He also urged them to intercede for him, and he gave them the lines along which they were to intercede:
1. for open doors for the ministry of the Word,
2. for a capacity to declare the mystery of Christ,
3. for ability to make it clear.

One thing comes through in all these requests for prayer. The apostle Paul did not count on his experience, commitment, God's mighty anointings of the past, spiritual gifts, zeal, and hard work, good as these were. He counted on the power of God released in prayer. He counted on God and He counted on God alone. He believed that God acts in answer to prayer. He believed that if men prayed, God would answer and that there were many things that God would do in answer to prayer that He would not do without prayer. He was fully persuaded that God heard the prayers of people on behalf of others (intercession), and so he pleaded with believers to intercede for others and for himself.

To Paul it was "pray or perish," "intercede or another perishes." He knew too well that although the Lord had given him a great ministry and he was in the centre of God's will and labouring very much in prayer, he could not accomplish his ministry, unless others prayed for him. So he laboured to have them pray constantly, without ceasing, and with all prayer, to strive in prayer, toil in prayer, labour in prayer, wrestle in prayer, press on in prayer, and win in prayer. He knew that the successful spiritual warrior first conquered the enemy in prayer before he faced him on the field. He knew that behind the visible enemy were mighty spiritual enemy forces in the unseen realm that yielded only to prayer. He knew that once these were overthrown, the battle was already won in the seen realm. He knew that believers were prevented from entering into their full inheritance by satanic forces which, once overthrown, left the believer to respond readily to the call of God. With this knowledge he prayed and invited people to pray before he acted. He prayed and invited people to pray while he was acting, and he prayed and invited people to pray after he had acted.

THE CONTENT OF THE APOSTLE'S INTERCESSION

We have seen that the apostle Paul had a goal and a burden to see the goal attained. He interceded and he acted. It is obvious that if he were to succeed, the contents of his intercessions must be related to the goal in view. It will be proper for us to examine the contents of some of his intercessions in order to know what we too ought to ask God to do in the lives of the saints. We shall limit ourselves to the two intercessory prayers in Ephesians, but we encourage the reader to study the others, so as to derive profit from them.

In the prayer recorded in Ephesians 1:16-23 we learn the following:

1. Intercession is to be wrapped in thanksgiving.
2. Intercession for the saints should be an unceasing activity.
3. Intercession should be addressed to God.
4. Intercession should be preceded by a worship of God.
5. The believer needs a spirit of wisdom in the knowledge of Him.
6. The believer needs a spirit of revelation in the knowledge of Him.
7. The Father gives the spirit of wisdom and revelation in

response to prayer, either by the person needing it or by the prayers of another (intercession).

8. The believer needs to have the eyes of his heart enlightened by the Lord.

9. The enlightened eyes will lead to a knowledge of the following: the hope to which the believer has been called by the Lord; the riches of the glorious inheritance that God has made available to the saints; and the immeasurable greatness of his power in us who believe. This power that is in the believer is according to the working of His great might.

10. The working of God's great might was accomplished in Christ when He raised Him from the dead and made Him sit at His right hand in the heavenly places—far above all rule, authority, power, dominion, and every name that is named in this age and that will be named in the age to come.

11. The working of this great might and the exaltation of Christ mean that God has put all things under His feet and has made Him the head over all things.

12. God has made Him the head over all things for the Church.

13. The Church is the Body of Christ, the fullness of Christ, who fills all in all.

In interceding this way, the apostle divides the needs of the believer into two groups. One group consists of things that God is yet to do, like giving the believer a spirit of wisdom and revelation. The second group has to do with things chat God has already done but the believer is blind to or ignorant of, and therefore God needs to open the eyes of the believer's heart to see what He has done in him and for him.

It is now understandable why Paul interceded and interceded. It is now understandable why Paul interceded and interceded for the believers. It is understandable why he interceded for all believers. He saw that their need was a spirit of wisdom and revelation in the knowledge of the Lord. He pleaded that the Father should give it to them, for how else could they have it? He also saw that they needed to have the eyes of their hearts enlightened as to the greatness of the power of God that was in them, the hope to which they had been called and the assured grounds of the exaltation of Christ from which all was subject to them.

Paul saw that those who went astray did so because they were blind and ignorant. He thus prayed for all and invited believers to pray. If he was to accomplish his goal, he had to have all the believers have a spirit of wisdom and revelation and know the hope to which they have been called and the immeasurable greatness of God's power that has been lodged in them. He also prayed that the believers would have their eyes open to the fact that they have also been raised with Christ and made to sit with him in the heavenly places in Christ Jesus far above all rule, authority, power, dominion, every name that is named in this age and will be named in the age to come.

In thus praying, Paul wanted the Lord to open the eyes of the believer to see the greatness of His authority now and use it now and, thereby, show principalities and powers now the manifold wisdom of God.

When this happened, a very significant part of his goal would already have been accomplished.

In the intercessory prayer recorded in Ephesians 3: 14-19 we learn the following:

1. Intercession is purposeful—"for this reason."
2. Intercession is carried out in utter humility—"I bow my knees."

3. Intercession is before the Father.
4. Intercession is in a spirit of worship and adoration—"The Father, from whom every family in heaven and on earth is named."
5. Intercession has specific goals: that according to the riches of His glory He may grant you to be strengthened with might through his spirit in the inner man; that Christ may dwell in your hearts through faith; that you, being rooted and grounded in love, may have power to comprehend with all the saints what is the breadth, length, height, and depth of the love of Christ; that you, being rooted and grounded in love, may have power to know (experience) the love of Christ, which surpasses knowledge; and that you may be filled with all the fullness of God.

It is quite obvious that the desire and the burden of the apostle that is expressed in these words of intercession was that the saints might come into spiritual experience. They needed strengthening in the inner man (the spirit); they needed to experience the indwelling of Christ in all fullness in their spirits through faith; they needed power to understand in their spirits the limitless love of Christ and to experience it. Finally, he prayed that they might be filled with all the fullness of God.

A TOTAL WORK BY A TOTAL GOD LN A TOTAL MAN

The apostle Paul had before him the limitless way in which God had given Himself away to man in Christ Jesus. He knew the limitless power of the Cross in undoing the works of the devil. He knew the glorious power of the resurrection. He knew the mighty power that was lodged in the believer's spirit by the Resident Holy Spirit. He knew the mighty effectiveness of the Almighty Intercessor on the throne and the great might of the Resident Intercessor. Knowing all this, he was certain that all God's purposes for the believer could be realized. He not only believed that all God's purposes for the believer could be realized; he believed that all God's purposes for the believer will be realized. He thus interceded that believers, all believers, each believer, should be filled with all the fullness of God.

Do you see the far-reaching extent of that prayer? Paul could have prayed that some believers should be filled with all the fullness of God, but he did not do that. He could have prayed that all believers should have something of God. He could have prayed that all believers should have the fulness of God. That would already have been great. However, he did not stop at that which is great. He pressed on and asked that all the believers should be filled with all the fullness of God.

That was total asking. Paul pressed on right to the fullness of God being manifested in all fullness in man. He pressed on for a total work by all of God in all of man. He reached the heights of intercession and asked nothing short of all of God for all of man.

Was it just words? Certainly not. The Lord Jesus will soon be here. He is coming for a Bride that will be presented to Him by Himself in splendour, without spot, without wrinkle, without blemish, with all holiness and with all purity.

That Bride will be made a pillar in the temple of His God. She will never go out of the temple of His God. He will write on her the name of His God and the name of the city of His God, the new Jerusalem that will come down from His God out of heaven, and He will write on her His own new name.

Soon the Lord will be here and it will be obvious that the apostle Paul did not intercede in vain for the Bride of Christ, who will be filled with all the fullness of God. So Paul concentrated in the inward work of God in the believer's spirit, fully persuaded that what happened in a man's spirit would penetrate his soul and body. May we too, like Paul, make the work of God in the spirit of man central in our lives and ministry. May we, like Paul, stretch out in intercession and lay hold of God's all for all of God's Church. Amen.

2

EPAPHRAS'S MINISTRY OF INTERCESSION: LABOURS FOR THE MATURATION OF THE SAINTS

"As you learned it from Epaphras our beloved fellow servant. He is a faithful minister of Christ on our behalf and has made known to us your love in the Spirit"
(Colossians 1:7-8).

"Epaphras, who is one of yourselves, a servant of Christ Jesus greets you, always remembering you earnestly in his prayers, that you may stand mature and fully assured in all the will of God.
"For I bear him witness that he has worked hard for you and for those in Laodicea and in Hierapolis"
(Colossians 4: 13).

"Epaphras, my fellow prisoner in Christ Jesus, sends greetings to you"
(Philemon 23).

We have looked at the intercessory ministries of Daniel, Moses, Abraham, Nehemiah, and Paul. We shall look at the intercessory ministry of the Lord of all glory the Lord Jesus and that of the Blessed Holy Spirit. We see clearly that Daniel, Moses, Abraham, Nehemiah, and Paul were very outstanding servants of God. They were mighty leaders and influenced many. We fear that people may be deceived into thinking that intercession is the work of spiritual leaders and not that of other members of the Body of Christ. We have, therefore, decided to end this section on the intercession of the men of the Bible by a study of the intercessory ministry of one whose ministry to the Lord did not bear the same proportion before men as that of the people we have already studied. For this reason we now turn to the intercessory ministry of Epaphras.

EPAPHRAS: BELOVED FELLOW SERVANT

Epaphras was a fellow worker, a co-labourer of the apostle Paul. He was a servant of the apostle Paul. He did not seek an independent ministry of his own. He gave himself without reserve to the apostle and to the apostle's ministry. He was a servant of the apostle. He was also a servant of the Lord Jesus. Or, to put it more accurately, he served the Lord Jesus by serving the apostle Paul.

Epaphras was loyal to the apostle and forgot himself, abandoning his own interests that he might advance the ministry that the Lord gave the apostle. He sought no greatness before man. He only laboured to ensure that the apostle succeeded.

Such men are great. Such men receive the honour that comes from God. They are people who have asked crucial questions: "In what direction is the Holy Spirit moving at the moment? With which minister is the Lord's Spirit identifying Himself?" Having asked these questions and received guidance from the Lord, they pour all that they are and all that they have into the life and ministry of another, and become his servant for Christ sake.

Such people are promoted by the Lord. They are leaders before God. Because they are servants of the servants of the Lord, they are great before God. They are beloved of the Lord. The apostle

Paul was certainly one of the Lord's be-loved. Epaphras was Paul's beloved co-labourer. It is certain that Epaphras was beloved of the Lord!

EPAPHRAS: FAITHFUL MINISTER OF CHRIST

Epaphras was not only a beloved fellow-worker of the apostle Paul. He was a faithful minister of Christ. Two thoughts are raised here. First of all, he ministered personally to the Lord Jesus. He ministered to Him in praise, worship, adoration, song, thanksgiving, et cetera. There was a deep and intimate relationship between him and the Lord Jesus. He did not only have occasional fellowship with the Lord Jesus, but he entered into and maintained sustained communion with Him. It was a deep relationship that started when Epaphras first believed in Him, and it continued to grow and deepen over the years. He was satisfied in the presence of the Lord Jesus. He would have been fulfilled if he had not had to intercede but had to spend his entire life in praise and adoration of Him.

It is out of such a relationship with the Lord Jesus that any ministry of service to the people of God can be born. Anyone who has never truly ministered to the Lord can never be sent by the Lord to minister on His behalf. Anyone who has never worshipped God in spirit and truth can never stand in the gap between man and Him. Epaphras was qualified to intercede.

The second aspect of it is that Epaphras ministered to the apostle as unto Christ. He ministered to him in the same way that he ministered to the Lord. He was as loyal to him as to the Lord. Although he served the apostle, he did so in the name of the Lord and for the glory of the Lord. He did everything as if unto the Lord. He expected no reward from the apostle but that the Lord would reward him. Thus he considered everything done for the apostle as done unto the Lord. In this way there was no conflict in his heart between serving God and serving man.

Epaphras was thus a minister of the Lord Jesus and a minister of the apostle Paul. What sort of ministry? His was a faithful ministry. He was a faithful servant of the Lord and of the apostle. What does it mean to say that he was faithful to the Lord and to the apostle? I think it means that:

1. He believed the Lord totally. He had faith in the Lord. No one who lacks implicit faith in the Lord can truly serve Him. He can certainly never intercede; for an intercessor must believe in God absolutely.

2. He believed the apostle. He believed that he was sent by the Lord and that his ministry was God-ordained. He believed that the apostle was totally sincere. He refused to judge, criticize, or censor his motives or acts. No one can become a fellow-worker who does not believe the one with whom he is to work. Anyone who demands perfection from anyone before he can become his helper will go nowhere. Those who believe the Lord also believe others. They have faith in the Holy Spirit who indwells them.

3. He believed himself. He was not perfect, but he was fully assured that his life had been changed and that the Holy Spirit dwelt in him. He was assured that God would receive his ministry of praise, worship, adoration, thanksgiving, song, et cetera. He had confidence to enter the sanctuary by the blood of Jesus, by the new and living way that He opened for us through the curtain, that is, "through his flesh" (Hebrews 10: 19-20). He was fully assured that this ministry as a servant and fellow-labourer of the apostle was pleasing to God. He was assured that God would hear him as he interceded for others. Without faith in the Lord's work in a person's life, the person cannot minister to the Lord or to the Lord's people. Those who doubt themselves, in a sense, doubt the work of the Lord in

their lives. They are also doubting the Lord and cannot intercede; for if they doubt what the Lord clearly says He has done, how can they turn to Him to plead with Him to work in others?

Because Epaphras believed the Lord, because he had faith in the Lord, the apostle and himself, he acted accordingly. He did everything that the Lord wanted him to do. He also did everything that the apostle wanted him to do. Finally, he did everything that he knew he ought to do. He was faithful to the Lord, the apostle, and himself. He was faithful in big matters and in small ones. He did everything to satisfy the heart of the God before whom there was no small or big thing. He was thus able to intercede, pleading for the people of God in every way.

EPAPHRAS: FELLOW-PRISONER

The apostle Paul was often in prison for the Lord Jesus. It was the normal consequence of his consecration. Epaphras was faithful and loyal to him, and when it was time for the apostle to go to prison, he went with him. In this way, he entered more fully into the experiences of the apostle. He was prepared to become anything for the Lord. He was prepared to suffer anything for Him. He was prepared to share the ministry of the apostle in both its popularity and its unpopularity before men. Like the apostle Paul, he could say:

"We put no obstacle in any one's way, so that no fault may be found with our ministry, but as servants of God we commend ourselves in every way: through great endurance, in afflictions, hardships, calamities, beatings, imprisonments, tumult, labours, watchings, hunger; by purity, knowledge, forbearance, kindness, the Holy Spirit, genuine love, truthful speech, and the power of God, with the weapons of righteousness for the

right hand and for the left; in honour and dishonour, in ill repute and good repute.

We are treated as impostors, and yet are true; as unknown, and yet well known;

as dying, and behold we live;
as punished, and yet not killed;
as sorrowful, yet always rejoicing;
as poor, yet making many rich;
as having nothing, and yet possessing everything"

(II Corinthians 6:3-10).

There was nothing that Epaphras withheld from the Lord. There was nothing that he was not prepared to do for Him! There was nothing that he was not prepared to suffer for Him! Thus Epaphras found himself in prison with the apostle for the Gospel. He was identified in this way with his suffering Saviour Jesus and with his prisoner leader Paul. He was thus qualified to intercede; for intercessors are people who have counted everything as loss that they may win Christ. They are people who are prepared to sacrifice everything for the sake of those for whom they are interceding. As prisoners of God, they are better able to intercede for those who are captives of the enemy. They are also able to intercede so that all who belong to the Lord Jesus may become His prisoners in every way, having no liberty of their own. Having been prisoners, they can wrestle others into permanent bondage unto the Lord Jesus.

EPAPHRAS: INTERCESSOR

We have seen clearly that Epaphras had a clear standing before God. He was, first of all, a man after God's heart by life and spiritual experience before he became a man pleading for others to enter into what he had entered. He could not plead that the Lord should bring people into that about which he was resisting the Lord. Having attained spiritual maturity and having been fully assured in all the will of God, he could labour for others to become what he had become.

"One of yourselves"

Epaphras was initially of the Church in Colossae. He was one of them. It is as if God sought for a man from among the Colossians who should stand in the gap and plead for them so that they might stand mature and fully assured in all the will of God. It is heart-warming to know that when the Lord sought for a man from among them who could intercede for them, He found one. Because He found one, the Church in Colossae could enter into God's riches. If none had been found, that Church could not have entered into the riches that it did.

"Always Remembering You"

Epaphras began the work of interceding for the Colossians. He not only began it, He kept at it. He was faithful at it. It was his preoccupation. He prayed for them in the morning, in the afternoon, and in the evening. He continued at it all day and night. His heart was welded to theirs. He took no rest. He could not rest. He gave God no rest. He could give God no rest. He kept at it. It possessed him and he gave all of himself to interceding for them. True intercessors never stop interceding until they have received what they asked by faith. They are always at it.

Earnestness

Epaphras not only remembered the Colossians in his prayers to the Lord; He remembered them earnestly. He gave his whole being to it. All of himself was involved. His spirit, soul, and body were involved. All intercessors are earnest. They pour their entire being into the task. They know that failure may mean that the Lord will pour out his indignation upon them. Therefore they pour out their entire being to the Lord on behalf of those for whom they are interceding. They pour out their spirits, they pour out their souls, and they pour out their bodies. They are consumed by a holy desire to see the will of God done. Their whole being is aflame for God's purpose to be done in the lives of those for whom they are interceding.

Epaphras was earnest. He longed for God, and he longed for the Colossians to enter into the fullness of God. He fainted after the Lord, and he fainted with desire that the Colossians might become all that the Lord saved them for and all that He wanted them to be. He loved the Lord with all of his heart, soul, and body. Because of his love for the Lord, he also loved the Colossians with all of his heart, soul, and body and, therefore, interceded for them with his total being spirit, soul, and body.

There are people who sleep on their knees in prayer. There are people whose bother and fear about a long prayer session is that they may fall asleep. It is obvious that none such are intercessors. Such is the lot of men and women at ease; such is the lot of men and women who "say their prayers." Intercessors are different. They are like men who have woken up from sleep to find out that the building in which they are is on fire. Such men do not need artificial stimulants to keep awake. They are awake. The house is on fire; the burden to save all that can be saved, the knowledge that all that is not saved would be lost completely, and the knowledge of the limited amount of time before them drives away all sleep, all fear, and all reserve, and imparts to them strength, boldness, courage, and power that they did not hitherto seem to possess. They become their true selves. All intercessors know this supernatural release of power in the spirit, soul, and body. The power of the Lord comes upon them in the critical hour and, because the burden of the Lord is upon them, they give the Lord maximum co-operation and are changed into other people people with the very power of God.

Therefore, no intercessor needs to count on his own natural resources. He must count on God. The angel Gabriel said to Mary,

"*The Holy Spirit will come upon you, and the power of the Most High will overshadow you*" (Luke 1:35). Every intercessor can look up to the Lord and count on the Lord's Holy Spirit and on the power of the Most High and not on himself. That is why it is so important that he be a man totally yielded to God; so that all of God's power should find a free course in him and through him. We repeat that without total consecration of all to the Lord Jesus, a person cannot become an intercessor; for God's fullness will not find a free course in him and through him. All who are not totally yielded to the Lord should not bother to intercede. God will not hear them. Their unyielded lives will stand in His way.

Mature and Fully Assured in All the Will of God

It is impossible to separate a man's prayers from:
1. the depth of his consecration,
2. the extent of his consecration,
3. the extent of his faith in the Lord and in himself,
4. the degree of his faithfulness to the Lord and to himself,
5. his vision of what God has purposed to do, i.e., God's perfect will for the object of intercession.

If an intercessor accepts God's permissive will for the people and yields to it, he will not be able to carry the people beyond that point. If, on the other hand, he sees clearly what God's original purpose(His perfect will) was, he will labour to ensure that that purpose and nothing else comes to pass.

An intercessor must know what God's best is. He must also know what God's worst could be. He must know what the people of God will become if they enter into God's best. He must also know what they will become if they miss God's best and, consequently, have His worst.

The Lord never leaves people in doubt as to what His best for them is and as to what His worst for them could be. He clearly told the children of Israel:

"And if you obey the voice of the Lord your God, being careful to do all his commandments which I command you this day, the Lord your God will set you high above all the nations of the earth. And all these blessings shall come upon you and overtake you, if you obey the voice of the Lord your God.

Blessed shall you be in the city, and blessed shall you be in the field. Blessed shall be the fruit of your body, and the fruit of your ground, and the fruit of your beasts, the increase of your cattle, and the young of your flock.

Blessed shall be your basket and your kneading-trough. Blessed shall you be when you come in, and blessed shall you be when you go out ...."

(Deuteronomy 28: 1-4).

Anyone interceding for Israel knew that he should intercede that she should obey the Lord fully and thus be blessed. He knew that if he did not intercede and she went astray, the worst would come to her.

Epaphras knew that to which the Lord had called His own. He knew that He had called them to be as perfect as He was. He believed that this was possible, because God calls people to that which He can enable them to do. He knew that the whole counsel of God was to be known. He knew the dangers of babyhood after many years in the Christian life. He knew the importance of knowing God's will. He knew the problems associated with being uncertain as to the will of God. He knew that none could move ahead and do great things for God until he was fully assured about God's will and his personal call to it. He knew that believers who were uncertain about God's will were a ready source of temptation to Satan.

With this knowledge Epaphras settled clearly what was the priority of the Church in Colossae. That priority was:
1. stable maturity, an experience of spiritual heights and spiritual glory entered into and maintained,
2. a full knowledge of the will of God,
3. full assurance and walking in the will of God.

Epaphras then concentrated on these three things and their implications in the lives of the saints of Colossae. His intercession was goal-directed. He knew clearly what He wanted God to do, and so he could tell when it was done. Knowing clearly what God had to do in order that His will for the believers in Colossae might be done, he gave himself to it and fought the good fight. He laboured with the Lord, pleading that He might do it. He also saw the activity of the enemy in blocking God's action. Thus Epaphras, like Nehemiah, battled with God so; that He might do His work in them, and battled at the same time with the enemy, who was bent on destroying what God was doing. He thus saw not only what God wanted to do so as to stand with Him, but also what the enemy planned and thus stood against him. Nehemiah, who built the city wall under violent opposition from the enemy, wrote:

"Those who carried burdens were laden in such a way that each with one hand laboured on the work and with the other held his weapon.

And each of the builders had his sword girded at his side while he built" (Nehemiah 4:17-18).

EPAPHRAS': A PERFECT MINISTRY

The depth, breadth, and height of a man's ministry is governed by how far the person has gone with the Lord. Deep calls for deep. Those who have had deep transactions with God will of necessity have a deep ministry, and those who have only touched the Lord superficially will of necessity have a superficial ministry. Epaphras had risen high with the Lord. He knew spiritual heights. He saw God's position. He saw all of God's position. He therefore prayed as God would have prayed. He not only wanted God's best, but he wanted God's all for those for whom he prayed. He did not only pray that they should be assured in the will of God. He prayed that they should be fully assured. He knew clearly that it was one thing to be assured and another to be fully assured. He wrestled for God's best for them, which was that they might be fully assured. In addition, he did not pray that they should be fully assured in the will of God. He prayed that they might be fully assured in all the will of God. Again he realized that there was a difference between the will of God and all the will of God. He did not want people who were fully assured in some aspects of God's will and not in the others. He wanted people who knew all the will of God, were fully assured in all the will of God, and did all the fully assured will of God.

He sought God's all. He knew God's all and he pressed for God's all. May God raise up in His Church today people who are like that. May He raise up people who possess both spiritual power and spiritual character. May He raise people who have put on all of Christ in character and manifest all of his power in ministry. May He raise up people who will be like Him in life and service. There is no choice in this. It is a desperate need of the hour.

However, if such men and women are to arise in the Church, they need to be preceded by intercessors who see God's total and perfect picture and are experiencing it in their lives, and are committed to interceding until that has become the normal way and walk of the average believer.

Lord, where are such people? Lord, how much longer must the Church wait far them to appear on the horizons of Your world? Lord, won't You act quickly? Lord, won't You act now?

EPAPHRAS' EXPANDING MINISTRY

It is in the purpose of God that the Gospel of the Lord Jesus should spread as far as the curse is found. It is in the heart of God that those who have conquered one individual—themselves, for the Lord should move out and conquer two individuals, then three individuals, then ten individuals, then one thousand individuals, then one city, one nation, twenty nations, one continent, many continents, and one planet, et cetera.

God wants to promote those who are faithful in small things and thus give them responsibility over much. He, however, wants to do it step by step; so that a person's heart may expand according to the work that he is to do for God. This is also so because God cannot give a man a work that is larger than his heart can bear. He may have a big mind, but spiritual work is given on the basis of the capacities of the heart and not those of the soul (mind, will, and emotion). As the heart grows, so does the work grow. As a knowledge of the Lord grows, so does the work grow. Any work that grows out of proportion to the growth of the heart of its leader has gone wrong. The growth may not be of the Lord, and that growth will soon stop.

It may be just an outward growth with no relationship to intimacy with God.

Epaphras' ministry of intercession grew. It must have started with a ministry of intercession for the apostle Paul. Then it grew to include the co-workers of Paul. Then as his heart grew Godwards and his knowledge of the Lord deepened, God reached out and added the Colossians on his heart. He was thus able to fully satisfy the Lord in praying for Paul, Paul's co-workers, and the Colossians.

As Epaphras continued to grow in the knowledge of God, the Lord laid upon him the additional burden of praying for the Church in Laodicea, and with more spiritual progress Godwards the Church in Hierapolis was added to him by the Lord, and he bore the burden of interceding for her. Because he depended on the Lord for the increase in burden, because the burden was added in proportion to his knowledge of God and his power to intercede, he bore the burden and was not crushed by it. He continued to minister to the Lord as a priority. His life remained a sweet-smelling offering to God. He remained in control of what happened at Colossae, Laodicea, and Hierapolis as he bore them before the Lord in intercessory prayer and in destroying all the plans of the devil.

I believe this is God's way of expanding a ministry. May He teach us His ways. May we abandon the man-made methods that are a burden to the Church today. May He, out of love for His name and His people, bring to nought all that has risen on the horizon of Christian service as His work but is the product of the carnal manipulations of people who have long since ceased to worship Him in spirit and truth and are therefore led by their depraved souls.

Lord, do it quickly. Lord, do it now. Lord, start with my own ministry. Take away all in it that has its origin in me. Take away, pull down all that has my honour and my glory as its goal. Only spare that which is in Your perfect will and for Your glory and Your glory alone. Lord, do it as an act of deep love for me. Amen.

EPAPHRAS: A GRADUATE OF PAUL'S SCHOOL OF INTERCESSION

We have seen the way in which the apostle Paul interceded. We know something of the depth of his consecration to the will of God and the work of God. We saw what the objects of his intercession were. We can truly say that Epaphras interceded as he learnt from the apostle Paul.

The apostle Paul operated a mobile school of intercession. The school was present wherever he was. The school was not made up of a building and a written curriculum. The school was his life. He was given to intercession. His co-workers, like Epaphras, saw the priority he gave to intercession. They heard him intercede and they saw the consequences of his intercession in the lives of the people in the Churches.

It is likely that he invited the young, inexperienced, but consecrated Epaphras to intercede with him. It was during such periods that the young man learnt the art of intercession from the experienced intercessor. So the apostle imparted the art of intercession by being an example. He must have taught intercession by words, but above all, he taught by life.

The shortage of real intercessors in the Church today is an exposure of the quality of men who are betraying the sheep of the Lord, instead of watching over them. If the apostles, prophets, evangelists, pastors, and teachers of today were intercessors, the whole scene would be different. The tragedy is that the Christian horizon is influenced by lovers of human company and not by lovers of God's companionship. Church-planters, prophets, evangelists, pastors, and teachers who intercede, are hard to find. Much of the work today is accomplished in the power of human showmanship, and not in the power of the Holy Spirit. Many depend on man and not on God. They depend on techniques and not on the power of the Most High. A great deal know how to manipulate men to make large offerings, but do not know how to move God through prayer.

The human beings who are the products of such "ministries" are like their masters—prayerless men or men of too little praying. They do not know how to intercede. They do not hunger for the ministry of intercession; for it will not bring immediate applause from men. There are no Epaphrases among them.

Lord God, deliver me from such a ministry. Lord, do not allow my ministry to expand beyond the extent of my union with You, my knowledge of You, my hunger for You, my consecration to You, my fasting life, my prayer life, my devotion to You, my love for Your Word, my obedience to Your Word, my example as a man sold out to You, and my satisfaction in Your heart.

Lord, put to nought all that is hay, wood, and stubble; so that I should not waste my time and life. Help me to grow in union, knowledge, hunger, consecration, devotion, love, obedience, and satisfaction in You. Help me to make an impact on others by the quality of my life and service for You. Help me to be a living Bible School, a school of holiness, power, intercession, and cross-bearing.

Lord, do it urgently. Lord, do it now. Lord, do it in all whom You have called to serve You. Amen.

PART 7

God in the ministry of intercession

1

THE LORD JESUS AS AN INTERCESSOR WHLE ON EARTH

"*And in the morning, a great while before day, he rose and went out to a lonely place and there he prayed* ".
(Mark 1:35).

"*Now it happened that as he was praying alone the disciples were with him; and he asked them, 'Who do the people say that I am?'* "
(Luke 9:18).

He was praying in a certain place, and when he ceased, one of his disciples said to him, "*Lord, teach us to pray, as John taught his disciples*"
(Luke 11:1).

"*Now about eight days after these sayings he took with him Peter and John and James and went up on the mountain to pray. And as he was praying, the appearance of his countenance was altered, and his raiment become dazzling white*"
(Luke 9:28-29).

"In these days he went out to the mountain to pray; and all night he continued in prayer to God"

(Luke 6:12).

"But so much the more the report went abroad concerning him and great multitudes gathered to hear and to be healed of their infirmities. But he withdrew to the wilderness and prayed"

(Luke 5: 16).

"Simon, Simon, behold, Satan demanded to have you, that he might sift you like wheat, but I have prayed for you that your faith may not fail; and when you have turned again, strengthen your brethren".

(Luke 22:31-32).

"When Jesus had spoken these words, he lifted up his eyes to heaven and said,

'Father, the hour has come;

glorify thy Son that the Son may glorify thee, since thou hast given him power over all flesh, to give eternal life to all whom thou hast given him.

And this is eternal life, that they know thee the only true God, and Jesus Christ whom thou hast sent.

I glorified thee on earth, having accomplished the work which thou gavest me to do;

and now, Father, glorify thou me in thy own presence with the glory which I had with thee before the world was made.

'I have manifested thy name to the men whom thou gavest

me out of the world;

thine they were and thou gavest them to me, and they have kept thy word.

Now they know that everything that thou hast given me is from thee;

for I have given them the words which thou gavest me, and they have received them and know in truth that I came from thee; and they have be-

lieved that thou didst send me.

I am praying for them; I am not praying for the world but for those whom thou hast given me, for they are thine; all mine are thine, and thine are mine, and I am glorified in them.

And now I am no more in the world, but they are in the world, and I am coming to thee.

Holy Father, keep them in thy name, which thou hast given me that they may be one, even as we are one.

While I was with them, I kept them in thy name, which thou hast given me; I have guarded them, and none of them is lost but the son of perdition, that the Scripture might be fulfilled.

But now I am coming to thee; and these things I speak in the world, that they may have my joy fulfilled in themselves.

'I have given them thy word; and the world has hated them because they are not of the world, even as I am not of the world.

I do not pray that thou shouldst take them out of the world, but that thou shouldst keep them from the evil one.

They are not of the world, even as I am not of the world. Sanctify them in the truth; thy word is truth.

As thou didst send me into the world, so I have sent them into the world.

And for their sake I consecrate myself, that they also may be consecrated in truth.

'I do not pray for these only, but also for those who believe in me through their word, that they may all be one; even as thou, Father, art in me, and I in thee, that they also may be in us, so that the world may believe that thou hast sent me.

The glory which thou hast given me I have given to them, that they may be one even as we are one, I in them and thou in me, that they may become perfectly one; so that the world may know that thou hast sent me and hast loved them even as thou hast loved me.

Father, I desire that they also, whom thou hast given me, may be with me where I am, to behold my glory which thou hast given me in thy love for me before the foundation of the world.

O righteous Father, the world has not known thee; but I have known thee; and these know that thou hast sent me.

I made known to them thy name, and I will make it known, that the love with which thou hast loved me may be in them, and I in them"

(John 17:1-26).

The Lord Jesus prayed! He was given to prayer. He laboured at it. He went to the temple at the age of twelve and astounded those who spoke with Him. He was well able to start public ministry then. Why then did He wait until He was thirty? What did He do between twelve and thirty? My own feeling is that He spent those eighteen years interceding for the ministry that He was to carry out later on. He spent eighteen years preparing through intercession for a three-and-a-half-year ministry. He therefore invested about five years of preparation for every year of public ministry! Oh, that we would learn from Him!

During the actual exercise of the public ministry, much time was spent in intercessory prayer. Once the devil asked that He might be permitted to sift Peter like wheat. The Lord interceded for him, and even though the devil did sift him, Peter repented and continued with the Lord. Had the Lord not prayed for him, Peter would have been lost permanently. The intercession of the Lord made all the difference. An intercessor is a person who, by his praying, changes things in the spiritual realm and the changes are manifested in the visible realm.

However, it is in John 17 that the Lord permits us to see something of what prayer meant to Him and what He went through. We shall look at it briefly; for it opens our eyes to in-tercession as it ought to be.

INTRODUCTION

The Lord addressed His intercession to the Father. He was very caught up with Him. He was as if removed from those around Him. He lifted His eyes towards heaven. There was a burden, a consuming passion, in His heart. He hoped that the Father might glorify Him. He confessed the power that the Father had given Him over all flesh. He confessed to the Father what the power given Him, was. He declared to the Father what He already knew—what eternal life is.

The next thing that Jesus did was to confess to the Father the fact that He had been faithful. He said:

1. "I have glorified thee on earth."
2. "I have accomplished the work which thou gavest me to do."
3. "I have manifested thy name to the men whom thou gavest me out of the world."
4. "They have kept thy word."
5. "They know that everything that thou hast given me is from thee."
6. "I have given them the word which thou gavest me:"
7. "They have received it."
8. "They know in truth that I came from thee."
9. "They have believed that thou didst send me."

So the Lord clearly presented to the Father the fact that He had been faithful. He told Him very clearly that the work had been accomplished and that it had borne fruit in the lives of the disciples. He also told the Father clearly how the fruit was manifested: "They have kept thy word, they know that everything that thou hast given me is from thee, they have received thy word, they know in truth that I came from thee, they have believed that thou didst send me." So as one who had received a commission from the Father and fulfilled it He was in a position to intercede.

The unfaithful can never intercede. God will not hear them!

THOSE FOR WHOM JESUS WAS INTERCEDING

The Lord was not interceding just for everybody. He had a clear burden for a particular people. He did not leave this in His heart. He made sure that He told the Father those He had in mind. He put it plainly, as follows:

1. "I am praying for them."
2. "I am not praying for the world."
3. "I am praying for those whom thou hast given me."
4. "I am praying for thine."
5. "I am praying for those in whom I am glorified."
6. "I am praying for mine who are in the world and cannot come with me as I am leaving the world."
7. "I am praying for those who will believe in me through their word."

Real intercessors have a clear burden and a clear object of intercession. The Lord refused to pray for the world. He prayed for His own. To what extent do we follow suit?

WHAT JESUS ASKED THE FATHER FOR HIS OWN

1. That they may be kept in the Father's name. He pleaded with the Father, "Keep them in thy name." He assured the Father that while He was with them, He kept them in the Father's name. He continued to tell the Father what He had done: "I have given them

thy word. The world has hated them. They are not of the world." He made sure that the Father understood that He was not asking Him to keep them by taking them from the world. He stated this clearly: "I do not pray that thou shouldst take them out of the world but that thou shouldst keep them from the evil one." Then he reminded the Father that He had to do so because they were not of the world.

One thing that is interesting is the fact that in the Lord's intercession, He told the Father what He was asking and plainly stated what He was not asking. It reflected such a burning desire to ensure that things were understood exactly as He wanted them to be: "I do not pray for the world." "I do not pray that Thou shouldst take them out of the world."

2. That they might be sanctified in the truth. The Lord was burdened that all should be in the truth. He stated clearly that God's Word was the truth. Throughout His intercession He talks of the word:

1. "They have kept thy word."
2. "I have given them the words which thou gavest me."
3. "They have received them."
4. "I have given them thy word."
5. "Sanctify them in the truth."
6. "That they also may be consecrated in truth."
7. "Those who believe in me through their word."

One thing becomes clear: Real intercession is standing on the Word of God. There is no other basis for intercession. The Lord knew this too well, and He used it fully. He desired that His might be sanctified in the truth. He was desiring that they might be set apart from sin unto God in all truth. He desired this so that they might not be swept away into false concepts of sanctification. He knew that unless they were sanctified, their ministry would be ineffective. He did not leave it at that. He told the Father, "*And for their sakes I sanctify Myself, that they also might be sanctified by the truth*" (John 17:19, KJV). He set the example. He sanctified Himself. He separated Himself from sin, He separated Himself from the common, He separated Himself from the good, He separated Himself from the better, He separated Himself from the best, and He separated Himself unto the demands of the Father on Him. He asked the Father to do for them what He had done in Himself. He provided a model and then said to the Father, "Father, do in them what I have done in Myself."

I find this thought very wholesome and very provocative. An intercessor cannot ask the Father to do in others what he has not allowed the Father to do in himself. He must be different from those for whom he is interceding. He cannot step into the gap for others while he himself is bound by the things that hold them in bondage. The Lord was most clear about this. He said, "They are not of the world even as I am not of the world ... As thou didst send me into the world, so I have sent them into the world.• ... For their sake I consecrate myself, that they also might be consecrated in truth. , . the glory which thou has given me I have given to them, that they may be one even as we are one ... that the world may know that thou hast sent me and hast loved them even as thou hast loved me .... Father, I desire that they also whom thou hast given me, may be with me where I am ... the world has not known thee, but I have known thee and these have known thee ... that the love with which thou has loved me, might be in them, and I in them."

The Lord, therefore, sought the Father to do in the disciples what had already taken place in His life; He sought for them to experience what He had already experienced, and He sought the Father to make them into what He was. Do you then see why only a few people can really intercede? Do you see the demands that an intercessor must satisfy? Do you see then that intercession is not learning to say what another person has said and trying to say it the way in which he said it? Do you see that intercession is the reflection of a position reached and maintained with God? Do you see then that there are things for which an advanced intercessor can intercede and for which an advancing intercessor cannot intercede? Do you see that there are other things that an advancing intercessor can intercede for that a beginner in the school of intercession dare not intercede for?

It is obvious that the level of intercession and the things, places, and people that may be interceded for are closely linked to progress in the school of God. Those who have made progress in knowing Him and being transformed by Him can also progress in the school of intercession. Babes dare not repeat the phrases of adults. They will offend God. A man must have experienced in his own life what he wants God to do in another or in others. Anything less than that is hypocrisy, and God does not listen to hypocrites. That prayer that His might be sanctified in the truth needs to be answered in the life of each believer. It is a prerequisite for intercession at all levels. Without a separation from all known sin, without a separation from the world that is deep, thorough, and perhaps harsh, all attempts at intercession are noise-making. The Lord will not hear anyone who harbours any sin in his heart, regardless of what that sin may be!

3. That they might be one. The Lord prayed that they might all be one. He gave the Father an example of how the oneness was to be-"even as thou, Father, art in me and I in thee." He went on, "That they also may be in us." He went further to give a reason why they should be one. "So that the world may believe that thou hast sent me." He did not even leave it there. He told the Father what He had contributed to ensure that they might be one: "The glory which thou hast given me I have given to them, that they may be one even as we are one." He went further to explain the depth of unity that He wanted the Father to work out in them: "I in them and thou in me, that they may become perfectly one." He again told the Father why He wanted it so:

"So that the world may know that thou hast sent me and has loved them even as thou hast loved me."

Do you see how the Lord was insisting? Do you see how He went to lengths to explain everything to God? Do you see how He laboured to ensure that He gave the Father all the details? Praise the Lord.

4. That they might be with him.

5. That the love with which the Father loved him might be in them. The Lord was totally unselfish. He wanted all that He had to be given to His disciples. He had no desire to leave them behind; rather, He laboured that the Father might raise them to where He was. He did this Himself, saying, "I have given them the words which thou gavest me; as thou didst send me into the world, so I have sent them into the world," et cetera. He pleaded for them, asking the Father, "I desire that they also whom thou hast given me may be with me where I am." He finally asked that the love with which the Father had loved Him might be in them and He in them. What utter unselfishness! What utter commitment to the glory of others!

I consider this total forgetting of self and commitment to the interests of another a basic quality of all intercessors. Anyone who does not want the very best for another, so that he is prepared to labour and sacrifice himself so that that one may enter into God's best regardless of what happens to him, cannot truly become an intercessor.

We can say that intercessors have to die to themselves, to all their honour, to their glory before man, to what they could become before the eyes of a watching and congratulating world. Without such dying, the many words of prayers heaped at God will produce little fruit. The Lord Jesus said:

"Truly, truly, I say to you, unless a grain of wheat falls into the earth and dies, it remains alone; but if it dies, it bears much fruit.

He who loves his life loses it, and he who hates his life in this world will keep it for eternal life" (John 12:24-25).

This dying to self will enable an intercessor to plead that another may be given God's best, regardless of what he himself has received from the Lord. It will enable him to rejoice when the Lord promotes the one for whom he has interceded and apparently leaves him unpromoted. John the Baptist knew and possessed such a spirit. When it was reported to him that everyone was turning to Jesus, he said:

"Therefore this joy of mine is now full. He must increase, but I must decrease"
(John 3:29-30).

For anyone's joy to be full at the decrease of self and the increase of another is greatness. It is that which is characteristic of real intercessors.

THE LORD JESUS' ART OF INTERCESSION

1. He Was Sometimes Repetitive

The Lord was not afraid to say the same thing to the Father more than once. He said many times for example:

"I am coming to thee."

"I am not of the world." "They are not of the world."

"The men whom thou gavest me." "Those whom thou hast given me." "Which thou hast given me."

"They also whom thou hast given me."

"That they may all be one."

"That they may be one."

"That they may be perfectly one."

The burden on His heart could not allow Him to be satisfied with having said something once. He was desperate that the Father should hear and understand Him. He therefore put the same thing in slightly different words. For example, He prayed:

1. "That they may all be one, even as Thou, Father, art in me, and I in thee, that they also may be in us, so that the world may believe that Thou hast sent me."

2. "That they may be one even as we are one, I in them, Thou in me, that they may become perfectly one, so that the world may know that Thou hast sent me and hast loved them even as thou hast loved me."

2. He Pleaded with the Father

Jesus used the typical words of an intercessor: "Father," "Holy Father," "Thou Father," and "O righteous Father." He did not take it for granted that the Father would hear Him because He was the Son. He did not take it for granted that the Father would do it because it was His will. He laboured as if it all depended on His intercession, and indeed, all did depend on His intercession.

He knew that although the Father could act without His intercession, the Father had decided never to act unless there was intercession or praying. He knew that no matter what the intentions, desires, and will of God were, He never moved until someone prayed. He knew that without prayer there was no action on God's part.

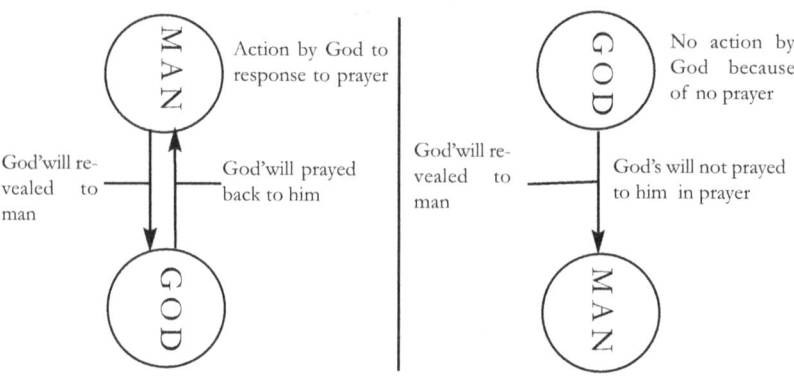

Knowing this fully well, he pleaded and pleaded. I am amazed that the laws of prayer bind even God the Son. If He needs to plead His cause through, would it not be total folly for anyone not to pray and pray? I find here the greatest encouragement and provocation to pray.

3. He Explained Things to the Father in Detail

The Lord prayed as if the Father knew nothing. He did not say, "Well, He knows everything because He is God and I will not bother Him." He explained things. He went into detail. He told Him the same thing in other words. He spoke to God as if God were meeting the situation for the first time. He did not even say, "Father, as You already know," or "Father, I just want to remind You." It was all done as if God was being brought into the situation for the first time. He spoke to God about the things that God had done as if God was being made aware of them for the first time. He more or less gave God the background to the situation. He did not leave out anything that He wanted the Father to do, saying that He would understand or reason out what He meant. He left nothing in His heart, saying, "God sees My heart. He knows the needs and the burdens in it." He was a supplicant. He presented all that He could present. He added to the initial thought and developed it as fully as possible, until he had expressed fully and clearly all that He wanted the Father to do. We can take just one example. He said to the Father, "*I do not pray for these only, but also for those who believe in me through their word*" (John 17:20). If He had left it at that, it would have implied that He wanted the Father to keep them and consecrate them. He went ahead to specify, "That they may all be one." He did not just ask that they be one; He asked that they might all be one. He made sure that the Father understood that He wanted all. He did not leave it there either. He went ahead to explain the way the unity that He wanted was to be expressed: "Even as thou Father, art in me, and I in thee." He thus used the example that the Father "understood" most. But that was not all. He went on to explain, "That they also may be in us." By this He got the Father to be involved not just as the One being petitioned but as the One in whom, along with Christ, the disciples were to be united.

The Lord from heaven had not yet finished that point. He did not consider that He had pressed His point home enough. He went ahead to tell the Father why it was necessary that they be one, and He did not choose just any of the possible correct reasons that were open to Him. For example, He could have said, " so that your children may live at peace with each other." He carefully chose the reason that involved the Father's deepest interest, honour, and name! He said, "so that the world may believe that thou hast sent me." It was a kind of "holy blackmail." He was more or less saying, "Father, You sent Me. You wanted the world to believe that You sent Me. If that is still in Your heart and for as long as that is in Your heart, keep them one; so that what You had and have in Your heart may be realized."

The Lord was not yet through with the point. He was not yet satisfied. He had not yet prayed it "through." He had not yet reached the point where asking gives way to receiving and petitioning gives way to praise. The burden was still on Him that all His would be one. He therefore continued to talk to the Father about the same issue. He told the Father what that unity had cost Him. He said, "The glory which Thou hast given me I have given to them, that they may be one." He was telling the Father, "I am not praying cheaply. Concerning what I desire that You do, I have done all that I could do. I am asking You to do that which I cannot do; for there is nothing that I could do about it that I have not done." He continued to explain why He gave them the glory that was given to Him. It was so that: "They may be one even as we are one." Again He went ahead to explain to the Father the way He wanted them united: "Even as we are one, I in them and thou in me." Then He added something concerning the unity: "That they may become perfectly one." Before, He had just asked that they be one. Now, very quietly but very purposefully, the Lord introduced the matter of all being perfectly one as something to which the Lord was being asked to bring them. Having reached the apex of His own desire and request for the unity of His, He gave the Father the most solid reasons why He had to do it and both reasons involved the Father's honour and integrity.

1. "so that the world may know that thou hast sent me." This is tied to the reason He gave before.
2. "so that the world may know that thou hast loved them even as thou hast loved me."

Do you see the matter of "ascending in intercession"? The Lord Jesus developed His arguments and presented His point, building them up steadily in such a way that, to use human words, "He put God in a corner." God, therefore, had to act. He always acts when treated like that in intercession. Is that not a part of the whole matter of "taking no rest and giving God no rest"? It must be. Glory be to God!

PERSONAL LESSONS FROM JESUS' INTERCESSION

There are a number of things that come across forcefully to my heart as I study the Lord's intercession. I will outline them as follows:

1. I must intercede or perish in the ministry that the Lord has given me. I cannot have God move except by prayer.
2. I must live a very holy life. To sin and pray is an abomination.
3. In intercession I must not take for granted that God knows anything. It is my duty to tell Him everything. I am to consider that He does not know what I have not told Him in prayer. I must tell Him everything.
4. It is folly for me to expect God to do what I have not asked in prayer. He will not do it. I dare not take Him for granted.
5. What has not been protected in prayer is in "no man's land." The devil has a claim to it, and he will claim it. Why shouldn't he?
6. Intercession is arguing a case with God. It is presenting it neatly and thoroughly in such a way that God is compelled to act. There is a sense in which the Lord will gladly not act, unless I compel Him to. Intercession is the holy act of compelling God to do the things in His will that He has decided will not be done, unless the compelling is done by prayer and fasting.
7. I must put in all that I have, all that I can put in, before I can intercede honestly. If I am asking God to save a certain nation, I must put in all that I can put in to further their evangelism. The Lord gave the glory that the Father gave Him to His own; so that they should be one. It was very costly. After He had done that He prayed that the Father should maintain the unity. He put in His all, and then

He interceded. If I intercede in any situation in which I have not done all that I could do or in which I am not willing to do all that I could do or in which I am holding back a part of the price, I am making noise, and the Lord will not hear me. I am being a hypocrite, and what can He do with such, except to turn away His ears?

8. God must be begged. He must be petitioned in prayer. He is the King of kings and the Lord of lords. He is not my servant. Although I must come to Him with boldness because of the shed blood, I must always come with fear and trembling, for He is God and I am mere man, and as the hymn writer puts it: "Even the dust upon thy feet outweighs me utterly." This attitude will give me the right spirit in which to intercede. Glory be to His name!

WHAT CAN YOU LEARN FROM JESUS' INTERCESSION?

Have you as an individual learnt anything from Jesus' intercession? Will you outline it below as I have done above? God bless you!

2

THE LORD JESUS AS INTERCESSOR IN HEAVEN

"The former priests were many in number, because they were prevented by death from continuing in office; but he holds his priesthood permanently, because he continues for ever.

Consequently he is able for all time to save those who draw near to God through him,

Since he always lives to make intercession for them.

For it was fitting that we should have such a high priest, holy, blameless, unstained, separated from sinners, exalted above the heavens.

He has no need, like those high priests, to offer sacrifices daily, first for his own sins and then for those of the people; he did this once for all when he offered up himself.

Indeed, the law appoints men in their weakness as high priests, but the word of the oath which came later than the law, appoints a Son who has been made perfect for ever"

(Hebrews 7:23-28).

THE INDISPENSABILITY OF INTERCESSION

We saw that one of the last things that the Lord Jesus did on earth was to Intercede for His own. We saw that He therefore ranked intercession as a must in His life and ministry. We know that after He interceded publicly for His own, He gave Himself to His enemies and they crucified Him. We also know that on the Cross He said that it was finished; that was to say that His work on earth was finished. He had done that which had to be done for the salvation of sinners. He had given the enemy a decisive blow and won the victory. It was all settled. The full price was paid and the Father bore testimony to the fact that it had been done perfectly by raising Him from the dead. The Lord Jesus returned to the glory of heaven, even as He had prayed, saying, "*Father, glorify thou me in thy own presence with the glory which I had with thee before the world was made*" (John 17:5).

We know that the Lord Jesus paid the whole price for man's salvation. When He got back to heaven, He could have settled there to perpetual enjoyment of the glory of heaven. He could have said, "I have done my part. If anyone wants my salvation, holiness, and glory, let him do his part as I have done mine." This would have been perfectly logical. It could have been perfectly acceptable.

However, the Lord Jesus did not do that. He knew that God works in answer to prayer. God only acts in answer to prayer. He knew that the human heart yields to the power of the Holy Spirit in response to prayer. He knew that even though He had done all that needed to be done on earth for the salvation and perfection of His own, all would be lost if the Father did not act to bring it to pass. Knowing this and knowing that the Father always acted in response to prayer, He made intercession His priority in heaven.

It all becomes clearer to me as never before. We know that the Lord Jesus will never waste His time. He never spends one second on formalities. He will never carry out things just for the sake of carrying them out. If the Lord Jesus continues to intercede in heaven, we can be sure that intercession is most indispensable. The Father still wants the intercession of the Son before He can act on earth.

We can plainly say that if the Father receives no intercession from the Son, He will not carry out many things on earth in the Church and in the world on behalf of the Church. The Father does not understand the intentions of the Son to intercede. The Father actually wants, looks for, and expects the intercession of the Son before He can act on behalf of the Son's interests on earth.

Because this is so, the Son, the glorified Lord Jesus, has given Himself to an unceasing ministry of intercession. The Lord Jesus has been before the Father carrying out active, vigorous, and moving intercession twenty-four hours every day, from the time He got to heaven until now. He is constant and He is persistent. It was said to the watchmen:

"Upon your walls, O Jerusalem, I have set watchmen; all the day and all the night they shall never be silent.

You who put the Lord in remembrance, take no rest, and give God no rest until he establishes Jerusalem and makes it a praise in the earth"

(Isaiah 62:6-7).

The Lord Jesus is doing the same thing in heaven. He is the heavenly Watchman. God can say also of Jesus, and actually says of Him: "Upon the throne of heaven I have set a watchman all the day and all the night. He shall never be silent. You who put the Lord in remembrance take no rest and give Him no rest until he establishes the Church and makes it a praise to God."

If it were not absolutely necessary for the Lord Jesus, the Father would not demand it. If God could carry out His purposes for the Church, in the Church, and through the church without the intercession of the Son, He would do it and spare the Son the labours and agony that are a part of intercession. However, without the intercession of the Son, the Father is grossly limited. There is a divine law that demands that the Father should move in response to intercession. That law is binding on the Father. There is no way in which He can waive or break it. It is established. Intercession is a must for the Lord Jesus in heaven even as it was on earth.

JESUS: FAITHFUL HEAVENLY INTERCESSOR

The Lord Jesus knows the laws of heaven about prayer and the Father's action. He submits Himself to those laws absolutely. He refused to absolve Himself. He refused to say, "I have been to earth. I have suffered there. I died on a cruel cross. I am back to glory now. I interceded while on earth. Let another or others intercede now." He did not say that. He is not saying that. He has submitted to the Father and committed Himself to intercession. He is living to intercede. He is always interceding. While on earth, He said, "My food is to do the will of him who sent me, and to accomplish his work" (John 4:34). Now in heaven He says, "My life is to do the will of My Father by intercession and accomplish His work by intercession." The Lord Jesus has so yielded and welded Himself to the ministry of intercession that it is as if He would "die" were He not interceding. It is as if He had nothing else to do but intercede. Intercession is His one preoccupation, and he never departs from it. For nearly two thousand years He has been at it, turning neither to the left nor to the right. He has been utterly faithful. He has been faithful to His Father: He has been faithful to the people for whom He came to earth. He is a Faithful High Priest. He is a faithful Intercessor.

The Lord Jesus has been interceding for twenty-four hours every day for nearly two thousand years. He has put all His time into it. He is not bored and the Father is not bored. The Father has not yet granted all the requests that He has been making. How then can

He stop interceding?

This knowledge says that that local assembly that has one hour of intercession per week is joking! That individual who throws a few requests at God while going into his car or for a few minutes just before he eats, saying, "Lord, save Mr. ---; Lord, save our---; Lord, move mightily in that campaign," is not serious at all.

The Lord Jesus is putting all His time into intercession.

The Lord Jesus taught on earth about persistence in prayer. He talked about "wearing out God" by pressing and pressing and pressing. He was not just preaching to others. He believes His message and is practising it. He was speaking from His heart, and in heaven He is doing that. Trillions upon trillions of times He has prayed, "Father, sanctify My Bride." So He may be using the same words over and over.

Someone could ask me, "Is it not a lack of faith that someone should pray the same thing over and over?" Well, I do not know. I only say, 'Jesus prayed for His own on earth. Was that not enough? He has been interceding for that Church for two thousand years. Is that a lack of faith? No intercessor can dare stop short of the answer. No intercessor dares stop before God has told him, Pray no more."

WHAT WAS THE SUBSTANCE OF JESUS' HEAVENLY INTERCESSION?

The Lord interceded for the Church while He was on earth that the Father might keep the Church in the Father's name, that she should be one, that she might be kept from the evil one and from evil, that she might be kept in the truth, that she might be sanctified, that Jesus' joy might be "fulfilled in them, that they might be in the world, even as He was in the world, that she might be consecrated in truth, that she might one day be with Him to behold the glory that the Father had given to the Son and, finally, that the love with which the Father has loved Him might be in them.

It is obvious that these remain the topics of the Son's intercession. He has been interceding this way for nearly two thousand years. He intercedes for everyone who believes from the moment he believes until the moment he sleeps in the Lord. He is interceding for those of us who are His and who are alive and will do so until His trumpet blows and we are caught up to meet Him in the air.

As we get nearer and nearer the time of Jesus' return, one topic of intercession that must weigh very heavily on His heart and be most frequent on His lips is: "*Father, I desire that they also, whom thou hast given me, may be with me where I am, to behold my glory which thou hast given me in thy love for me before the foundation of the world*" (John 17:24). There must be this burden on his heart, and He must be pressing it in intercession with the Father unceasingly. He well remembers the promise that He made, saying to His own, "*And when I go and prepare a place for you, I will come again and will take you to myself, that where I am you may be also*" (John 14:3).

Oh, that there might be many lovers of the Lord Jesus on earth! Oh, that they too might be so burdened to see Him! Oh, that those who are babies in the faith would hunger for Him! Oh, that there might be the young thirsting after Him and the old panting for Him! Oh, that all would with violent intercession plead, "Father, let the Lord Jesus come back now"! Oh, that they would turn and pray, saying from their hearts and then through their lips, "Come, Lord Jesus."

NO INTERCESSION, NO FINISHED WORK!

Often a preacher prepares his message in prayer and delivers it in prayer and after that, considers his work accomplished. Often an evangelist prepares in prayer and preaches in prayer and after that considers his job as done and finished. Often an apostle plants churches, appoints the leaders, and considers his job finished. Often a writer conceives a book in prayer, writes it in prayer, and when it is produced and is being distributed, considers his task to have been well done in prayer to the glory of God.

The truth is that these are all unfinished projects. We suggest the following outline for any work of God:

1. Reception of the divine order.
2. Reception of the divine method.
3. Labour at the work until it is «practically" finished.
4. Labour at the work until it is spiritually finished through intercession.

The Lord Jesus finished the "practical" aspects of His work on the Cross and declared it so. However, the "spiritual" aspects were far from finished. He prayed while He did the "practical" aspects. After these were finished, He gave Himself to the "spiritual" aspect of intercession. The truth is that there is a real sense in which the work of the Lord Jesus is not yet finished. His work cannot be finished until all the desired effects of His death have been realized. Each believer just needs to look at himself and the Church to know that a lot of the desired work is not yet realized. We must honestly confess that "we do not yet see everything in subjection to Him" in the Church. We must confess that we have not yet come to perfect unity, sanctification, separation from the world, as He desires. The Church is not yet that spotless Bride, without blemish, without wrinkle that she must be. Because these were on the Lord's heart from the beginning and, having through His death on the Cross provided all that is necessary, He now intercedes so that the Church may respond as she should. Intercession for Jesus is not only necessary, it is a must; so that the work on the Cross may have full effect. If He did not intercede, He would in a sense have done an incomplete work. He would in a sense have failed. Praise the Lord! He is interceding. He will accomplish all His purpose. Glory be to His name!

It becomes obvious that after a preacher has preached, an evangelist evangelised, an apostle planted a Church, a writer written a book, a counsellor counselled, a helper helped, only a part of the work has been done. Each must labour in intercession; so that his work should produce the right effects to the glory of God. Without this, it might soon be found that most people are dull of hearing and that little or no impact has been produced that will last until Jesus comes. I have heard of pre-crusade prayer meetings but I rarely hear of post-crusade prayer meetings. The result is that there is very little that abides out of many large-scale crusades that report thousands or hundreds of thousands of decisions. Oh, for evangelists who pray during the crusade alone twelve hours each day for, say, four weeks before a crusade, pray six hours each day alone during the crusade, and withdraw for another month of praying twelve hours each day alone! Such a man may conduct three or four campaigns at the most in one year, but the results of those campaigns in eternal weight and glory will exceed fifty years of crusades in all the nations of the world that are carried out as more evangelists do today.

May God help us! Open our eyes, O Lord! Open my eyes, O Lord! Make us obedient to what You are saying, O Lord! Make me obedient to what You are saying, O Lord!

COMPLETING THE PRACTICAL AND THE SPIRITUAL ASPECTS OF A WORK: THE TIME ELEMENT

The Lord Jesus accomplished His earthly ministry in about three years. He did the "practical" aspect of the work in that short period of ti1l1e.•How long is He taking to accomplish the "spiritual" aspect? How much time is He putting into intercession? We do not know how long He will take to accomplish that aspect of His work. We have deep-seated desires in our hearts that He should come soon and we pray to that effect. However, we cannot be sure as to when He will burst through the sky and meet us in the air. One thing, however, we do know. Today is the twelfth of March, 1988. The Lord has been gone about 1,957 years. He has been labouring at the ministry of intercession so that His work might be truly finished for that long. Some mathematics will help us. He took 3.5 years to do the "practical." For every "practical" year the Lord has put in about 559 intercession years. If we are to follow the Lord's example, then we recommend that if a preacher preaches for I hour, he should spend 559 hours in intercession. The same thing applies to the evangelist, the apostle, the writer, et cetera. This would mean that a man intercedes for twenty-four days and then preaches one sermon. I am confident that such a sermon will have the divine effects of pulling down strongholds and bringing every thought captive to obey Christ. This is what spiritual leadership ought to do. This is what is not being done. There are multitudes of sermons, but the effects are minimal. A new day must come. O Lord, grant that it should come. Grant that the ministers of the word should spend their time interceding. Grant that the time spent in intercession should far outweigh the time spent preaching. O Lord, grant that the time spent before You in intercession should far outweigh that which is spent before man in preaching. O Lord, do it as a matter of urgency.

INTERCESSION AND THE END OF THE TASK

For how long must a person intercede? The answer is simple. Intercede until the purpose of intercession is accomplished. If you are interceding for the salvation of a person, do it until he is saved. If he is not saved after one year, pray until he is saved. If he is not saved after ten years, pray until he is saved. If he is not saved after twenty-five years, are you to give him up because he has not responded? Certainly not! You must continue until he is saved, even if he is saved at seventy-five. The purpose of the intercession was his salvation. When he is saved, you have accomplished the purpose of that intercession, although you may set a second goal in intercession to wrestle until he is presentable to Christ—without spot, blemish, or wrinkle.

As we can see from the example of the Intercessor from the throne, there is no substitute for going on in intercession until the work is accomplished practically and spiritually. Jesus' work has already taken Him about 1,957 years. He has not grown weary. He is pressing on. He will not grow weary. He will press on until it is accomplished. A day will come when He will leave the heavenly Intercessor's throne. That day will be the end of His ministry as the heavenly Intercessor. From that throne He will set out for the earth and meet His Church in the air, and then there will never be any need for intercession. Praise the Lord!

WHAT DOES ALL THIS MEAN TO ME AND YOU?

To me the intercessory ministry of the Lord Jesus from the throne tells me that my priority is prayer. There is no substitute for intercession. The success of any ministry that I may carry out for God depends upon how much time I am prepared to put into intercession and what the quality of the intercession is. It tells me that I must make intercession my priority. It insists that I must intercede before a work is done and intercede while the work is being done, and after the work is finished I must plunge into intercession and labour at it for long hours, days, and maybe months. I have been thinking about this matter for some time. I have been thinking about the priorities of my life as a minister of the Word. It is obvious that I have spent more time before man than I have before God. Even with an average of four hours in prayer daily, I have to face the fact that I am ministering to people, preparing sermons, preaching them, conducting leadership courses, and writing for an average of eight hours a day. If I add to this the two hours I spend in meditation each morning, then I am spending six hours before God and eight hours for God before man. Will such a minister like me obtain a full prize at the Judgment Seat of Christ? Of course not! Certainly not!

I will do something about it. I have before me plans to preach Christ in South India, the United States of America, and Zambia from the fourth of August to the fifth of September 1990. I must abandon them. I abandon them. I will withdraw from all else between those dates. I will withdraw from people. I will withdraw from ministering to man and to men. I will go apart and intercede. I will intercede for twelve hours every day. I will seek God. I will labour in His presence. This is the first response to this message. Other reactions will follow. May the Lord help me to be like the heavenly Intercessor. I enroll in His school. I will learn from Him. I must water all that I have done for the Lord in the past in violent intercession, and then by God's grace things will happen as the Lord intended: there will be fruit, abundant fruit, to the honour

and glory of His all glorious name. Amen.

What does this all mean to you? Does it say anything to you? What will you do about it? What must you do about it? What is the practical step to take now?

WHAT DOES ALL THIS MEAN TO THE CHURCH?

We have seen that the Lord Jesus has been interceding for nearly two thousand years. Why has the Church not made more progress than she has made? Is the Father not responding fully to the Son's intercession? Are the Son's intercessions defective in quality or quantity?

We know too well that the intercessions of the Son are perfect in every way. We also know that the Father always responds to the Son. The delay is elsewhere. The problem is that the Lord Jesus as Head of the Church decided to have the Church, which is His Body, as His co-worker. He became involved in a kind of "three-legged race" with the Church as partner, His intercession is perfect, but He is held back by His partner the Church. He is doing all that He must do, but He cannot fully succeed without the full co-operation of the Church. The Church is therefore limiting the Lord.

For how long must this continue to be?

For how long must He be hindered?

What does this say to you as an individual member of the Church? What does this say to you as an apostle?

What does this say to you as a leader of a work of God? Are you doing what you should do as a leader?

Is your assembly doing what she should do in intercession?

Are the Churches you have planted doing what they should do in prayer warfare for God's local and global interests?

Will you repent?

Will you pray and plan intercession?

Will you start a prayer chain in your local assembly and have the people pray without ceasing until the work is done?

May the Lord lead you to obedient action.

May you not stand in the way of the people of God. May you not stand in the way of the Lord.

May you be committed to the most important job on Planet Earth, which is intercession, and then the heavenly Intercessor will come for us and we shall be gone.

Glory be to His holy name! Amen.

3

THE HOLY SPIRIT: THE RESIDENT INTERCESSOR

"*Likewise the Spirit helps us in our weakness; for we do not know how to pray as we ought, but the Spirit himself intercedes for us with sighs too deep for words.*

And he who searches the hearts of men knows what is the mind of the Spirit, because the Spirit intercedes for the saints according to the will of God"

(Romans 8:26-27).

"*And I will pray the Father, and he will give you another Counsellor, to be with you for ever, even the Spirit of truth,*

*Whom the world cannot receive because it neither sees him nor knows him, you know him, for he dwells with you, and will be with yo*u"

(John 14: 16-17).

"*O Lord, thou hast searched me and known me!*

Thou knowest when I sit down and when I rise up, thou dis-cernest my thoughts from afar.

Thou searchest out my path and my lying down, and art ac-quainted with all my ways.

Even before a word is on my tongue, lo, O Lord, thou knowest it altogether" (Psalm 139: 1-4).

WEAKNESSES IN INTERCESSION

It is obvious to anyone who has begun to make progress in the school of intercession that he is weak at best. The most potent intercession of the greatest praying saint is weak compared to the needs of the moment. Part of the reason for this is that there are too few who really intercede and if we work on the promise that in a sense God acts as if He knows nothing about the needs of people and situations until He is told, we can be sure that He is told little. When that little is spread out, it is very thin, because most believers do not pray.

Another thing to look at is that sometimes the burden is too much for the intercessor. Think of someone who is burning to have the heathens saved. Before him are nearly 2 billion communists and nearly 1 billion Muslims, not to mention the other unsaved peoples. He will realize that if he is to do justice to the Muslims, he should pray round the dock for them and continue at that rate until there is a breakthrough. But what then would become of the communists? What then would become of those who are caught up in the web of pseudo-Christianity and paganism? What of true believers who need to be built up and are the most potent arm for all these things of intercession? It is certain that a person with these burdens, even if he has prayed, feels a deep sense of inadequacy. He is not equal to the task.

There are other times when the intercessor seems to be wasting his time. He prays, but his words appear so weak. They seem to have no power for breakthrough. The words seem to bounce on the ceiling and come back to the intercessor. His body seems to be in rebellion. His soul seems to be totally uninvolved and his spirit totally weak and un able to take control of soul and body and thus lead in prayer. At such moments the thinking is scattered and the force of concentration seems totally lacking and the interceding saint seems to jump from one thing to another in confusion as he tries to pray.

At other times there will be real burdens on the intercessor's spirit, but the spirit of the intercessor is so weak that he cannot pray them through. The flow from the spirit to the soul seems to be totally blocked.

To sum up, the intercessor, even at his best, does not know how to pray as he ought. He is praying below the mark. It is sublevel praying. A helper is needed.

THANK GOD THERE IS A HELPER AVAILABLE

The Bible says: "The Spirit helps us in our weakness; for we do not know how to pray as we ought." The Lord is committed to intercession. He is also committed in intercession. He has promised the intercessors a helper to help him in all his weakness in intercession. When the intercessor has come to the end of himself, he should remember that he has a Helper. When he is so confused and disintegrated in praying, he should remember that he has a Helper. That Helper is the Holy Spirit. He is resident in the intercessor to provide help from inside. When you as an individual get to that point where there seems to be no breakthrough, when there seems to be a real impasse, do not give up. There is a Helper around. He is resident in your spirit, and wants to help you. He is helping you. Because He is helping you, you should press on. Soon the cloud will be over and the weakness gone and you are through to communion and battle again.

LACK OF KNOWLEDGE TO PRAY AS WE OUGHT

The spiritual dimensions are huge. The dimensions are not easily fathomable. The Bible warns us that we are not fighting with flesh and blood but with spirits—principalities, powers, wicked hosts of darkness in heavenly places, et cetera. The battle being spiritual, that is, against spirits, we cannot fight with the arms of the flesh or soul. We cannot merely use our wills, minds, and emotions. Our spirits have to be released. We must have our intuitions fully sensitized by the Holy Spirit; our consciences must be fully developed and totally pure all the time. Now we have to admit that this is not the daily, hourly, and minute-by-minute condition of each intercessor. There are moments when things are cloudy, when the communion with God, even though not broken by any known sin, is not deep and fully satisfying. There are moments when there is failure in the intuition-when there are errors. There are moments when what is received in the in-tuition is not being correctly communicated to the soul, where action is. The sum total of this is that we do not know how to pray as we ought. We do not know how to pray as each situation demands.

There is another side to the issue. Even if our spirits were normal all the time and our souls responding perfectly to what is released from the spirit, we would still see only in part. Believers like the apostle Paul, who made a very high degree of progress in every area of Christian growth and was very close to perfection, confessed, "For now we see in a mirror dimly, but then face to face. Now I know in part; then I shall understand fully, even as I have being fully understood" (1 Corinthians 13: 12). Because of this limited knowledge, which is the lot of all the saints, there are things, many things, about which the sincere, consecrated, advanced intercessor cannot intercede as he ought.

We have said earlier that God has to some extent decided that He will not move except in response to prayer. He does not compromise this decision. Normally it means that where the believer cannot pray as he ought, the Lord will do nothing! This, being true, leaves a lot of gaps in which God will do nothing and openings in which the enemy will do a lot of things!

THERE IS A HELPER TO HELP

The Bible tells us that when we do not know how to pray as we ought to pray—that is, when we pray and fall short because of our weakness and limitations through seeing only in part—the Holy Spirit prays for us.

THE INTERCESSOR FOR INTERCESSORS

The Holy Spirit intercedes for intercessors! This is wonderful! He does not intercede for those who are too lazy to intercede, too sleepy to intercede, too busy to intercede. He intercedes for those who, having put in all the time, energy, effort, and drive, still fall short of fulfilling their ministry as intercessors and still fall short of the successful moving of God's hand to move the hand of man. The Holy Spirit helps in weakness. He does this in two ways. First of all, He renews the strength of the intercessors and gives them more knowledge to see things God's way. The Bible says:

"He gives power to the faint, and to him who has no might he increases strength.

Even youths shall faint and be weary, and young men shall fall exhausted; but they who wait for the Lord shall renew their strength, they shall mount up with wings like eagles, they shall run and not be weary, they shall walk and not faint"

(Isaiah 40:29-31).

So the Holy Spirit helps the weak but pursuing intercessor. He strengthens him and gives him power. He renews his strength. He causes Him to mount up with wings like those of eagles, being carried up by the Spirit to explore realms of intercession hitherto untouched and unreached. He causes him to run in full strength, pressing on to God and pressing on God in intercession until the

Lord is moved to act. Even at his weakest, when others faint and give up, the Holy Spirit gives him the enabling to keep pressing on, walking ahead with the Spirit and interceding. This is one way in which the Holy Spirit helps intercessors.

PRAYING WITH SIGHS TOO DEEP FOR WORDS

The Holy Spirit not only helps the intercessor by strengthening him; He also intercedes for him. He prays to the Father for the intercessor. He prays to the Father what the intercessor has in his heart but cannot pray. He also prays what He knows is the will of the Father, but which the intercessor does not know so that what is lacking is made up for.

We can, therefore, say that the intercession of the Holy Spirit is for:

1. the renewal of the strength of the weak and weary intercessor,
2. the strengthening of the intercessor,
3. the lifting of the intercessor to new heights of intercession,
4. the things that the intercessor has left out in error,
5. the things for which the intercessor has prayed too inadequately,
6. the things that are in the will of God but which the believer does not know about,
7. the plans of the devil that are unknown to the intercessor.

This sevenfold coverage assures the sincere intercessor that after he has done all that he could, he should not be swept away by discouragement and worry about what has not been done, but rest in the Lord and count on the ongoing work of the Holy Spirit to put the finishing, enabling, and transforming touches on his efforts. What an encouragement! His needs are being presented to the Father according to His will. Does that not explain the reason why you have received so many blessings and had so many of your needs for which you have not prayed met? Does it not explain why the Church has been enabled to keep going on, even though it prays so little either for herself or for the world? The intercessory ministry of the Holy Spirit is God's answer, and we give Him praise and glory for it.

The glory of the whole matter is that the Holy Spirit not only intercedes, He intercedes at the highest height and at the deepest depth. We know that there are three planes at which one can intercede. These planes are:

1. with known words (with the human mind),
2. with unknown words (with the human spirit, which receives utterance from the Holy Spirit),
3. without words (with sighs, groans, et cetera).

It is at the third plane, the highest, that the Holy Spirit intercedes for the saints according to the will of God. He intercedes with groans and sighs that are too deep either for words that are known or for words that are unknown. The needs of the intercessor are transformed into groans and sighs. These can of course only be understood by the Lord, and He understands them. The Spirit searches the heart of the intercessor, sees what is there, perfects it, and completes it. He then prays it through to God in sighs and groans that are too deep for words. He is doing that for each intercessor twenty-four hours each day. This to me is really wonderful and very encouraging. The knowledge that I have one intercessor on the throne that does not cease to intercede for me and in addition I have another intercessor resident within me who intercedes for me with sighs too deep for words, comforts and assures me. Does it comfort and assure you? The Lord Jesus said, "*I will pray the Father, and he will give you another Counsellor, to be with you for ever*" (John 14: 16). The Lord Jesus is the first Comforter. He is in heaven interceding. The Holy Spirit is another Comforter. He is in us interceding. We are in good hands. Glory, glory, glory, be to God, the Son, and the Holy Ghost.

RESIDENT INTERCESSOR! PRESIDENT INTERCESSOR?

We have said that the Holy Spirit is the Resident Intercessor. He resides in the believer. However, if anyone is to make progress in the school of intercession, he must know the Holy Spirit not only as the Resident Intercessor, but as the President Intercessor. He must be the absolute Lord of that life in every way and in every sense. He must possess the intercessor in such a way that he is His prisoner. His will must be sought, known, and done in everything. When this is the case, He will carry out His duty as Resident Intercessor unhindered. If He meets a rebellious, unyielded heart, He is severely limited and cannot do what He would.

It is for this reason that the Holy Spirit searches the hearts of men. He tries their hearts. He knows all that is there. He does not just listen to the intercessor's words before God. He is particular about the type of heart from which such words issue. If the heart is yielded and true, He co-operates with what is coming forth, strengthens, adjusts, and perfects, and then brings the demands to God. If the heart is divided, unmoved, pretentious, and false, He is unmoved. He cannot groan and sigh that the desires of a lustful, covetous, and worldly believer be realized. He can only intercede against these desires.

THE INDISPENSABLE CONSECRATION!

We have said throughout this book that the unchanging condition for a life that is invested in intercession is absolute consecration and absolute purity. Have you laid your all on the altar? Did you bind your sacrifice with cords on the altar; so that it may remain there? Is your all still on the altar? Can God testify to the fact that you are not holding anything back? Does the Holy Spirit testify to the fact that your all has been surrendered for all time and that the surrender is irreversible? If your answer to these questions is, "Yes," you can count on the Holy Spirit to intercede for you and with you. You are not alone. He is by you. He is in you. He will not abandon you. He will strengthen, lead, and teach you. He will bless you and lead you into new heights of intercession. He will show you things to come and enable you to intercede for them. He will show you things that are God's perfect will and cause you to pray that they should come to pass. He will show you the plans of the enemy and enable you to bring them to nothing. You will have Him as your Partner in intercession, and how blessed you will be! Amen.

MY PRAYER

My Lord, You are the Lord of the harvest. You have caused Your servant to read the message in this book. You spoke to his heart while he read it. You convicted him. You showed him what You wanted done.

Lord, I pray that You should hide the word in his heart. Lord, grant that the enemy should not snatch it away. Lord, open his heart to see that the devil will take away everything that You have said to him, unless he co-operates with You to hide it from him.

Lord, lead him to obedience. Cause him to begin to pray for himself and to intercede for others. Make him willing to pay the price that it entails. Lord, cause him to believe You. Cause him to believe that You are able to make of him an intercessor of consequence. Lord, deliver him from discouragement. Cause him to see that the weak can become strong in You.

Lord, do these things and more for the glory of the Lord Jesus and the edification of Your Church. Amen.

Very Important

If you have not yet received Jesus as your Lord and Saviour, I encourage you to receive Him. Here are some steps to help you,

ADMIT that you are a sinner by nature and by practice and that on your own you are without hope. Tell God you have personally sinned against Him in your thoughts, words and deeds. Confess your sins to Him, one after another in a sincere prayer. Do not leave out any sins that you can remember. Truly turn from your sinful ways and abandon them. If you stole, steal no more. If you have been committing adultery or fornication, stop it. God will not forgive you if you have no desire to stop sinning in all areas of your life, but if you are sincere, He will give you the power to stop sinning.

BELIEVE that Jesus Christ, who is God's Son, is the only Way, the only Truth and the only Life. Jesus said, *"I am the way, the truth and the life; no one comes to the Father, but by me" (John 14:6). The Bible says, "For there is one God, and there is one mediator between God and men, the man Christ Jesus, who gave himself as a ransom for all" (1 Timothy 2:5-6). "And there is salvation in no one else (apart from Jesus), for there is no other name under heaven given among men by which we must be saved" (Acts 4:12). "But to all who received him, who believed in his name, he gave power to become children of God..."* (John 1:12). BUT,

CONSIDER the cost of following Him. Jesus said that all who follow Him must deny themselves, and this includes selfish financial, social and other interests. He also wants His followers to take up their crosses and follow Him. Are you prepared to abandon your own interests daily for those of Christ? Are you prepared to be led-in a new direction by Him? Are you prepared to suffer for Him and die for Him if need be? Jesus will have nothing to do with half-hearted people. His demands are total. He will only receive and forgive those who are prepared to follow Him AT ANY COST.

Think about it and count the cost. If you are prepared to follow Him, come what may, then there is something to do:

INVITE Jesus to come into your heart and life. He says, "*Behold I stand at the door and knock. If anyone hears my voice and opens the door (to his heart and life), I will come in to him and eat with him, and he with me* " (Revelation 3:20). Why don't you pray a prayer like the following one or one of your own construction as the Holy Spirit leads ?

> "Lord Jesus, I am a wretched, lost sinner who has sinned in thought, word and deed. Forgive all my sins and cleanse me. Receive me, Saviour and transform me into a child of God. Come into my heart now and give me eternal life right now. I will follow you at all costs, trusting the Holy Spirit to give me all the power I need."

When you pray this prayer sincerely, Jesus answers at once and justifies you before God and makes you His child.

Please write to me and I will pray for you and help you as you go on with Jesus Christ

***

If you have received the Lord Jesus-Christ after reading this book, please write to us at the following addresse :

For Europe :

> Editions du Livre Chrétien
> 4, Rue du Révérend Père Cloarec
> 92400 Courbevoie
> Courriel : editionlivrechretien@gmail.com

For Africa :

> Christian Publishing House
> B.P. 7100 Yaoundé
> Cameroun
> Courriel : cphyaounde@yahoo.fr

Made in United States
Orlando, FL
05 May 2025